International Practice Theory

Christian Bueger • Frank Gadinger

International Practice Theory

Second Edition

palgrave
macmillan

Christian Bueger
Department of Politics and International Relations
Cardiff University
Cardiff, UK

Frank Gadinger
Centre for Global Cooperation Research
University of Duisburg-Essen
Duisburg, Germany

ISBN 978-3-319-73349-4 ISBN 978-3-319-73350-0 (eBook)
https://doi.org/10.1007/978-3-319-73350-0

Library of Congress Control Number: 2018930250

Printed on acid-free paper

This Palgrave Macmillan imprint is published by Springer Nature
The registered company is Springer International Publishing AG
The registered company address is: Gewerbestrasse 11, 6330 Cham, Switzerland

Acknowledgements, 2nd Edition

Since the first edition of *International Practice Theory* was written, the practice theoretical debate in international relations has matured significantly. It seemed reasonable to drop the "new perspectives" sub-title, considering that practice theory is now a well-established perspective.

What sparked our ambition for this significantly revised and extended edition was, firstly, to include many of the great practice theoretical works published in the last years. New answers to the challenges we set out in the first edition, such as questions of change and materiality, have been published and require attention. We were, secondly, delighted to see that the first edition was received as an accessible overview and entrance point to the practice debate in international relations. In this new version, we have aimed at living up to the promise of providing a gateway to practice by further adding clarity and elaborating more fully on some of the intricate theoretical and practical challenges of international practice theory.

Some of the original concerns of the first edition remain. Fortunately, the international practice theory debate has not been narrowed down to one version of practice theory, but has instead become more pluralistic in recent years. It remains an important goal of the book to open up the debate and seek connections between practice theories within international relations, as well as, importantly, beyond it. Ensuring a fruitful dialogue with our neighboring disciplines of sociology, science studies, anthropology, international law, or geography is of continued importance. Articulating the differences between practice theoretical accounts more clearly and discussing them as useful tools in empirical analysis is another ongoing concern. Further efforts in exploring the relations to other ways of doing IR are required, whether the traditional rationalist or constructivist approaches, or the wide range of other turns, such as the discursive, aesthetic, visual, pragmatic, or performative turn that have influenced theorising lately. Last but not least, in this second edition we emphasise our understanding of practice theory as a methodological orientation to an even greater extent. What we hope to enable with this book is not theoretical debate, but thick praxiographies of the international, producing stories of what international practices are.

The juggling symbol on this 2nd edition's cover represents many of the core concerns of the book. Juggling is an ancient practice that lives on in today's era of computer games. It is a physical skill that requires objects as well as practical experience. While it is a good example of a practice, it also represents the concerns of practice theory. In the metaphorical sense, juggling implies coping with and balancing several activities at the same time, or organising an object in a certain manner. Moreover, juggling points to the creative and playful character of many activities in our everyday lives. The practice theoretical work we discuss in this book is juggled and moves with vocabulary, ontology, research tools and actual practices, while emphasising the importance of creative research.

Several people helped us in producing the second edition. People with whom we had extended discussions about the first edition in part or whole include Emanuel Adler, Rebecca Adler-Nissen, Claudia Aradau, Pol Bargués Pedreny, Niklas Bremberg, Alena Drieschova, Alejandro Esguerra, Katja Freistein, Nina Graeger, Gunther Hellmann, Ted Hopf, Jef Huysmans, Jonathan Joseph, Friedrich Kratochwil, Milja Kurki, Jorg Kustermans, Merje Kuus, Max Lesch, Daniel Nexon, Holger Niemann, Vincent Pouliot, Hilmar Schaefer, Sebastian Schindler, Klaus Schlichte, Christopher Smith, Jan Stockbruegger, Peter Sutch, William Walters, Tobias Wille, Antje Wiener, Dvora Yanow, and Taylan Yildiz. We are grateful for their advice and suggestions. We like to further thank Daniel Orders for his superb editorial and stylistic work, Elena Simon for brilliant editorial assistance, and Sarah Roughley from Palgrave Macmillan for supporting the project and instantly recognising the importance of a second edition.

Christian Bueger acknowledges the support of the research leave scheme of Cardiff University that facilitated the writing up of the manuscript. He further thanks the University of Seychelles, where parts of the book were written.

Frank Gadinger wishes to thank colleagues and fellows at the Centre for Global Cooperation Research, University of Duisburg-Essen, for continuing to provide him with an inspiring work environment while writing this manuscript. He would also like to express his gratitude to his wife, Anna, for her unwavering support and encouragement during the preparation of this book.

Parts of Chap. 2 draw on Bueger, Christian and Frank Gadinger. 2015. The Play of International Practice, *International Studies Quarterly* 59(3): 449–460.

Cape Town and Duisburg, November 2017

Acknowledgements, 1st Edition

This book is the outcome of an intellectual journey that brought us to different places and led us to discover thinkers across disciplines. Various conversations have shaped our thinking about what practice theory is and what we can do with it in International Relations (IR). The first ideas for writing this book emerged from a discussion in a corner bar in the suburbs of Florence. Back then, both of us were fascinated by the alternative universe that contemporary social theory provides to understand international politics, especially if compared to the narrow spectrum that classical IR theory has on offer. However, when first embarking on this intellectual quest, we occasionally thought we were heading in diverging directions by thinking about different problems such as materiality, practical knowledge, reflexivity, justification or narrativity and in discovering new authors from other disciplinary contexts. Ultimately we always noticed that the sometimes hidden intellectual spirit behind our search was the priority of practice in social life. "Practice theory" in IR has seen a similar evolution to our own experience. What was once a sort of intellectual stranger is now seen increasingly as a familiar body of thought whose core insights are of immediate relevance for the discipline. It is our impression that the connections that the idea of centering theory in practice provides are, however, still underestimated. With this book we hope to be able to make some of these connections more visible and indeed also more plausible. Often we find that researchers prefer to develop niches, in arguing for the superiority of this or that perspective – whether it is Bourdieusan praxeology, Actor-Network Theory, Relationalism or Narrative theory – rather than elaborating on the grander picture. While our interpretation of what practice theory is, or perhaps should be, is, of course, also restrictive, the goal of this book is to outline how perspectives hang together, and how a set of common challenges – whether ontological or methodological – exists. These challenges provide a common ground, and are an invitation to appreciate the tensions between different theoretical perspectives and positions. At the same time we hope that this book also provides an intelligible introduction for those new to practice theoretical thought. Our goal is to make the core assumptions and insights from international practice theory accessible and provide guidance of how to pursue a practice-theoretical research project. Finally, with this book we hope to spark more dialogue between IR, and the different disciplines concerned about practice, including, but not limited to, sociology, cultural studies, policy studies, organization studies or anthropology.

Conversations with a range of individuals have been instrumental in writing this book. We had the pleasure to talk over different aspects reflected in the book in discussions with Emanuel Adler, Morten Skumsrud Andersen, Trine Villumsen Berling, Richard Freeman, Inanna Hamati-Ataya, Gunther Hellmann, Friedrich Kratochwil, Xymena Kurowska, Jorg Kustermans, Anna Leander, Maximilian Mayer, Christian Meyer, Iver Neumann, Vincent Pouliot, Peer Schouten, Ole Jacob Sending, Peter Sutch, Hendrik Wagenaar, William Walters, Dvora Yanow, and Taylan Yildiz. Felix Bethke, Elisa Wynn-Hughes, Holger Niemann and Sebastian Jarzebski have provided detailed comments on parts of the manuscript. We are grateful to Christopher Smith and Jan Stockbruegger not only for research assistance, but also for providing detailed comments on the entire manuscript.

Christian Bueger acknowledges the support from the Centre for Advanced Security Theory, Copenhagen University where parts of this manuscript were written. Writing up moreover benefitted from the support by the Economic and Social Research Council [ES/K008358/1] and the Department of Politics and International Relations, Cardiff University.

Frank Gadinger would like to thank his colleagues and fellows at the Centre for Global Cooperation Research, University of Duisburg-Essen, for providing him with a stimulating work environment and rich discussions while writing this manuscript.

Parts of Chaps. 5 and 6 draw on Bueger, Christian, Pathways to Practice: Praxiography and International Politics, *European Political Science Review* 6(3), 383–406, 2014

Cardiff and Düsseldorf, August 2014

Contents

List of Tables

CHAPTER 1

Introducing International Practice Theory

Matt Sweetwood from Liberty, in the US state of Missouri, fell in love with a German girl he met at university. He followed her to Germany, where they are now happily married and living with three sons in Potsdam. Sweetwood has lived in Germany for over ten years, but the country's people and their culture remain something of a mystery to him. Professionally, he writes, directs and edits documentary films. In his most recent feature, he set out to discover the essence of the German people. He decided that the key to German identity lies in understanding one of its best-known cultural assets: beer. For his documentary *Beerland,* he spent months travelling around, visiting breweries, drinking clubs, and ordinary taverns. He found that Germans can be serious and silly, tradition-bound and visionary, all at once.

The idea that we might be able to understand the German people by studying and experiencing one of their most recognisable habits and cultural goods – drinking beer – seems intuitive; anyone who has had the opportunity to spend an evening at a German tavern will understand this immediately. What appears obvious for a documentary maker or the everyday traveller seems to be of limited value when we seek to understand world politics, however. Although international relations (IR) theory is also concerned with national identities, we are nonetheless advised to look elsewhere when studying the discipline. 'Go and study the speeches of famous politicians!', we are told. 'Examine national interests!' or 'calculate power and balancing behaviour!' are just some of the conventional guidelines that

C. Bueger, F. Gadinger, *International Practice Theory*,
https://doi.org/10.1007/978-3-319-73350-0_1

any student of IR will be familiar with. And yet, is there anything we may learn from Sweetwood's eye-opening quest? Can the account of a documentary filmmaker suggest new directions for IR scholars?

Whilst working at the Norwegian Ministry of Foreign Affairs, Iver Neumann faced a similar problem to Sweetwood. How does one come to understand what the work of a diplomat actually involves? Hardly anyone had written about what these mandarins do when they undertake their *métier*. And yet, wasn't it obvious that IR should be able to say something about what diplomats do?

Searching for an argument that would be intelligible for IR researchers, Neumann (2002) introduced a body of thought that he described as 'practice theory' in a 2002 article. He declared it to be vital that IR return to studying the doing and sayings of those involved in world politics. Neumann was certainly not the first to highlight the importance of turning to practice; indeed, earlier generations of IR scholars had already proposed that practice should be a core category in IR theory. His article sparked interest in giving centre stage to the concept of practice, however, as well as rethinking how it may be theorised and studied empirically.

Neumann was not on his own. A broad movement of scholars from across the social sciences had started to think about practice and how the investigation of doing and sayings can provide us with a better understanding of the world. Together, these scholars suggest that the attention to practice requires a 'turn'; that is, a practice turn. This metaphor suggests that practice theory is not merely a new theory, but involves substantial shifts in thinking about the world and the nature and purpose of social science.

What, then, does it mean to study international relations through the lens of practice? Scholars focusing on practices as a core unit of analysis do not want to begin with fixed assumptions of what people are like, how they behave or what logic they follow. Nor do they start with claims about the nature of the international system or of global politics. Instead, they consider an account that starts by paying attention to what actors do and say, and how these activities are embedded in broader contexts. They ask what knowledge is required to perform world politics, and how actors work together to make the international. They attempt to pay attention to the things and technologies used in producing the international. To focus on practices is also an attempt to break with some traditional assumptions and distinctions of 'level of analysis' usually taught in introductory IR courses. Practice theorists argue that many of our traditionally learned dichotomies are more of a hindrance than a help. These include the division between agency and structure, micro and macro, subject and object, individual and society, mind and body or the ideational and the material.

How then, may we conduct meaningful research if these are unproductive assumptions? Does practice theory seek to throw all received wisdom overboard?

Both Matt Sweetwood and Iver Neumann naturally began their investigations with background knowledge of their 'cases'. They had clear objectives: Sweetwood wanted to understand German identity, while Neumann addressed diplomacy. Sweetwood prepared for his movie in reading about the historical evolution of beer as a cultural aspect of German life. Neumann relied on literature on diplomacy in world politics, for instance, Ernest Satow's *Guide to Diplomatic Practice*, widely regarded as the authoritative text in the world's foreign ministries (Neumann 2012: 1–3).

Satow defines diplomacy as "the conduct of official relations between the governments of independent states" (quoted after Neumann 2012: 1). Yet, for Neumann, definitional or theoretical knowledge was not sufficient in understanding how diplomacy works. Sweetwood dealt with the same problem; the cultural history of Germany provided him with an overview of the range of national brewing and beer drinking traditions, but it did not lead him to a richer understanding of German culture as lived experience, and told him little about how to understand the German people.

Sweetwood and Neumann recognised that to understand their objects, books were not enough. Rather than trying to be 'objective' and 'distant' observers, they had to engage with their objects of investigation. This required not only observing practices, but also learning, adapting and becoming active. Sweetwood not only learned how to drink beer, he also studied in a small brewery in Bavaria. Through this experience, he began, for instance, to understand why an established family tradition of independence may be stronger than the drive for profit by contracting out to a major company. The survival of small independent breweries over several decades was an issue that had puzzled Sweetwood, since he was used to the monopolised US beer market.

Neumann, meanwhile, became a diplomat, working for the foreign ministry. Through this experience, he learned, for instance, that writing a diplomatic speech is not an isolated action of one individual thinker, followed by forwarding the piece to a higher political level. Instead, it is a group undertaking that involves talking with different individuals and slowly finding a common thread through bureaucratic procedures and routines. Practice theory involves observing the practices of others, talking about these practices, participating in and reflecting upon them all at once. The aim is not to reduce and present abstract explanations of social phenomena, but to come to a deeper understanding of how the world works in and through practices.

If 'practice theory' has only recently been introduced to IR, the concept of 'practice' is certainly nothing novel. The term 'practice' is part of everyday language and is used colloquially in IR. Often, practice is also contrasted with theory. In this case, by practice, we mean what 'normal' people are doing, and by 'theory' we refer to abstract generalisations – or what academics are doing. The notion of 'practice theory' breaks down this separation, and indeed argues that practice and theory are intrinsically linked: Without practice there can be no theory, and vice versa. We will come back to the relation between practice and theory, and how 'practice theory' forges new recombinations more substantially when we discuss the methodology of practices later in the book (Chap. 6).

Practice was also being developed as a distinct concept long before the conversation on practice theory began in IR. Advanced understandings of practice began to emerge in the early 1990s with the introduction of constructivist thoughts. Many of the early constructivist works drew substantially on authors we describe today as practice theorists. For instance, in the so-called agency-structure debate of the 1990s, Anthony Giddens' 'structuration theory' became influential. In this debate, 'practice' was identified as an important intermediary of agents and structures (Doty 1997). In these earlier proposals, 'practice' did not take centre stage, however. It was primarily a supporting concept, and remained only weakly conceptualised. Practice theory is quite different in this regard; here the concept of practice is promoted from a supporting function to the lead role. We provide a more detailed discussion of the history of the concept of practice in IR in Chap. 2.

Over the past decade, practice theory has become increasingly prominent in IR. In this book, we describe this endeavour as the common project of international practice theory. We will explain and expand what we mean by this expression and what it implies for IR over the chapters that follow. We will in particular explore a range of distinct approaches to international practice theory (Chaps. 3 and 4), but also the conceptual challenges they face (Chap. 5). Given the rise and extent of the international practice theory project, we think it deserves an acronym. Throughout the book we refer to IPT.[1]

IPT comes with a range of promises. These include the potential for getting closer to the actions and lifeworlds of the practitioners who perform international relations, to producing knowledge that is of relevance beyond an intimate group of peers and may even address societal concerns or contribute to crafting better policies, avoiding and overcoming (traditional) dualisms, such as structure and agency, developing a perspective that is receptive to change as well as reproduction, to more fully integrating material aspects, ranging from bodily movements to objects and artefacts. These promises and prospects require detailed attention, and in our conclusion, we assess how far IPT has already lived up to them.

To understand the unique character of IPT, it is important to gain a sense of the kind of empirical phenomena and issues scholars aim to address. What IR scholars are interested in differs from other disciplines. Although in no way limited to them, four issue areas have been particularly important in the discussion of IPT, namely, diplomacy, the production of insecurity, transnational governance, and state building and intervention.

Asked what the core practices of global politics are, many answer by pointing to diplomacy. The study of bilateral and multilateral diplomatic practices has become one of the most crucial issue areas where practice theory was developed. Two of the first major studies in IPT were concerned with understanding diplomatic practices (Neumann 2002, 2005, 2012; Pouliot 2008, 2010b). Understanding diplomatic culture and actions continues to be one of the main fields of investigation, with a rich number of studies on diplomatic practices having been published recently (e.g. Pouliot and Cornut 2015; Sending et al. 2015).

A second issue area concerns the study of security and the production of insecurity. In many ways, critical security studies has been one of the innovators and drivers of IPT. Critical security studies' core point was that the meaning of security is not fixed, but socially produced and as such inherently political and contingent. Consequentially, scholars investigate the practices through which security and insecurity are produced (Balzaq et al. 2010; Bueger 2016). Influential studies such as those by Bigo (2005), Huysmans (2006), or Berling (2012) draw on practice theory and argue in favour of understanding security politics as a field of practice constituted by the actions of experts who give security meaning and identify threats, as well as devices such as technology, algorithms, databases, and risk analysis tools.

The study of transnational and global governance processes is a third major issue area. In the 1990s, IR addressed the question of which actors other than states matter in global governance (Avant et al. 2010). The emphasis soon shifted to the modes of governance, and today a significant number of scholars study the diverse range of governing practices, including, for instance, benchmarking (Fougner 2008; Porter 2012) or quantification through indicators and statistics (Davis et al. 2012a, b). Devices, such as documents or databases, and material activities ranging from negotiating to calculating or filling out forms, have also become the focus of such research (Walters 2002; Bueger 2011; Sending and Neumann 2011). Practice theories therefore offer a renewed understanding of what it means to govern, and of how authority is distributed.

Finallys, state-building and peacebuilding is a field of international activity that has increasingly been scrutinised from a practice-theoretical viewpoint, accompanying the growth of interventions and peace operations since the 1990s. Practice theoretical studies were, on the one hand, introduced to provide a better understanding of international activities geared at building peace and reconstructing states. Scholars became interested in the everyday work of peacebuilding (Mac Ginty 2014) and in conceptualising interventions as a rich and heterogeneous set of practices (Olsson 2015). On the other hand, practice theoretical ideas also allowed scholars to re-describe the situations that international programs aim to respond to (Schouten 2013; Koddenbrock 2016).

Studies in these four issue areas were pivotal drivers in the development of IPT. They provide the context and the 'problematic situations' for which practice theory aims to develop responses. Over the course of this book, we will come back to these issue areas and the above studies. We introduce them here briefly, since we require some understanding of what international practices are before we can set out to explore IPT.

1.1 Chapter Overview

To gather a better understanding of what international practice theory consists of, we provide an initial approximation of practice theory and what we can do with it in IR in Chap. 2, drawing on a range of strategies to do so. Our first strategy is to provide a brief overview of how practice theory has been introduced across the social sciences. This discussion reveals that practice theory is a heterogeneous set of ideas and concepts; to grasp this complexity, we introduce the metaphor of a 'trading zone'. This implies thinking about practice theory not as a cognitive construct, but rather as an intellectual space in which scholars 'trade' ideas on how to study practices and cooperate to further develop the project. The trading zone gives us a basic metaphor to grasp the character of practice theory as an intellectual project.

Our next strategy is to situate practice theoretical thinking in the wider landscape of social theory and philosophy. We introduce a mapping technique that contrasts practice theory with other social theories, such as rational choice, and with different expressions of culturalist theorising such as discourse theory. Drawing on the work of Andreas Reckwitz, we show how in ideal-typical form practice theory differs from cultural theories that foreground either the mind and beliefs or discourses and structures of meaning. This also grants us a map for understanding how IPT relates to other theoretical developments in IR, such as constructivism. We gain a strong picture of how IPT is related to and differs from other attempts to theorise international relations. Our third and final strategy of introducing the basics of practice theory is to move to more positive and programmatic heuristic. We argue that practice theory entails a number of commitments of how to think about and perform social science, and about the core characteristics of international politics. We summarise these commitments under the concepts of process, knowledge, learning, materiality, multiplicity, performativity and empiricity. These commitments can be interpreted in differing ways; we therefore need to discuss how different practice theoretical approaches interpret and develop them. This is a task we take up in the two following chapters.

In the Chaps. 3 and 4 we zoom in on distinct approaches of IPT. We provide a detailed discussion of seven approaches, each of which provides a distinct conceptual vocabulary and interpretation of the core premises of practice theory. We discuss the origins of each approach, their core concepts, and how they have been used in IR. Our focus is on approaches that have already shown great promise in interpreting international politics differently, and have attracted a significant range of scholars. These approaches are, to some degree, the cornerstones of IPT, and together they broadly document the different directions one can take. Our intention is not to narrow down IPT to these seven approaches, since this spectrum certainly does not cover the full spectrum of approaches. Indeed, as we emphasise in the conclusion, other approaches are being developed and used in IPT.

(1) We start with the praxeology of Pierre Bourdieu. Bourdieusian research has been most directly associated with the label of practice theory; his concepts are therefore an important reference point in the debate. Beginning with early contributions by Ashley (1987)

and Guzzini (2000), Bourdieu's praxeology has received significant attention. Key concepts from Bourdieu – habitus, capital, doxa, field – are used to study international practices of diplomacy, security policy or political economy (Balzaq et al. 2010). The majority of Bourdieu-inspired studies investigate the emergence of and power relations within transnational fields, understood as social spaces constituted by practices in which actors cooperate and compete (e.g. Berling 2012; Williams 2007). Bourdieu's praxeology has not only attracted considerable attention as it provides the most elaborate (and indeed highly complex) conceptual apparatus, but also because it intends to bridge subjectivist and objectivist methodology.

(2) Michel Foucault's concepts of governmentality, problematisation and genealogy have inspired a broad range of studies on different practices of governing and knowing the international. Although Foucault's body of work is often not directly associated with the term practice theory, our discussion intends to correct this misunderstanding in arguing that Foucault is first and foremost a practice theoretical thinker who, in particular, allows us to conceptualise and study historical practices and configurations of very wide scope. A wide range of technologies and practices have been studied on the basis of Foucauldian vocabulary, meanwhile. This includes works on benchmarking, statistics or indicators, with strong empirical emphasis placed on global governance and the diverse power effects of international organisations (Merlingen 2006; Fougner 2008; Jaeger 2010).

(3) We continue by discussing the concept of community of practice. This approach originates in organisation studies, and was originally developed by Etienne Wenger as a concept to study learning in organisations. The framework was translated to IR by Emanuel Adler (2005) and is a powerful device for rethinking various forms of transnational communities. The community of practice framework emphasises a social collective that shares a repertoire of practices and knowledge, and foregrounds processes of learning practical knowledge. Adler principally used the framework for revisiting security communities (Adler 2008), though it is increasingly used to study other practice collectives ranging from diplomats to pirates (Gilson 2009; Lachmann 2011; Bueger 2013a).

(4) Theodore Schatzki has provided a sophisticated practice theoretical outline, and his definitions have become quite influential in the debate. Although the use of his vocabulary in IR remains limited, his approach deserves to be explored more fully. In particular, Schatzki's idea of practice as composed of performance and pronouncements organised by practical understandings, rules and teleo-affective structures, as well as his concept of arrangements, are of interest. So far, Schatzki's vocabulary has primarily been employed by Cornelia Navari (2010) to lay out the English School's concept of international practice.

(5) We elaborate on an approach that puts emphasis on narrative as the concept that binds together practice across time and space. This approach is not directly associated with a single theorist, and we discuss a broader range of authors together. Narratives can be understood as configuration devices by which actors make sense of the world and order it in particular ways. The focus becomes the elements of narratives and how these are told and narrated in particular situations. Narrative approaches have become particularly influential in the analysis of foreign policy (Devetak 2009; Krebs 2015a), as well as the study of peacebuilding and post-conflict situations (Buckley-Zistel 2014).

(6) Actor-network theory is our next approach. Developed in science and technology studies, this approach foregrounds the practices of making relations as well as the importance of non-human, or material aspects. This approach represents, perhaps, a more radical shift from conventional IR theories. Drawing on the works of theorists such as Bruno Latour, John Law, or Michel Callon, scholars emphasise performativity and contingency. For them, international politics is a world continually in the making that requires significant effort and maintenance work (Acuto and Curtis 2013; Best and Walters 2013). Studies attempt to disentangle the socio-technical networks that perform international phenomena and knowledge in fields ranging from international economy to climate change or security. They investigate the effects of technologies, attempt to disentangle the practical relations that produce world politics, or develop an understanding of international politics as controversy between different arrangements.

(7) The final approach we discuss is the pragmatic sociology initiated by the work of Luc Boltanski. Like Schatzki's work, the approach holds significant potential for studying international practices, but has not been widely employed to date. The focus of the approach is on the study of controversies and the justifications that actors provide. The approach is particularly interesting in the way that it reclaims insights from the classical pragmatism of John Dewey and others. Central themes such as creative capacity, situations of controversy as moments of change, and the notion of order as the outcome of everyday negotiations are taken up from pragmatism and turned into empirical research approaches. The first studies to have drawn on this approach in IR have focussed on UN Security Council debates (Niemann 2015), US Congress debates around the "war on terror" (Gadinger 2016), or global health governance (Hanrieder 2016).

For each of these approaches, we provide an introduction to their core ideas, main concepts, strengths and weaknesses, and discuss ways of using them in IR. Together, they give us a theoretical repertoire for the study of practice.

In the subsequent chapter, we ask what the relations between the approaches are, and argue that the differences between them provide for a range of productive tensions. Scholars take different positions on issues, such as how contingent the world is, when and how practices and larger constellations change, or how to conceptualise the varying scale of international practices. They also offer varying understandings of core concepts in international relations and give differing perspectives on normativity and the function of norms, the role of the materiality of a practice, and conceptualisations of power.

Taken together, these questions point us to a range of challenges for the development of practice theory. We elaborate on each of these, and sketch out the various options to address them. These challenges, or perhaps even puzzles, are principally philosophical in character, and therefore there are no straightforward intellectual answers or even 'optimal solutions' to be presented. Instead, we suggest that these puzzles should be taken as starting points for empirical research. In the absence of actual practices, it makes little sense to discuss them at length or to try to find solutions. This leads us to a range of methodological reflections in the subsequent chapter: what are the modalities of initiating a practice theoretical research project? Where does one start? What methods are available?

Underlining the importance of more and better empirical research, we discuss the methodology and methods of international practice theory in Chap. 6, starting by outlining a number of methodological guidelines that spring from practice theory, and the fact that undertaking social science is a practice. We introduce the notion of praxiography to speak about the methodology and methods of practice theory-driven research. In the chapter, we discuss the status of 'theory' and why practice theory calls for novel understandings of it, whether and how one can generalise with praxiography, as well as the significance of recursive and abductive reasoning. There follows a discussion of where to anchor and start a praxiography. We argue that the seven core approaches imply differing research strategies and productive starting points. The largest part of the chapter is, however, devoted to the discussion of concrete research techniques (or methods).

Our argument is that praxiography implies carefully considering how practice can be observed directly. Arguing against the conventional wisdom that international relations is not open to participant forms of field work, we show how different forms of such work, including participant observation, event observation and shadowing can be adopted in an IR context. Some situations, for example the study of historical practices, will nevertheless continue to require alternative techniques, and we point to interviews and different forms of text analysis as options. We provide a short sketch of each of these techniques, how they can be employed in praxiography, and introduce some paradigmatic examples. Together these techniques provide a rich repertoire for praxiography that can be blended in various ways depending on the demands of the phenomenon studied.

Our final section is concerned with the writing of a praxiography. This is not only an issue that has received relatively sparse attention, but it is also a challenging one. Writing about practice implies controlling for the unruliness of practices, and ordering them into a more-or-less coherent narrative. We argue that, firstly, we should also think about writing as a practice, that is, as a particular practice that is not separate to producing knowledge, but is a fundamental part of it. In practical terms we consider writing about practices to be primarily about the problem of intelligibility. How can a narrative about practice be written in a way that makes sense to a distinct audience? We argue that praxiography requires experimentation and creativity, and introduce ideas from ethnography and filmmaking as inspirations.

Our concluding chapter attempts to zoom out. We ask whether IPT has lived up to its promises, some of which are clearly on the way to be realised, while others leave us with a more mixed evaluation. The practice turn is far from being completed, but what will it imply as and when that comes to pass? What will the status of practice theory be in the future? We end by speculating about this future, and re-investigate three scenarios originally outlined in the first edition of this book. Is IPT becoming an ever-growing and thriving trading zone, a paradigm, or will it soon begin to disappear into the annals of IR theory?

Note

1. We are aware that this acronym has attracted some criticism. Some might think that there is not enough substance to grant international practice theory an acronym, while others may point out that IPT is already reserved for international political theory. We find the first critique misleading; this book showcases how IPT has flourished. The latter concern is, of course, valid, but we consider that the discipline can cope with having the same acronym for two different intellectual fields.

CHAPTER 2

Situating Practice in Social Theory and International Relations

In 2001, Theodore Schatzki et al. (2001) published a seminal edited volume entitled *The Practice Turn in Contemporary Theory*. This book became influential not only because it demonstrated the diversity of practice theoretical work already produced in different branches of the social sciences, but also through introducing the idea that the new focus on practices implied a 'turn', that is, a shift in how we think about and undertake social sciences.

Across the social sciences, similar attempts have been made to argue for a practice turn, attracting a growing number of scholars in a range of disciplines. Sociologists analyse organisation, learning and strategy-making through the lens of practice (e.g. Miettinen et al. 2009; Nicolini 2013), for example. What has become known as 'strategy-as-practice' research is now a well-established approach in organisation studies, not least as documented by a handbook published on the subject (Golsorkhi et al. 2010).

In other areas of sociology, researchers study, for example, consumption behaviour through the lens of practice (e.g., Halkier et al. 2011). In many ways, researchers in science and technology studies have been at the forefront of the practice theoretical project (e.g. Pickering 1992; Rouse 1996). Indeed, the majority of contributors to the *Practice Turn* volume hailed from this branch of the social sciences. The study of practice has also gained a strong foothold in policy studies, and scholars draw on the concept to study the practices of policy making and implementation (e.g. Hajer and Wagenaar 2003a).

C. Bueger, F. Gadinger, *International Practice Theory*,
https://doi.org/10.1007/978-3-319-73350-0_2

Across these disciplines, and others such as history, geography, environmental studies, gender studies or cultural sociology, the number of scholars embracing the concept of practice and demonstrating its value has been growing consistently; one finds an astonishing range of practices that have been studied, whether it be cooking, cycling, running, driving, walking, negotiating, organising, writing, reading, or experimenting.

The metaphor of 'turning', while attractive for some, tends to be off-putting for others, however.[1] Given the proliferation of so-called turns, including the cultural, linguistic, material, performative or pictorial ones, the appetite for them seems to have ebbed. However, referring to a practice turn remains a powerful reminder that the introduction of practice theory implies more than the introduction of just a new theory or paradigm. While practice theory develops new types of approaches and frameworks, it also involves significant shifts in thinking about the world and the nature and purpose of social science. These shifts involve epistemology, ontology, methodology, methods, and indeed rethinking how social science and IR relate to and are situated in the world.

In the following sections, we provide an approximation of practice theory, and adopt three strategies to bring us closer to an understanding of what practice theory is, and the commitments it consists of. Firstly, we provide a brief review of the intellectual ancestors of practice thinking, and argue for understanding IPT as a social space or a trading zone in which various scholars exchange ideas and data. Secondly, we draw on the work of German social theorist Andreas Reckwitz to situate practice theoretical thinking in the wider landscape of social theory and philosophy. We show how, in ideal-typical form, practice theory differs from cultural theories that foreground either the mind and beliefs or discourses and structures of meaning. We then discuss how IPT relates to other theoretical developments in IR, such as constructivism, and finally, we outline the commitments implied by IPT in terms of how to think about and undertake social science, and about the core characteristics of international politics.

2.1 A First Approximation: Practice Theory as a Trading Zone

Practice theories position themselves towards or in opposition to numerous recent "paths of thinking, including intellectualism, representationalism, individualism (e.g. rational choice theory, methodological individualism, network analysis), structuralism, structure-functionalism, systems theory, semiotics, and many strains of humanism and poststructuralism" (Schatzki 2001: 2).

In IR, practice theories have primarily been introduced by outlining differences with rationalism and various kinds of constructivism and post-structuralism. The intent is to show how core phenomena of IR, including power, state behaviour, identity, international organisations, transnational collectives, norms and rules, or war and peace can be studied differently. IPT thereby makes decisive contributions to the study of international relations and world politics across the sub-disciplinary issue areas.

The opposition of practice theories to other approaches should not be overemphasised, however. Differentiations are important for introducing new ways of doing things, providing theoretical orientation, and complying with the expectations of a discipline that favours contributions arguing for theoretical superiority, but if overstated, they may easily lead to unproductive dualisms and misunderstandings, and in the worst case, to mutual ignorance. There is an ongoing risk that this characterises the relation of practice theory to constructivism, post-structuralism, feminism or post-colonialism. These perspectives, pluralist in their own right, share many concerns with practice theories. While differences need to be respectfully articulated, cultural turf wars must be avoided.

Practice theories do not offer a unified approach; differing concerns, types, forms of opposition to other approaches, and vocabularies are clustered around the notion. A core of practice theories conceives of practices as "embodied, materially mediated arrays of human activity centrally organised around shared practical understandings" (Schatzki 2001: 2). Differences arise among scholars over how to conceptualise practical understandings, which additional supporting concepts are required, how practices are interwoven or mediated by non-human elements, machines and objects, or what the methodological consequences of practice thinking are. Some place stronger emphasis on repetition and routinisation, such as the social theories of Anthony Giddens and Pierre Bourdieu, while others foreground fluid processes of recurrent "situated accomplishments" structured through practices (cf. Lynch 2001: 131) or describe practice as "infrastructure of repeated interactional patterns" (Swidler 2001: 85). Large parts of the following exploration of IPT aim at understanding these varieties and divergences, and investigating why they matter when we study international relations.

Coping with the diversity of practice theories implies taking a view on how these perspectives manage to hang together. For the anthropologist Sherry Ortner (1984), who was among the first to consider the notion of practice theory, practice was no more than a 'symbol'. As she put it, 'practice' is "a new key symbol of theoretical orientation [...]. This is neither a theory nor a method in itself, but rather, [...] a symbol, in the name of which a variety of theories and methods are being developed" (Ortner 1984: 127). Given the vast energy that has gone into defining consistent practice approaches and the growing number of attempts to extrapolate the differences between them, practice has certainly become more than a symbol, however.

For others, practice theory is primarily unified by a shared intellectual history. Miettinen et al. (2009), for instance, suggest speaking about a "re-turn to practice", given that current practice theory, to a large extent, rediscovers understandings that have a *de facto* historical tradition.

Indeed, the concept of practice, or praxis, is anything but new. Richard Bernstein (1971), whom Miettinen et al. (2009) allude to, lays out a history of the concept stretching from the Hegelian tradition and Karl Marx's outline of the idea of practice or 'objective activity' to the American pragmatist philosophers Charles Pierce and John Dewey and their notion of habit and actions. Joseph Dunne (1993) develops a different history, which takes the Aristotelian concepts of different types of practical knowledge – *techne* and *phronesis* – as a starting point. From there, he explores thinkers such as R.G. Collingwood, Hannah Arendt, Hans Georg Gadamer and Jürgen Habermas, for whom practical knowledge was a crucial category. In other debates, a historical line is drawn from the seminal works *Time and Being* by Martin Heidegger and *Philosophical Investigations* by Ludwig Wittgenstein (Schatzki 1996; Stern 2003). These studies developed accounts of the primacy of practice in the making of the social world. Heidegger's practice-based ontology and Wittgenstein's understanding that rules and meaning are grounded in social practices moreover had a clear impact on current practice approaches.

Another way of thinking about practice theory is to identify it as an intellectual space. As historian Gabrielle Spiegel (2005b: 25) points out, "the very looseness and theoretical incoherence [of practice theory], may prove to be of [...] benefit, carving out a space where the differential concerns of a broad group of historians, anthropologists, sociologists, and philosophers can find a common space within which to address each other". A productive way to approach this space is through Peter Galison's (1997) concept of 'trading zones'. Galison introduced the notion to scrutinise how scientists can cooperate and exchange results and concepts, while simultaneously disagreeing on their general or global meanings. In his words (1997: 46),

> subcultures trade. Anthropologists have extensively studied how different groups, with radically different ways of dividing up the world and symbolically organising its parts, can not only exchange goods but also depend essentially on those trades. Within a certain cultural arena – what I called [...] the 'trading zones' – two dissimilar groups can find common ground. They can exchange fish for baskets, enforcing subtle equations of correspondence between quantity, quality and type, and yet utterly disagree on the broader (global) significance of the items exchanged. Similarly, between the scientific subcultures of theory and experiment, or even between different traditions of instrument making or different subcultures of theorising, there can be exchanges (co-ordinations), worked out in exquisite local detail, without global agreement.

The turn to international practice theory can be understood as such an intellectual trading zone. It is a space bound together, not by fish or baskets, but by a shared understanding of the value of studying 'practice'. In this space, different (IR) practitioners meet and trade ideas of how to conduct intelligible IR research relying on concepts of practice. Whilst engaging in this exchange, IR practitioners may still continue to fundamentally disagree over the meaning of core concepts.

In an IR context, the work of Emanuel Adler and Vincent Pouliot has notably become associated with the label of practice theory. In a practice theoretical manifesto and the introduction to an edited volume, (Adler and Pouliot 2011a, b, c) they argue for a similar understanding to that of a trading zone. They project practice theory as a joint enterprise that will strengthen IR's inner-disciplinary dialogue and allow researchers to overcome any paradigmatic boundaries within the discipline. Adler and Pouliot's (2011a: 28) understanding submits that "taking international practices seriously leads not to synthesis but to dialogue" and promises "cross-fertilisation" between different IR theories. They describe the modus of dialogue in the following way:

> For example, realists can analyse the lifecycle of the balancing practice from a material power perspective, while liberals can emphasise the choices of institutions and individual choices. Alternatively, English School scholars can emphasise the historical processes via which emerging practices aggregate into social societies, while constructivists and poststructuralist scholars may emphasise transformation in collective meanings and discourse as a result of practice. (Adler and Pouliot 2011a: 28)

Adler and Pouliot thus invite all students of IR "to approach world politics through the lens of its manifold practices" (Adler and Pouliot 2011a: 1) and suggest that the notion of practice is a "focal point" that makes "interparadigmatic conversations possible" (Adler and Pouliot 2011a: 3).

Our understanding of IPT as trading zone differs in two important regards. Firstly, the very looseness and incoherence of the field of international practice theory is its strength, not its weakness. Rather than directing efforts towards cross-fertilisation and agreement, the exchanges and tensions between different practice approaches need to be preserved. As Mol (2010a: 262) phrases it, the strength "is not in its coherence and predictability, but in what at first sight, or in the eyes of those who like their theories to be firm, might seem to be its weakness: its adaptability and sensitivity."

Secondly, not every IR theorist can be or should be considered as a trader in the practice theoretical forum. In Adler and Pouliot's initial outline, IPT is a project to which anyone can subscribe, independently from theoretical positions. We disagree with Adler and Pouliot that it makes sense to include all IR theories in the practice endeavour, however, and doubt that a division of labour as sketched out in the above paragraph is possible. Not every IR theorist is a practice theorist, can be a practice theorist or is engaged in practice-oriented research; even many self-proclaimed constructivists do not do practice theory.

There may be good reasons why someone does not want to be (or should not be) an international practice theorist. The reason for this is simple: many IR scholars, although writing about practice, do not share the epistemological and ontological commitments that practice theories imply, such as a performative understanding of the world, or an understanding of science as one cultural domain among others. Sharing a set of commitments is required to trade in the practice theoretical zone. We come to these commitments at the end of this chapter.

Rather than turning practice theory into an overcrowded circus, the ontological and epistemological commitments that give practice theory its distinct value must be safeguarded to some degree. This is not an isolationist argument, and does not imply that practice theorists cannot (or should not) cooperate and converse productively with other theorists and other trading zones of international relations, including post-structuralism, discourse theory or the many varieties of constructivism. Very much to the contrary: such cooperation, collaboration and dialogue, notably in empirical work, is very promising. The precondition for such cooperation is, however, a clearly laid-out set of commitments.

Understanding practice theory as a trading zone also implies taking trans-disciplinary trade and exchange seriously. Research in other disciplinary contexts is often much more relevant to IPT than the contents of many 'must-read' IR journals. Indeed, the practice theoretical programme is in large part about making such trans-disciplinary connections; whether it be with organisational sociology, social theory, science and technology studies, geography, anthropology or policy studies, IPT benefits from trans-disciplinary conversations. These disciplines have much to contribute to understanding international politics, though the empirical material they deal with may at times be unfamiliar. The challenges of conceptualising practice and conducting empirical research on that basis provide common problems across disciplines, however. As we will elaborate upon during a discussion of the core approaches to IPT, many of these understandings have been developed through exchange with other disciplines.

Before proceeding further, we require a better understanding of what practice theory is and how it can be situated in the grand landscape of theoretical reasoning. The trading zone gives us a basic metaphor with which to grasp the character of practice theory as an intellectual project. Our next step is to situate practice theoretical thinking in the wider landscape of social theory and philosophy. In the next section, we contrast practice theory with other social theories, such as rational choice, and with different expressions of culturalist theorising, such as discourse theory. Drawing on the work of Andreas Reckwitz, we show how in ideal-typical form practice theory differs from cultural theories that foreground either the mind and beliefs or discourses and structures of meaning. This moreover grants us a map for understanding how IPT relates to other theoretical developments in IR, such as constructivism, a discussion that we take up in the following section. Overall, we gain a clear picture of how IPT is related to, and differs from, other attempts to theorise international relations.

2.2 Practice Theory and Social Theory

For Andreas Reckwitz, practice theories represent a "family" of theory. Using this metaphor, he points to Wittgenstein's concept of family resemblance, defining similarities through relations. To better outline this family, Reckwitz mapped out the social theoretical landscape.

The table below presents the core distinctions and categories of this map. Reckwitz (2002, 2004a) firstly argues that social theory can be categorised according to three ideal types (Reckwitz 2002: 245–246): rationalism, norm-orientation, and cultural theory. Secondly, he suggests that practice theory falls in the realm of cultural theory, and therein can be differentiated from what he calls mentalism and textualism. The intention of this mapping is to provide orientation to better navigate the jungle of social theories, and therein position practice theory.

As summarised in Table 2.1, Reckwitz (2002, 2004a) suggests that three different types of theorising prevail in social theory, each of which suggest different central elements of meaning and develop quite distinct explanations for behaviour. Rationalist theories are based on methodological individualism, taking the individual as the most basic unit. These individuals are conceived of as acting in accordance with their own self-interest, guided by subjective forms of rationality and cost-benefit calculations. Given the focus on calculations, this actor type has been described as *homo oeconomicus*. From the perspective of rationalism, the world of *homo oeconomicus* is mainly composed of individual actions (Reckwitz 2002: 245); actors are driven by interests and the individual beliefs by which these interests become formulated.

Norm-oriented theories, Reckwitz's second category, place more importance on social relations. For such theories, the social primarily consists of normative rules. These rules designate what kind of action is possible at all; that is, they allow actors to identify what behaviour is allowed or prohibited,

Table 2.1 Map of the social theory landscape

	Central elements of meaning	*Behaviour as an explanatory problem*
Rationalism	Interests and beliefs	Individual actions
Homo oeconomicus		
Norm-oriented theories	Normative order	Intersubjective coordination of action
Homo sociologicus		
Culturalist theories	Collective orders of knowledge	Repetitive patterns of action
Mentalism	Cognition, mind	
Textualism	Discourse, structures of meaning, symbol systems	
Practice theory	Practices	

Adopted and revised from Reckwitz (2004a: 318)

legitimate or illegitimate, and worthwhile or worthless (Reckwitz 2002: 245). Actors consent to a normative order that consists of these rules; consequently, this actor type has been described as *homo sociologicus*. Norm-oriented theories tend to understand the social world by focusing on the intersubjective coordination of potentially contradicting actions of diverse actors. How can a constant clash of opposing interests be avoided? Norm-oriented theories answer this question by pointing to the creation and acceptance of normative expectations and roles. Such theories then add another dimension; the world is comprised of more than individuals and their rationalities.

Reckwitz's third and final category of culturalist theorising makes a similar move in that it foregrounds the importance of collectivity. There is a fundamental difference, however. *Homo oeconomicus* and *homo sociologicus* both dismiss "the implicit, tacit or unconscious layer of knowledge which enables a symbolic organisation of reality" (Reckwitz 2002: 246). Culturalist theorising adds an additional layer that is concerned with the driving forces behind actors' conception of how the world is ordered, and what enables them to act to begin with. The ability to understand that the world is ordered assumes that there is an established set of symbolic and meaningful rules in the form of culture; as such, culture is the domain that gives meaning to actions and objects, and provides the means with which to make sense of them (Reckwitz 2002: 246).

Culturalist theorising addresses questions of underlying social order that often go unnoticed in the two other types: Rationalist perspectives tend to gloss over broader questions of social order by reducing them to an issue of unequal distribution of resources and tend not to address collective patterns of action. Through a focus on shared norms, norm-based theorising is better situated to understand the complexity of collective actions and ensuing change. The assumption is that actors are driven by norms, and the focus then turns towards examining how and why a certain social order came to be. Such theories, however, often fail to offer explanations of how these norms appear and are established.

Culturalist theorising differs on this point: the core idea is that the patterns that structure action in the world are the result of common orders of meanings, cues, symbols, and knowledge that function as rules for action. Culturalist theories therefore aim at studying repetitive patterns of actions by understanding collective orders of meaning and how reality becomes organised by symbols and knowledge (Reckwitz 2002: 246–247).

Reckwitz maps out three directions that culturalist theorising can take, distinguishing between mentalism, textualism and theories of practice. If these strands of culturalist theorising agree on the importance of a focus on shared orders of knowledge, they diverge on where this knowledge is situated. In mentalism, shared orders of knowledge are conceptualised as being processed in the human mind, while culture is conceived of as a cognitive phenomenon residing therein (Reckwitz 2002: 247). The main objects of analysis are shared cognitive-mental schemes, and these are seen as the smallest unit of analysis. Reckwitz (2002: 247) points to theorists and concepts such as Max Weber and his notion of *Weltbilder* (world images), French structuralism as developed by thinkers such as Claude Lévi-Strauss and Ferdinand de Saussure, and the phenomenology of Edmund Husserl and Alfred Schütz as representative of such an understanding.

Textualists go in the opposite direction. Instead of looking inside the mind, they focus on the 'outside' and attempt to identify culture in discourses, structures of meaning, texts or communication (Reckwitz 2002: 248). Reckwitz here refers to a tradition comprised of poststructuralism, constructivist system theory, radical hermeneutics, or semiotics as conceptualised by theorists such as Clifford Geertz, Michel Foucault, Jacques Derrida, Niklas Luhmann, Paul Ricœur and Roland Barthes. Despite considerable conceptual differences, these culturalist theorists emphasise extra-subjective structures of meaning, attempting to understand collective knowledge through shared social procedures and cultural codes. For Reckwitz, Geertz's *The Interpretation of Cultures* or Foucault's *Archeology of Knowledge* are prime examples of such work.

Reckwitz then situates practice theory by contrasting it with these two ideal types. For practice theorists, it is in practice that one needs to identify collective knowledge. The notion of practice meshes the inside and the outside; collective knowledge resides in the mind (since humans transmit practices) and in texts and structures of meaning (since practices result in some form of patterns of action and extra-subjective structures). Practice theorists assume that shared knowledge is practical knowledge; there is consequently a strong focus on situations of day-to-day life. In such situations, individuals perform common practices and thereby establish and (re-)produce orders. Any assumed incentives underlying actions are of less concern for practice theorists; rather, the analytical focus shifts to concrete activities and enacted performances, and the situations are much more important than the actors themselves.

Reckwitz (2002: 249) defines practice as "a routinised type of behaviour which consists of several elements, interconnected to one another: forms of bodily activities, forms of mental activities, 'things' and their use, a background knowledge in the form of understanding, know-how, states of emotion and motivational knowledge". The interconnectivity of all of these elements in action defines a practice, which cannot be reduced to any single one of them.

Activities and everyday situations are core categories for practice theorists. For practice theorists, mentalist and textualist accounts over-complicate and over-intellectualise the world, since they underplay the importance of everyday action. Too much importance is placed on complex abstract structures, and the ability of any actor to criticise and competently evaluate the social world is largely dismissed.

2.3 Practice and the Discipline of International Relations

The Reckwitzian map provides a useful tool for situating practice theories in the social theory landscape. It is worth keeping in mind that, like any other map, the Reckwitzian one operates to a defined scale. It gives us the broad picture, but glosses over many details and differences. Moreover, it also faces the difficulty that the terrain it seeks to represent is shifting, as social theory constantly evolves through movements, mutations and the birth of new theoretical schools. Keeping these caveats in mind, the social theory map also helps if we zoom in on international theory and try to situate the emergence of IPT within it.

If we operate on similar level of abstraction, IR has also seen a diversification in rationalist, norm-oriented and culturalist theories. That much of international theory of the past decade either relies on the model of *homo economicus* and the logic of consequences or *homo sociologicus* and its logic of appropriateness has been frequently noted (e.g. Fearon and Wendt 2002). Though proposed as a label in the 1990s by Yosef Lapid and Friedrich Kratochwil (1996), cultural theory is a less-familiar denominator in international relations. The discipline of IR prefers the descriptors of 'constructivism' or 'critical theory' to describe the forms of theorising that Reckwitz terms as culturalist. In particular, the notion of constructivism is a peculiar IR construct, since it tends to grasp norm-oriented theories as well as culturalist theorising, particularly in the North American context.

This heterogeneity within constructivism has frequently been diagnosed.[2] As Guzzini (2000: 148) argued, "the sheer diversity seems to make the category of constructivism explode". Indeed, one of the faultlines within constructivist research is whether these centre on 'norms' and rely on the logic of appropriateness (Sending 2002).

Many descriptions of critical theory nevertheless come close to Reckwitz's outline. In an early description, Richard Ashley provided such an understanding, arguing that

> approaches meriting the label 'critical' stress the community-shared background understandings, skills, and practical predispositions without which it would be impossible to interpret action, assign meaning, legitimate practices, empower agents, and constitute a differentiated, highly structured social reality. (Ashley 1987: 403)

Putting aside labelling issues, the Reckwitzian map of mentalism, textualism, and practice theory usefully captures current international theory. We find expressions of the mentalist stream in IR, for instance, in early cognitive-psychological works or constructivist research on 'ideas' (although much of this research is inconsistent in so far as it remains committed to a positivist epistemology, Laffey and Weldes 1997).

Moreover, studies operating with concepts such as 'belief systems', 'world views', 'operational codes', or 'frames' rely on mentalist reasoning. They focus on mental 'sense-making' events as the object of analysis and explore, for instance, the impact of past experiences on future action. Although based on individuals' cognitive acts of interpretation, such studies adopt a mentalism perspective, focusing on the shared knowledge and meaning structures that coexist in a group's mind. However, they distance themselves from the rational actor models of methodological individualism (Goldstein and Keohane 1993: 7). Studies analyse the shared effects that 'experience' has on political actors in collective decision making, for example (Hafner-Burton et al. 2013), or draw on cognitive psychology to explain the link between personality profile and leadership style of world leaders (Steinberg 2005) or the mental schemas of terrorists (Crenshaw 2000).

Textualism has had an enduring effect on international theory, notably in European and Canadian IR. Introduced in the late 1980s by the "dissidents in international thought" movement (Ashley and Walker 1990), expressions of textualism have become well anchored in the discipline. We find them under labels such as 'post-structuralism', 'discourse theory', or 'discourse analysis'. In the aftermath of the so-called 'third debate' (Lapid 1989), the study of textual structures became particularly influential in foreign policy, European integration, and critical security studies. A range of seminal contributions draws on discourse analysis to study textual structures as preconditions for the actions of diplomats, regional cooperation, transnational identity, the identification of threats, or the development of security strategies.[3] If authors rely on different theorists – including Derrida or Foucault – their studies share the same objective: to understand world political phenomena by investigating extra-subjective structures of meaning through which agents achieve the capability to act. They show, for instance, that shared knowledge establishes authority, and that textual genres render distinct forms of knowledge acceptable (Hansen 2006: 7). Thus, language is "a site of inclusion and exclusion" and creates a "space for producing and denouncing specific subjectivities within the political realm" (Herschinger 2011: 13).

International relations theories develop their own disciplinary understandings of the Reckwitzian categories; the framework nevertheless allows us to capture the major lines in the field. This becomes clear if we consider how practice theory was introduced to IR theory.

A reconstruction of the development of the concept of practices in international relations is provided by Bueger and Drieschova (2017). As they show, the concept of practice has substantially influenced several discussions in IR; these constitute, to some degree, predecessors of practice theory, as well as productive connections to the larger discipline. A broad set of scholars labelled as constructivists are included in this overview, starting from those who relied on pragmatist thinking in IR, including the work of Karl Deutsch, Ernst Hass, and John Ruggie, relying on assertions concerning knowledge and action similar to practice theory. The influence of Wittgenstein on the discipline, as represented by the work of Friedrich Kratochwil and Nicholas Onuf on practical knowledge and speech acts, the introduction of the sociology of Anthony Giddens and its idea of practices as mediator of structure and agency by Alexander Wendt, as well as the neo-institutionalism of James March and JP Olson, Michael Barnett and Martha Finnemore, which understands institutions as settled practices, all are examples of constructivist scholarship in IR that worked with concepts of practice. According to the same study, the concept of practice was also significant in the feminist and post-structuralist debate, starting in the late 1980s. Indeed, an article from 1988 is credited as the first study that explicitly gave the concept of practices centre stage. Published in *International Studies Quarterly*, Michael J. Shapiro et al. (1988) developed the concept of "discursive practices" to emphasise the contingency of structures of meaning (discourse) and their reliance on enactments.

When Neumann (2002) introduced practice theory, he did so by contrasting it with textualism, arguing that studies of discourse remain too focused on structures of meaning and overemphasise language at the price of the material conditions. He thereby emphasised the continuities of practice theory with earlier discussions. Rather than contrasting practice theory with textualist accounts, Pouliot (2008) demonstrated the advantages of practices in contrast to constructivist approaches, in particular by exploring the differences with a logic of appropriateness.

The Reckwitzian map gives a sense of orientation. It allows for understanding practice theory by a strategy of 'othering'. Such a 'negative' strategy runs the risk of underplaying the commonalities between culturalist theorising and neglecting the many links that exist between *de facto* expressions of mentalism, textualism, and practice theory, however. This is notably the case for differing variants of post-structuralism that emphasise practice (e.g. Wodak 2011).

Carving out intellectual space through othering is a helpful, but also dangerous tool. We therefore also require a positive approximation of practice theory. This can be done by identifying the commitments that practice scholars rely on. In the next section, we outline these commitments, summarising them under the concepts of process, knowledge, learning, materiality, multiplicity, performativity and empiricity. The differing ways in which these commitments may be interpreted is then shown in the succeeding chapters, which outline the core approaches of IPT and the ways that these concepts present challenges to be addressed in empirical work.

2.4 The Commitments of International Practice Theory

The map primarily gives us an understanding of practice theory by distinguishing it from other perspectives. This is to provide orientation, but, as already discussed, such distinctions should not be exaggerated. Another strategy for better understanding what practice theories are and what they aim to do is to develop an outline of their core ideas. We attempt this below, arguing that practice theories share a number of core commitments to certain themes, rather than assumptions. Again, this outline needs to be taken with a grain of salt; as we will see in the following chapters, practice theorists share these commitments, but tend to prioritise and interpret them quite differently. In our view, there are seven core commitments that describe the idea of practice theory quite comprehensively: emphasis of process, practical knowledge, collectivity, materiality, multiplicity, performativity and empiricity.

Understanding practice theory as being composed by a number of core commitments provides a restrictive definition, limiting our understanding of what it should encompass to a narrower range than that suggested by Adler and Pouliot. Put another way, not everyone who studies practices is a practice theorist. That said, the approach is broader than what is conventionally understood in IR; most notably, different variations of pragmatist theorising are included. In adopting the notion of commitments, our claim is not to have found a definite core that every variant of practice theory or every practice theorist shares or 'believes'. Rather, we argue that conducting practice-theoretical analysis involves engaging with a number of themes and concerns. The commitments concern what one can achieve with a practice-theoretical approach and clarify the reasons for centring analysis on the unit of practice. Questions such as what a practice is remain open to continual interpretation and reconstruction in the conduct of actual practices of research, however (Kratochwil 2011: 37–43).

Firstly, practice theories emphasise process over stasis, foregrounding the procedural dimension of practice, and positing that any process requires activity. Practice theorists therefore prefer verbs such as 'ordering', 'structuring', and 'knowing' over the respective (static) nouns of 'order', 'structure', or 'knowledge'. With such a "prioritisation of process over substance, relation over separateness, and activity over passivity" (Guillaume 2007: 742), practice theories interpret the international through relational ontologies (Jackson and Nexon 1999). Scholars thereby bypass essentialist and static notions of the international and sideline distinctions that emphasise them, such as the one between agency and structure. Practices in this sense have no substance, but must be thought of as emergent.

Secondly, practice theories offer a distinct perspective on knowledge. They situate knowledge in practice and thereby develop a unified account of knowing and doing (Friedrichs and Kratochwil 2009). Connecting 'practice', 'acting', and 'knowing', implies understanding knowledge as "knowing from within" (Shotter 1993: 7). Such a conception of knowledge extends beyond conventional understandings of 'knowing that' and 'knowing how'. Practices cannot be reduced to background knowledge, however. While knowledge, its application, and creation cannot be separated from action, "it would be wrong to see the concept of practice as merely a synonym for action" (Hajer and Wagenaar 2003b: 20). In practice, the actor, his beliefs and values, resources, and external environment are integrated "in one 'activity system', in which social, individual and material aspects are interdependent" (Hajer and Wagenaar 2003b: 20). As a result, knowledge cannot be essentialised, but is instead a spatiotemporally situated phenomenon.

Thirdly, practice theories consider knowing and the acquisition of knowledge by learning as inherently collective processes. Members of a distinct group (for example, medical professionals, football players, or children in a nursery) learn and internalise practices as 'rules of the game' primarily through interaction. Practices as "repeated interactional patterns" achieve temporary stability because "the need to engage one another forces people to return to common structures" (Swidler 2001: 85). In the medical sphere, for instance, formal rules and algorithms provide guidelines in medical operations to guarantee standard practices. These prevent doctors from having to make every decision anew in complicated situations. However, performing a practice does not necessarily presuppose an interactional dimension. Human collectiveness is not a general criterion for the sociality of practices. Practices can also involve an "interobjective structure", for example, when actors learn a practice through interaction with a machine or computer without necessarily communicating with other people (Reckwitz 2010: 117).

Fourthly, practice theorists contend that practices have materiality; bodies are the main carrier of practices, but are not the only one: material artefacts or technologies can also fulfil this function. The materiality and embodiment of the world is an aspect that tends to be sidelined in other social and culturalist theorising, whereas for practice theorists, the world is "continually doing things, things that bear upon us not as observation statements upon disembodied intellects but as forces upon material beings" (Pickering 1995: 6). To stress the impact of objects, things, and artefacts on social life is not to merely add the element of materiality, it is an attempt to give non-humans a more precise role in the ontologies of the world.

Fifthly, social order is understood as multiplicity: instead of assuming universal or global wholes, the assumption is that there are always multiple and overlapping orders (Schatzki 2002: 87). There is never a single reality, but always multiple ones. This does not imply chaos, limitless plurality, or an atomised understanding of order; orderliness is, however, an achievement. It requires work, and emerges from routines and repetitiveness in "situated accomplishments" of actors (Lynch 2001: 131). As such, order is always shifting and emergent; the assumption is that actors are reflexive and establish social orders through mutual accounts. Thus, the permanent (re-)production of 'accountability' is preserved through ongoing practical accomplishments. Practices therefore have a dual role, both creating order through accountability, and serving to alter the 'structure' by the innovativeness of reflexive agents.

Sixthly, practice theories embrace a performative understanding of the world; the world depends on practice. This 'world of becoming' is the product of ongoing establishment, re-enactment, and maintenance of relations between actors, objects, and material artefacts. The concept of enactment turns the focus away from the idea that objects or structures have assumed a fixed, stable identity and that closure is achieved at some point. Enactment stresses the genuine openness of any construction process. Construction is never complete; objects, structures, or norms, therefore, exist primarily in practice. They are real because they are part of practices, and are enacted in them. Such a performative understanding avoids attempting "to tame" practice and to "control its unruliness and instability," as Doty (1997: 376) noted early on. In practice theory, "[...] practice must entail an acceptance of its indeterminacy. It must entail a decentering of practice" (Doty 1997: 376). This also clarifies that practice is not a substance; it is continuously emergent and dependent on performances.

Seventhly, practice theorists give primacy to the empirical, and call for a readjustment of the relation between theory and practice. Practice theory is best understood as a methodological orientation in which concepts provide starting points, allow one to problematise, and ask empirical questions. Praxiography – the methodology corresponding to practice theory – is akin to ethnography since it takes the observation of practices as its primary basis. Research, and, in particular, writing is seen as performative rather than descriptive. One is producing the phenomenon one is talking about.

These seven commitments stress that undertaking practice theoretical analysis implies engaging with a range of core themes and concerns. Laying out these commitments gives us a sense of how practice theory coheres and defines its limits. Our intention is not, however, to 'police' what practice theory is and what it is not. Considering these commitments nevertheless clarifies some of the boundaries.

Ringmar's (2014) general attack on the promises of practice theory, for instance, targets two studies. He criticises Abrahamsen and Williams' work (2011) as being nothing more than rational choice theory (Ringmar 2014: 10). Abrahamsen and Williams do indeed combine different approaches and do not follow Bourdieu dogmatically, but it is through this comprehensive practice-oriented approach that they successfully explain the growth of private security in globalisation as a complex relational phenomenon, thus overcoming the dualism of local and global. The study therefore relies on the outlined commitments. We agree, however, with Ringmar's (2014: 13) criticism of Patrick Morgan's study on practices of deterrence (Morgan 2011) that offers a "reconstruction of the intentions and aims of actors involved." Morgan's argumentation is rooted in methodological individualism and strategic action that has little in common with the concerns of practice theory.

The commitments outlined provide general criteria to bring coherence to international practice theory. As discussed in the next section, one should not read them as 'shared assumptions and beliefs'; practice-driven approaches draw on the commitments and develop them in different ways.

2.5 Introducing Key Approaches

In the following two chapters, we introduce a range of approaches to IPT. Our discussion shows that the outlined commitments may be interpreted differently. By the notion of approach, we do not want to argue that these are consistent 'theories' of practice; instead, they provide dedicated ways of dealing with practices, through the outline of a conceptual vocabulary and by providing strategies for research. Although a range of these approaches gravitate towards the body of work of an individual author, such as Pierre Bourdieu or Michel Foucault, being approaches for the study of practice, they are better understood as clusters of research and collectives of researchers concerned with a similar set of concepts and strategies. Phrased otherwise, in outlining the approaches, our concern is not with the exegesis of an author's work, but with discussing the purposes for which certain concepts and strategies have been developed, and how they have been translated to and advanced in light of international practices.

We offer a concise introduction to core approaches of IPT, and discuss their origins and use in IR. We discuss seven approaches: (1) the praxeology of Pierre Bourdieu, (2) the understanding of practice of Michel Foucault, (3) the communities of practice approach, (4) the practice ontology of Theodore Schatzki, (5) the narrative approach, (6) actor-network theory, and (7) the pragmatic sociology inspired by the work of Luc Boltanski. We do not want to limit practice theory to these approaches, but rather take these as a selection. Nevertheless, they are the ones that have been thriving in IR; their productivity has been proven and they show great promise in providing further insights on world politics. Together they showcase the spectrum and diversity of IPT scholarship.

We document how each approach introduces practice theoretical concerns and uses the concept of practice, and familiarise ourselves with their main principles and guidelines, drawing on examples of empirical research. Defining the contours of IPT is an ongoing controversy; we therefore intend to reflect on the advantages and drawbacks attributed to each perspective, providing us with a valuable picture of the broad repertoire of IPT approaches and their strengths and weaknesses. Table 2.2 provides an overview of the core concepts, relevant IR studies and the main weaknesses of each approach.

Table 2.2 Overview of main approaches in IPT

	Core concepts	*Exemplary IPT studies*	*Main weaknesses*
Bourdieusian praxeology	field, habitus, capital, doxa	Adler-Nissen (2013a, 2014); Berling (2012); Guzzini (2000); Guilhot (2005); Pouliot (2010a, b); Kuus (2015); Leander (2005); Abrahamsen and Williams (2011)	Overemphasis of the regularity of practice; Too strong focus on domination and reproduction of hierarchies; Lack of attention to agency and change; Downplays materiality.
Foucault's practice theory	governmentality, problematisation, apparatus, discursive practices	Sending and Neumann (2006); Merlingen (2006); Löwenheim (2008)	Focus on large scale formations; tends towards linguistic and discursive practices Overly concerned with power
Communities of practice	community, learning, mutual engagement, joint enterprise, repertoires	Adler (2005, 2008); Adler and Greve (2009); Bicchi (2011); Bueger (2013b); Hofius (2016); Graeger (2016)	Unclear if concept of community can be adopted to large scale; Silences questions of power and hierarchies; Idealizes collectives and overemphasizes social cohesion through "community metaphor".

(*continued*)

Table 2.2 (continued)

	Core concepts	*Exemplary IPT studies*	*Main weaknesses*
Schatzki's ontology of practice	teleo-affective structures; organisation; bundles and meshes; material arrangements; human agency	Navari (2010), Bially Mattern (2011):	Strong focus on ontology; Tends to turn practice into a substance; Difficult translation into empirical research.
Narrative approaches	narration, storytelling, plots, polyphony, metaphors, myths	Buckley-Zistel (2014); Devetak (2009); Neumann (2002, 2005); Gadinger et al. (2014b); Jarvis and Holland (2014)	Overemphasizes linguistic dimension; Risks introducing a new dualism between practice and narrative; Concept of 'narration' remains fuzzy.
Actor-network theory	actants, relations, translation, blackbox, passage points, laboratory, non-humans	Bueger and Bethke (2014); Mayer (2012), Schouten (2014); Walters (2002);	Lack of attention to history and social stability over time; Style of analysis raises questions of intelligibility; Anti-humanist stance raises ethical concerns.
Pragmatic sociology	controversies, situations, uncertainty, justification, critique, Orders of Worth,	Borghi (2011); Gadinger (2016); Gadinger and Yildiz (2012); Hanrieder (2016); Niemann (2015); Eagleton-Pierce (2014); Scheper (2015)	Overemphasizes the importance of justice and morality; Lack of attention for other practices than justification and critique.

Notes

1. As exemplarily argued by Nicholas Onuf (2015): "I have some reservations about the metaphor 'turn.' Do we imagine IR as a colossal ship that turns, however slowly, all of a piece? I've already used the ship metaphor, but in this context it's not appropriate – we're not that put together, and, besides, no one is steering (not even those legendary gate-keepers). Or a herd of wildebeests, in which all the members of the herd turn together by keying off each other once one senses danger and turns? I don't think so, even if we do sometimes see signs of a herd mentality."
2. See Guzzini (2000), Kratochwil (2000), Onuf (2002), as well as the more recent reconstruction by Kessler (2016).
3. See among others the contributions in Ashley and Walker (1990), Walker (1993), or Hansen (2006).

CHAPTER 3

Approaches in International Practice Theory I

In this chapter, we introduce four approaches that all have their origins in the work of a major intellectual figure in practice theory: Pierre Bourdieu, Michel Foucault, Etienne Wenger, and Theodore Schatzki. As already emphasised, our goal is not exegesis or a close reading of the respective body of literature, but a concise introduction to the conceptual vocabulary and strategies for the study of practice outlined in the discussion of the work. In leaving the question of interpretation of these authors to others, our objective is pragmatic and directed towards identifying meaningful ways of studying practices and their advantages and disadvantages.

3.1 The Praxeology of Pierre Bourdieu

Pierre Bourdieu is one of the most important theorists in the development of practice theory. His *praxeology* holds a prominent place, particularly because of the significance of his *Outline of a Theory of Practice* (Bourdieu 1977) and the tradition he established in French sociology. His thinking also occupies a central place in IPT. Indeed, until recently, IPT was virtually equated with Bourdieu's work. The attraction of Bourdieu lies not least in the fact that his approach comes closest to a coherent research programme for IPT. Moreover, the praxeological conceptual apparatus seems relatively easily adaptable to IR research. The key concepts of habitus, field and capital seemingly correspond to IR categories such as strategy, conflicts and culture (Adler-Nissen 2013a). Moreover, as Vincent

C. Bueger, F. Gadinger, *International Practice Theory*,
https://doi.org/10.1007/978-3-319-73350-0_3

Pouliot and Frédéric Mérand (2013: 36) suggest, "Bourdieu's thought is at its core a theory of domination". This makes his practice approach compatible with a discipline traditionally concerned with power relations, conflicts and hierarchical structures.

For Rebecca Adler-Nissen (2013b: 2), Bourdieu questions theoretical assumptions in IR by dissolving the agency-structure problem, offering an epistemological position between objective and interpretive research traditions, whilst dissecting the static notion of the state. By drawing on Bourdieu's key concepts, "it is possible to map political units as spaces of practical knowledge on which diverse and often 'unconventional' agencies position themselves and therefore shape international politics" (Adler-Nissen 2013b: 2). Didier Bigo and Mikael R. Madsen (2011: 220) argue along similar lines when they suggest that Bourdieu himself was not particularly interested in international studies, but this does not mean that his sociology and conceptual tools are not applicable outside of France and the discipline of sociology. With regard to global issues, Bourdieu's perspective is particularly useful, not in taking grand notions such as globalisation, internationalisation, or international community for granted or as a premise for research, but "to sociologically reconstruct these categories in light of their particular trajectories and histories" (Bigo and Madsen 2011: 220).

In the following, we firstly discuss a number of core concepts in Bourdieusian vocabulary, before turning towards the question of how they have been employed to study international phenomena. We then engage in a discussion of the advantages and disadvantages of the approach.

Bourdieu's conceptual apparatus is a complex one. It is comprised of a series of interrelated terms, of which 'habitus', 'field', 'capital' and 'doxa' are the most important. His main intention in developing this framework was for Bourdieu to overcome what he saw as the weaknesses of the subjectivist explanations committed to a methodological individualism, as well as notions of objectivism as identifiable in textualist accounts. The aim is to construct a dynamic vocabulary that enables an analysis of the emergence and reproduction of practice.

The concepts of habitus and field are the main pillars upon which Bourdieu's framework rests. Habitus is a concept that acts as the "work horse in his theory" (Berard 2005: 203). The concept refers to the intermediary element between agents and structures. It seeks to grasp the practical knowledge inscribed in individuals. For Bourdieu (1977: 82–83), the habitus is a "system of lasting, transposable dispositions which, integrating past experiences, functions at every moment as a matrix of perceptions, appreciations, and actions". Pouliot (2008: 273–274) eloquently summarises habitus in arguing that it has four dimensions: firstly, habitus is to be understood historically, and is marked by individual and collective trajectories; secondly, it relies on the internalisation of practical, tacit knowledge learned by doing, that is, from direct experience in and with the world; thirdly, habitus is a relational term, that is, collective dispositions are gathered through embodied traces of inter-subjective interactions; and fourthly, habitus is dispositional in the sense that it does not determine actions mechanically, but rather initiates distinct courses of action. The function of the habitus in social life, then, can be understood as a practical sense that gives actors implicit rules on how to behave in a specific situation in relation to their social position. A habitus is formed through similar conditions of socialisation in a distinct group or class, from childhood on.

The habitus is further strengthened by bodily habituation, which leads actors to refrain from questioning their social position, since it appears legitimate and self-evident. Bourdieu refers to this (1977: 164) as ***doxa*** or ***doxic practice***. The term doxa is closely related to the logic of habit (Hopf 2010: 545) and captures common-sense knowledge in contrast to true knowledge. Bourdieu took this opposition, as Anna Leander (2011: 304) argues, and endowed it with the implication that to gain true knowledge about the social world, it is necessary to understand the doxa, the common-sense understandings that underpin it. The "doxa is so central to the production of social hierarchies, politics and power precisely because it is common sense – and hence unquestioned/mis-recognised" (Leander 2011: 304). Habitus is primarily used as a concept to explain tendencies of social reproduction; for instance, when forms of practices are exceptionally stable or constant in certain milieus or classes despite obvious difficulties such as inequality or inefficiency.

The habitus provides a basis for the generation of practices, but it does so only in relation to a specific situation or a distinct ***field***. This leads to Bourdieu's second key term. A field is basically a social configuration structured along relations of power, objects of struggle and taken-for-granted rules (Pouliot 2008: 274). Fields such as art, politics or economics are characterised as hierarchical systems of positions in which some agents are dominant, and others are dominated. These unequal positions are defined through different forms of ***capital***, a term with which Bourdieu aimed to encapsulate power resources. Capital, therefore, includes material possessions and non-material sources of value such as prestige or authority that are converted into four different forms: economic, cultural, social and symbolic capital. The latter is, in fact, the main basis of domination, in that it carries with it the power of legitimation and the capacity to define what counts as common sense (Nicolini 2013: 59).

A field can be compared to a common social game in which distinct rules are learned as well as applied. In this game, agents attempt to establish or improve their position by maximising the accumulation of capital (Bourdieu and Wacquant 1996: 168–175). Being a successful player in a game requires one to generate a practical sense or a 'feeling for the game'. This sense is, in turn, dependent upon the relative strength of forms of capital of the agents and the dispositions of the habitus. The competence of practical sense is apportioned differently among the players, which leads to hierarchies and unequal preconditions to succeed in gaining profits. The tacit practical knowledge leads back to the doxa and the seemingly self-evident rules that regulate the legitimate or illegitimate character of practices. The games played in fields are significantly shaped by conflict and struggle through competition. With these concepts, Bourdieu develops a complex theoretical system, and it is important not to isolate the concepts from each other. Recognising the relationships between the concepts is important; that is, the relations between incorporated sociality and embodied history (habitus), current practices, and objectified sociality in systems of position (field).

The terms habitus, field, capital and doxa provide a productive relational framework for studying international practices. The advantage of the term 'field' is that actors are not studied in isolation, but through their practical relations to each other. Fields enable a distinct space of action for actors; while the field incorporates the objective component of a distinct hierarchical sphere such as art, economics or even European security, the habitus focuses on the experiences and strategies of individuals seeking to establish or achieve an advantageous position within it. The habitus is the origin of the practices that reproduce or change the existing structures of the field. These practices again shape the experiences of actors, form their habitus and stabilise power structures in the field. In this sense, Bourdieu succeeds with his relational framework by overcoming subjectivist and objectivist explanations of social life. His emphasis on critical reflexivity when doing research "helps IR researchers move away from the self-legitimising and descriptive accounts of international institutions and organisations, to a more sociologically informed analysis" (Adler-Nissen 2013b: 11). Such a notion of reflexivity also turns the production of scientific knowledge, including in IR, into an object of analysis (Berling 2011).

Bourdieu has been influential in IR since the late 1980s. Early on, authors such as Richard Ashley (1987) and Stefano Guzzini (2000) pointed to the contribution of Bourdieu's theory of fields in understanding transnational spaces. Bourdieu's terminology became increasingly used in IR in this way, with a range of transnational fields being studied. European security relations were described in critical security studies as a transnational field of (in)security experts by scholars such as Didier Bigo (2005), Jef Huysmans (2006), and Trine Villumsen Berling (2012). Such a view on European 'insecurity professionals' as an emerging field may explain, for instance, the high degree of hegemony over European security knowledge (Bigo 2002: 64).

Nicolas Guilhot (2005) proposed understanding the career of practices of democracy promotion through a "transnational field of democracy promotion". Migration as a transnational phenomenon can be also analysed by Bourdieu's field theory to describe the ambiguous role of migrants between their home and new state (Levitt and Schiller 2004). Pouliot (2008) suggested understanding the transatlantic security community as a field constituted by shared practices of regulating conflicts by diplomatic and non-violent practices. Leander (2005) relied on the field concept to interpret the emergence of private military companies, meanwhile.

Rita Abrahamsen and Michael C. Williams (2011) draw on the concept of field to describe privatisation in global security. They explain the emergence of the transnational commercial security sector as "a complex re-articulation of relations between public and private, global and local security actors, where the categories of public and private, global and local continue to have effects on security practices even as they are being transformed" (Abrahamsen and Williams 2011: 311). By using Bourdieu's forms of capital as resources of power, they demonstrate that the growth of private security is closely related to its increasing acquisition of forms of capital that provide private actors with new possibilities to play powerful roles in the security field. To be accepted as a key player in the field, it is not sufficient to acquire economic capacity alone. Instead, as Abrahamsen and Williams (2011: 315) argue, the acquisition of cultural and symbolic capital is "at the core of the increasingly recognised competence of private security actors, a status itself connected to wider social practices involving the commodification and technification of security" that has become accepted as a service or a commodity to be bought and sold in a competitive market place.

While the notion of the field provides a good methodological entry point for Bourdieu-based research in IR, the concept makes sense only in relation to habitus, capital or doxa. In Pouliot's (2010a, b) study of

NATO-Russia diplomacy, for instance, the notion of field is a starting point for describing an emerging political sphere in which new diplomatic practices are negotiated and established. Based on dozens of interviews and historical text analysis, he demonstrates that diplomacy has become a normal, though not self-evident, practice between the two former enemies. Accordingly, some situations such as the intervention in Kosovo, Ukraine's Orange Revolution or the Russia-Georgia conflict were resolved. During the height of the Cold War, such incidents would have typically led to serious crises. However, the concept of habitus is essential here as a driving force to explain this dynamic, but still fragile relationship of 'limited pacification', which is the result of ongoing symbolic power struggles. NATO's practices of double enlargement have contributed to the resurgence of Russia's Great Power habitus and the growing creation of hysteresis in the international security game, as well as its role description as a player. This habitus of Russia hinders the development of a common security community when, for instance, "Russian practitioners take for granted that as a Great Power they ought not to adopt others' procedures without a minimal amount of negotiation and compromise" (Pouliot 2010a, b: 235).

The changing field of European security is another major case illustrating the adoption of Bourdieu's framework in IR. Studies by Berling (2012) and Adler-Nissen (2014) have shown how revealing such an analysis can be. Berling draws on Bourdieusian concepts to explain profound and unexpected transformations in European security by understanding them as symbolic power struggles of security agents over legitimate definitions of security. Her concept of "doxic battles" points to the mobilisation of different forms of capital by security agents during the profound change in taken-for-granted assumptions (doxa) (Berling 2012: 471). While the European security field during the Cold War was structured by a belief that threats could be measured materially and ideologically, and that the 'nature' of the international system caused war to be a recurring phenomenon, these deep, doxic structures of European security were challenged by social science think tanks and academic experts. A number of European think tanks made strategic moves in arguing in favour of the centrality of the EU as opposed to NATO to overcome traditional strategic thinking centred on military capabilities. The European way was described as more productive in the long term, in contrast to the short-term military orientation of NATO. These newcomers acquired new forms of scientific and cultural capital, were accepted as legitimate speakers in the field, and succeeded in shifting the hierarchy of the European security field that had traditionally been structured by military capital and scientific capital based in realist IR conceptions (Berling 2012: 467f.).

In short, Berling's Bourdieu-based 'action framework' suggests understanding the European security field as a power struggle between agents seeking to reshape the definition of security. It also questions the distinction of theory and practice. Accordingly, "social scientific knowledge was recast as a type of capital in the hands of agents and social science agents entered the struggles as agents in the European security field" (Berling 2012: 473).

Struggles over symbolic power can also be observed in related fields, such as European diplomacy. Adler-Nissen (2014) shows that national diplomacy is challenged by the rise of non-state actors, from transnational companies to non-governmental organisations that struggle for dominant positions in the field. The EU's new diplomatic service (the European External Action Service), one of the most important foreign policy innovations in Europe to date, does not, on the one hand, challenge national diplomacy in a material sense. On the other hand, it symbolically questions the state's meta-capital and monopolistic position of symbolic power when defining, for instance, the "genuine diplomat" (Adler-Nissen 2014: 671).

Following this argument, Merje Kuus (2015) analyses symbolic power in diplomatic practice in Brussels by focusing on the intangible and incalculable 'feel for the game' that distinguishes a well-informed and relaxed insider from an ill-informed and ill-at-ease outsider in European Union diplomatic circles. Kuus identifies different features of diplomatic practices, centring on notions of reputation, presence, poise, composure, and elegance. Through interviews with several diplomats, it becomes clear that the acquisition of this practical knowledge does not depend only on elite education and other easily trainable skills. Rather, the "issue is ease; a certain attitude, an intangible and unquantifiable capacity to objectify the objectification of the social gaze" (Kuus 2015: 377). For Kuus (2015: 369), daily cultural practices are not mere icing on the cake, but a constituent component of power relations, in diplomacy as much as anywhere else. Studies such as those by Berling, Adler-Nissen, and Kuus focus on symbolic power struggles to show the limitations of existing approaches, which either overemphasise institutional capacities or oversimplify the structural forces of globalisation and interdependence.

Bourdieu developed his framework by studying religion, art and politics in France. On the surface, it would seem that his work is deeply situated in a local context, and has little to contribute to international politics. Bourdieu's praxeology is an open conceptual framework, however. His field terminology is flexible and avoids setting strict boundaries concerning who or what belongs to the field. A major promise of using the concept of field is the rejection of the opposition between society and individuals by instead providing a relational approach. The research objective focuses on the practices of transnational activities, which avoids simplistic boundaries between domestic and international arenas and explores the historical trajectories of fields of power in the global realm (Bigo 2011). This term can, therefore, as we have shown, be an invaluable device for the analysis of transnational space.

There are, however, several theoretical challenges associated with the term, since it was never fully defined by Bourdieu. These conceptual ambiguities concern, for instance, when shared practices constitute a field, whether there is a hierarchy between fields, and how they relate to each other. It is not clear how many fields there are, or where exactly the boundaries between the fields lie. However, the main proponents of Bourdieu in IR, such as Pouliot, Berling or Adler-Nissen, demonstrate that research on security, identity, community, and sovereignty can benefit from a Bourdieu-based perspective. Such research sheds light on overlooked aspects of international politics, for instance the knowledge practices of experts.

A major strength of Bourdieu's framework, therefore, lies in its ability to dissect symbolic power struggles in politics, which are more complex and subtle than is conventionally acknowledged in IR. As a result, studying power relations by drawing on Bourdieu takes IR research in new directions, as Adler-Nissen and Pouliot (2014) have demonstrated, and contributes to the debate on different faces of power, as initiated by Barnett and Duvall (2005). Pouliot (2016) describes multilateral diplomacy and the governance of international security as the production, reproduction and contestation of local diplomatic hierarchies that practitioners often call 'pecking orders'. Such a perspective is therefore less interested in primarily structural resources of material capabilities, and more in the distinctive forms of social stratification organised around a struggle for diplomatic competence in sets of practices like *esprit de corps* or reporting through brokering.

Ingvild Bode (2017), for instance, complements a Bourdieusian perspective by considering individual agency in a more substantial manner. By following Michel de Certeau, she analyses decision-making processes at the Security Council and examines reflective practices of a strategic or tactical nature. Portraying practices as reflective rather than as being based only on tacit knowledge highlights how actors may creatively adapt their practices to social situations, and furthermore shows that individuals become recognised as competent performers because of their personality, understood as plural socialisation experiences (Bode 2017).

Bode's work is a prime example of the increasingly mutual exchange between Bourdieu's praxeology and French pragmatism. There are some lesser-known Bourdieusian concepts, such as the *nomos*, which describes the underlying normative order structuring a field of interactions (Epstein 2013: 165), that are yet to be employed more fully in IR research, however.

In summary, Bourdieu's praxeology helps IR scholars move towards a theoretically informed empirical sociology. The most promising way could be, as Adler-Nissen (2013b: 13) states using a term of Leander's (2008), to employ Bourdieusian vocabulary as a 'thinking tool' that allows for a certain perspective, but needs to be developed further and adjusted to the needs of situated research contexts. Concepts like the field or habitus can also be accentuated in more dynamic terms of pragmatism (Leander 2011). This implies following Bourdieu's methodological dictum of constructing one's own interpretations in direct interaction with an empirical case (Adler-Nissen 2013b: 13).

This analytical strength, however, can also be turned into a criticism. Due to the explicit focus on domination, power and hierarchies, one could gain the impression that practice is always embedded in power struggles. Indeed, the focus of Bourdieu's vocabulary is on structures of power and domination, and less on the extensive range of other sociocultural practices (Hillebrandt 2009: 389). Another key criticism levelled against Bourdieu is his structural determinism (de Certeau 1984: 57–59). The main target of this criticism is the concept of habitus, which can be understood as a mechanism of reproduction (King 2000). These criticisms are, to some degree, misleading, since Bourdieu's dynamic understanding of habitus conceptualises it as being in a constant state of evolution through changing conditions in fields and forces of adaption (Jackson 2008: 170–171).

Bourdieu (1990: 55) emphasised that actors adopt a particular habitus only with a certain, albeit high, degree of probability, and that this habitus also allows for the possibility of behavioural variation, although in his major works the habitus tends to be constantly confirmed or reproduced (Joas and Knöbl 2009: 393). Nevertheless, it is fair to say that the emphasis of Bourdieu's praxeology is on the stability, regularity and reproduction of practices, and less on subversion and renewal.

For Bourdieu, routinisation and reproduction is the norm in social life (Reckwitz 2004a, b: 46). For instance, Bourdieu's two core praxeological studies – the everyday practices of the Kabyle community (Bourdieu 1977) and the cultural codes of the French bourgeoisie in *Distinction* (Bourdieu 1986) – concentrate mainly on understanding conservative mechanisms of repetition and stability. The fact that in both cases a high tendency of reproduction can be observed does not mean that this is a core feature for a general 'logic of practice' (Reckwitz 2004b: 49). Both cases depend on the specific cultural codes and the acquirement of practical knowledge and cannot, therefore, be used as a foil for generalisation.

Consequently, the structure of his theory tends to be rather static. This is less a result of one of his concepts, but is primarily caused by his tendency to assume the homogeneity of the world. This problem applies to the uniformity of habitus, the overlapping relationship of habitus and field, and the dichotomised conception of power struggles between newcomers and established actors in a field (Schäfer 2013: 116–120).

Bourdieu's practice thought provides few starting points for a theory of social change. Although he states that processes of change in the fields of literature and painting (Bourdieu 1996), for instance, are most likely to be triggered by newcomers entering the field for the first time, and that each field requires its own models of change, this does not provide for a genuine theory of social change, as Hans Joas and Wolfgang Knöbl (2009: 395) argue. As his studies focused on only a few fields, his work inevitably lacks general statements about social change.

3.2 Michel Foucault, Problematisation and Governmentality

Michel Foucault is one of the best-known French intellectuals and theorists. His influence on social theory is significant, and few disciplines have been left untouched by his work in one way or another. His studies have visibly influenced IR debates since at least the 1970s (e.g. Ruggie 1975), while the first article-length treatments of his ideas began to be published in the late 1980s (including Shapiro, Bonham, and Heradstveit 1988 in *International Studies Quarterly* and Keeley 1990 in *International Organizations*). Foucault's work has generally been received in IR (as elsewhere) as that of a theorist of discourse and power; in other words, he is understood as a textualist, rather than a practice theorist.

As Clive Barnett (2015), among others, notes, there are, however, different versions of 'Foucault' or what Colin Koopman and Tomas Matza (2013: 817) call "Foucaultisms" at work. These range "from a theorist of power, to a model of intellectual commitment, or an inspiration for new models of ethico-political practice" (Barnett 2015: 1). There is "also a hardening division of labour between an increasingly sophisticated field of exegesis and a longer standing tradition of application of Foucault's ideas. Cutting across this division is another, between readings of Foucault by "ontologizers" and by "empiricists." This division might also be characterised in terms of readings of Foucault's work in search of grand concepts (of power, of biopolitics, of discipline), and readings that find there a model of analysis, if not quite a methodology" (Barnett 2015: 2).

In reading Foucault as a practice theorist, we foreground a number of concepts and themes, some of which have not been treated in this manner by the Foucauldian literature in IR. Firstly, discussing Foucault allows us to further elaborate on the relationship and fluid boundaries between practice theory, textualism and discourse analysis. Here, it is particularly Foucault's concept of 'discursive practices' that is of interest, in that it can be read in a practice theoretical way. Secondly, we like to re-appropriate the pragmatist side of Foucault and emphasise that his theorising be concerned with contingency rather than order and structures. Seen from this perspective, his work needs to be understood not as providing a global theory of power or anything else, but as empirically specific inquiries that provide useful concepts and analytical methods (Koopman and Matza 2013). Thirdly, we recognise that Foucault introduces the problem of the historicity of practices in a unique way. We fourthly place particular emphasis on how he provides concepts for studying practices of governing (governmentality).[1]

'Discourse' and 'discursive practices' are two of Foucault's core terms. He develops these in the *Order of Things* and *Archaeology of Knowledge*. Given his focus on structures of meaning in these early works, they are often considered (e.g. by Reckwitz 2002: 248) as developing a textualist account that locates meaning in the structures, rather than the practical and material process of their production. By contrast, Foucault's later works, in particular his analytics of government, are seen to be much closer to practice theoretical concerns.

Recently, there has been a tendency to reinterpret his early works along practice theoretical lines, and to argue against a break in Foucault's work or a fundamental re-orientation. Reading the early works in such a way implies shifting emphasis from a focus on discourse as reproduction and stabilisation of order, to discursive practices as ordering and structuring. Foucault theorised discourse as discursive practices, that is, as configurations of statement-making sayings. For him, statements are performances (Dreyfus and Rabinow 1983: 74). However, rather than being interested in everyday speech acts, he limited his focus to those statements which represent efforts to make authoritative knowledge claims. Such statements function as knowledge through exhibiting regularity and being part of what he called 'discursive formations' (Dreyfus and Rabinow 1983: 77). In analysing discursive formations, he was focussed on the human sciences and their dynamic relations in larger historical orders of discourse.

As Nicolini summarises it, a discursive formation

> consists of a number of rules that bestow a certain order of the statements which belong to it. These rules of formation are obtained by assembling in a novel way existing discursive and non-discursive elements through the institutions of new social and discursive practices. In particular these rules of formation and practice determine what can be spoken of, who is allowed to speak (or write) and how, and a field of possibilities with regards to the creation of theories and themes; that is, how the discursive formation is used in the wider institutional and societal arena. (Nicolini 2013: 196)

As Schatzki (2017: 136) argues, Foucault was conscious of the fact that the sayings that composed the discursive formations always occurred amid doings and material contexts. However, in his early work he arguably decided to split the discursive and material dimensions and "took these sayings, together with what is said in them, as composing distinct entities" (Schatzki 2017: 136). Nonetheless, it is important to note that Foucault's notion of discourse and discursive formation and practice is not limited to language and sayings. Rather, discourse is a configuration of statements, rules, norms and technologies. Statements work together with forms of bodily discipline, training, and normalisation to constitute discursive formations.

This becomes more visible when Foucault turns to genealogy in his project of analysing apparatuses. While Foucault remains committed to the study of formations of significant extension and proportion, such as modernity, in his genealogical work, he is more explicitly concerned about materiality and contingency. With the concept of 'apparatus' (translated from the French *dispositif*) Foucault turns to analyses of systems of relations between various heterogeneous material and linguistic elements. Apparatus can be understood as an open concept that describes a "relatively durable network of heterogeneous elements (discourses, laws, architectures, institutions, administrative practices and so on)" (Walters 2012: 36). In this sense, the concept of apparatus has similar features to those proposed in other approaches, such as the notion of actor-network or Schatzki's bundles and material arrangements.

Foucault's move to the study of contingency is characterised by his turn to genealogy, writing histories of the present, as represented in *Discipline and Punish* (1977) and *A History of Sexuality* (1978). With this methodological reorientation, Foucault emphasised the importance of actions and practices, the objective of describing and explaining change without appealing to overarching principles and instead turning to how people reinterpret and modify their situations, and that change is the outcome of contestable processes (Bevir 2010; Koopman 2013).

The guiding term of his genealogy was that of 'problematisation'. That is, to study and reconstruct how problems were made in order to find new ways of dealing with them.[2] The objective of a historical reconstruction is, then, to identify those apparatuses that have been developed to respond and indeed make a problem and to investigate those contingent moments in which alternatives have been excluded. As Koopman (2013: 20) suggests, problematisation provides a "kind of master concept for Foucault's methodology".

In his 1978 lectures, Foucault turned to the analysis of political knowledge and proposed a set of concepts that have become very influential in politics and IR. With the concept of governmentality, he proposed a new way of analysing the exercise of power and political rule. "The term governmentality sought to draw attention to a certain way of thinking and acting embodied in all those attempts to know and govern the wealth, health and happiness of populations" (Rose and Miller 1992: 174).

Foucault developed the concept to account for a shift in governing he identifies in sixteenth century Europe, redefining the purpose of rule from control over territory to the governing of populations. Foucault did not reduce the notion of government to the state; rather government was taken to be "the historically constituted matrix within which are articulated all those dreams, schemes, strategies and manoeuvres of authorities that seek to shape the beliefs and conduct of others in desired directions by acting upon their will, their circumstances or their environment" (Rose and Miller 1992: 175). In what soon emerged as a body of research described as "governmentality studies" (Walters 2012), the goal became to analyse technologies of government. As Rose and Miller (1992: 183) set out, the scope of such studies

> is a question of the complex assemblage of diverse forces – legal, architectural, professional, administrative, financial, judgmental – such that aspects of the decisions and actions of individuals, groups, organisations and populations come to be understood and regulated in relation to authoritative criteria. We need to study the humble and mundane mechanisms by which authorities seek to instantiate government: techniques of notation, computation and calculation; procedures of examination and assessment; the invention of devices such as surveys and presentational forms such as tables; the standardisation of systems for training and the inculcation of habits; the inauguration of professional specialisms and vocabularies; building designs and architectural forms – the list is heterogeneous and in principle unlimited. (Rose and Miller 1992: 183)

As Rose and Miller describe it, governmentality studies are wide in scope and draw on the core commitments of IPT. It is the notion of governmentality and the corresponding analysis of technologies of government that have most directly influenced the discussion within IPT.

Foucault's work has been widely accepted in IR, and a burgeoning body of work engages with Foucauldian concepts. This includes a wide range of studies taking up the notion of discursive practices, which do not, however, always engage with the non-discursive side of practices. In particular, it is those drawing on the concept of governmentality that have made vital contributions to IPT. As Walters (2012: 83) argues, a rich field of "international governmentality studies" has emerged.

Those studies that treat governmentality as an analytical toolbox for the study of technologies of government, rather than an expression of a particular (neoliberal) style of political rule,[3] have particularly investigated global governance processes in the fields of development, aid, or political economy. Sending and Neumann (2006), for instance, show how the role of NGOs has changed under the new logic or rationality of government in global governance. By using the cases of the international campaign to ban landmines and international population policy, they illustrate that the self-association and political will-formation characteristic of civil society and nonstate actors do not stand in opposition to the political power of the state, but are a central feature of how power, understood as government, operates in late modern society. Both cases underline that NGOs are refined from passive objects into an entity that is both an object and a subject of government. Thus, NGOs are not necessarily a barrier to government, they are themselves part of it. Sending and Neumann give us an example that reveals how a Foucauldian analysis challenges taken-for-granted binaries, such as those between the state and civil society.

Other researchers have turned to analyse the practices of power of international organisations.[4] Laura Zanotti (2005) critically analyses the UN debate on democratisation and good governance as a dominating framework since the 1990s. UN 'good governance' discourses and programmes are read as elements of global governmentality. That is, instead of asking under which conditions and through what kind of interventions democratisation can best be achieved, Zanotti (2005: 462) uses the concept of governmentality to explore the conditions of emergence of good governance as the UN political rationale, the mechanisms of government it promotes, and the political effects it produces. In her empirical findings, she illustrates the processes by which, at the United Nations, the language of governance colonised the discourse on democracy, peace, and development, and demonstrates the governmental character of the mechanisms of government promoted within this approach.

The role of indicators as a tool of governance has become another focus of governmentality analysis. Oded Löwenheim (2008), for instance, employs the notion of governmentality to shed light on the political meanings and outcomes of the increasing tendency to rate and rank the governance capacities and performances of states. He shows how various political actors such as the World Bank and the US government 'responsibilise' developing countries as they construct the examined states as ethical subjects deemed capable of free and responsible choices and thereby neglect their own responsible role of reproducing global injustices and inequalities (Löwenheim 2008: 256). In the meantime, a wide range of studies has demonstrated how quantitative tools, such as indicators, benchmarks or indexes, are major techniques of government in international relations permeating all sorts of fields of global governance.[5]

The other field in which Foucauldian practice approaches have become widely adopted is security studies. Here it is the context of the war on terror that particularly spurred the interest in governmentality.

EU counter-terrorism is a good example. Usually, EU counter-terrorism is regarded as a response to the growing threat of terrorism. Stef Wittendorp (2016) analyses three technologies in counter-terrorism (the action plan, the timetable, and the Counter-Terrorist Coordinator) designed for shaping the conduct of government. However, as he demonstrates, these technologies are implicated in the (re)production of insecurity rather than locating the source of insecurity external to these institutions, as institutionalist accounts do. This mode of governing therefore fuels a circular logic whereby the need to perform better leads to calls for improved monitoring and vice versa. The concept of governmentality also sheds new light on EU security policy, in particular on its common security and defence policy (CSDP). Whereas CSDP is often analysed as a site of and contributor to processes of securitisation, Michael Merlingen (2011) applies the conceptual tools of governmentality theory to show the dynamics and functioning of internal and external CSDP governance in post-conflict societies. Andreas Vasilache's (2014) study on the changing US security policy under the Obama administration is a good example of using one crucial strategy document. The new strategic guidance for the Department of Defense entitled 'Sustaining US Global Leadership: Priorities for the 21st Century Defense' involves, as he shows in his analysis, two different security approaches that follow different logics in US history. For Vasilache (2014: 584), the guidance is remarkable because of the distinctiveness, immediacy, and clarity with which both sovereign security logics in the tradition of great power politics and governmental security logics are introduced, presented, and dialectically joined – precisely by not merging or bringing them together in a direct and explicit manner. By providing a governmental reading, he shows that such a document is an interesting and politically weighty demonstration and example of a separating but parallelised configuration of sovereign and governmental rationalities in US military policy.

Foucauldian concepts are important tools in the spectrum of IPT. It is not only his understanding of discourse with its emphasis on the material and heterogeneous nature of practices and order, and the way it foregrounds the centrality of discursive practices and power phenomena that provides an important bridge between textualist and practice accounts. Concepts such as apparatus, problematisation and governmentality bring the contingency of practice to the fore.

As Nicolini summarises it, Foucault "has the merit of emphasising that the appropriate units of inquiry for practice theories are not unique, coherent, and stable objects, as much as emergent nexuses of local diversities. For Foucault in fact the unity of discourse does not lie in repetition of the same activity [...] as much as in the delimitation of diversity" (Nicolini 2013: 198).

It remains puzzling why Foucauldian forms of analysis have not been interpreted as an important contributor to the practice theoretical trading zone more frequently. One answer to the puzzle is certainly the complexity of Foucault's writing and the different paths and interpretations it allows. Another is the particular focus on grand shifts and large-scale histories he invites us to take, which seem to run counter to the intention of many practice turners to seek their fortune in the smaller scale.

Indeed, engaging with the Foucauldian approach produces the risk that one does not read it as an invitation to study the intricacies of the material and linguistic relations of concrete apparatuses and the practices of power, but favours – contrary to the intention of much of Foucault's writing – grand narratives over the empirical study of practices. As Bevir (2010: 431) notes, studies of governmentality, in particular, can then slide into structuralism in that they "lose sight of the fact that people create meanings and practices" and start to "treat meanings as things that exist as part of systems of signs quite apart from the actors who make them".

3.3 Communities of Practice

The community of practice approach (hereafter CPA) was developed in organisational sociology and management studies, being proposed and outlined by Jean Lave and Etienne Wenger. The core question that Wenger and Lave addressed was how learning processes unfold, and how they can be facilitated. Working in a typical 1980s Silicon Valley laboratory, Lave and Wenger wanted to know how humans learn how to use machines, and how human-machine interaction and processes of 'learning to learn' could be improved. If Lave and Wenger's co-authored book *Situated Learning: Legitimate Peripheral Participation* was principally concerned with learning, Wenger's later single-author study *Communities of Practice Learning, Meaning and Identity* (1998) developed these insights into a broader social theoretical account that goes far beyond these initial concerns. Since the publication of these books, CPA has travelled widely across disciplines and become a mainstream framework in, notably, education studies, management theory and organisational sociology.

In IR, the framework was first introduced by Emanuel Adler in his introduction to *Communitarian International Relations* (2005), where he suggested it to be a productive reconceptualisation of prevailing concepts of 'community', providing promising routes to address core theoretical questions of IR, such as the relation between actors and structures, identity or change. Since Adler proposed it, the phrase 'communities of practice' has become widely used in IR. Many use the concept only in a loose sense, however.[6] Direct translations of Wenger's approach to IR concerns are yet more limited. CPA nonetheless gained a strong foothold in the study of security, particularly in infusing the concept of security communities with practice theoretical ideas, but also in study of the practices of bureaucracy, international law, diplomacy, peacebuilding, terrorism, and piracy.

Two ideas are central in CPA: firstly, that learning is a core mechanism of practice by which knowing and doing become related, and, secondly, that practice is organised in community structures. CPA offers a sophisticated outline of how such communities function, how they interact and how they can be studied as well as facilitated. In the following, we firstly introduce the core concepts and strategies of CPA and, secondly, review how these have been employed in IR. We conclude with a critical reflection of the limits of the approach.

Lave and Wenger developed their account through a critique of cognitive understandings of learning that emphasise the mental processes of individuals. CPA hence positions itself most directly in relation to mentalist accounts of culturalist theorising. As summarised by Alison Fuller (2007), this entailed three core elements. Firstly, CPA promotes collectives and groups as the core unit of analysis. Learning, therefore, is pivotally a social relation to others. Secondly, learning evolves through practice, that is, the co-participation of people in the shared practices of their community. Individuals form and are formed by these collectives. Thirdly, the question of what is learned is answered by Lave and Wenger in terms of identity formation.

Learning, then, is the process by which one becomes a full member and knowledgeable and skilled practitioner within a community. Lave and Wenger (1991) captured the process of learning with the concept of "legitimate peripheral participation". The term highlights the progressive participation of newcomers to a community whereby they gain the practical competency to participate and become members. The notion of 'peripheral' implies that there are certain social positions within a collective. New members do not necessarily have to take a certain route to become increasingly competent practitioners, as through their and others' participation they might also change what counts as legitimate knowledge. The notion of legitimate peripheral participation therefore also emphasises that learning is not a straightforward process. In activities of participation, meanings and understandings and what counts as relevant and legitimate knowledge might change quite fundamentally. With this emphasis, the community of practice approach integrates an aspect that is less prominent in other frameworks, the integration of individuals in practical contexts and the emergence of new practices. Actors become members of a community of practice though learning its respective practices. Learning is understood here as practical learning and as socialisation into the legitimate forms of action of a community. Any community of practice is produced by and re-produced in a collective process of learning.

In *Communities of Practice Learning, Meaning and Identity*, Wenger (1998) generalises the idea of community of practices as an organisation theory. Lave and Wenger conceptualised community in weak terms, suggesting that the term does not reflect an entity that shares culture or a clearly identifiable social group with set boundaries (Lave and Wenger 1991: 98). Wenger (1998) shifts this emphasis; in his reworking of the notion, communities become established as a container of practice with clearly identifiable boundaries and recognisable social coherence. He suggests that communities of practice are a distinct social entity, and proposes studying organisations as composed of such communities. Organisations should, therefore, not only be projected as formal structures and units, but also as informal ones. They host a wide variety of communities that are the main source of identity, within which meaning is negotiated, and knowledge is created and shared.

Wenger understands communities of practice as units of analysis that cut across formal organisations, institutions, and other forms of association such as social movements. It is, simply put, a set of relations among people doing things together (Wenger 1998). In Wenger and Snyder (2000: 139), communities of practice are identified as "a new organisational form", that are "groups of people informally bound together by shared expertise and passion for a joint enterprise".

Following Wenger, a community of practice entails a set of relations in three dimensions by which practice is the source of coherence: 'mutual engagement', a 'joint enterprise' and a 'shared repertoire'. A community is given coherence by practice, firstly, when "people are engaged in actions whose meanings they negotiate with one another" (Wenger 1998: 73).

A community of practice is not a simple aggregate of people that share some characteristic, such as having a title, or knowing other people. It is people who engage with each other. "They work together, [...] they talk with each other all the time, exchange information and opinions, and very directly influence each other's understanding as a matter of routine" (Wenger 1998: 75). Such a mutual engagement, a working together, creates a unique set of relationships between members of a community.

Secondly, communities of practice negotiate a joint enterprise. Members respond communally to situations and deliberate what their enterprise is constituted by. Joint enterprises also give rise to regimes of mutual accountability. These include "what matters and what not, [...], what to do and what not, what to pay attention to and what not [...], what to justify and what to take for granted, [...] when actions and artefacts are good enough and when they need improvement or refinement" (Wenger 1998: 81).

Thirdly, communities of practice develop a shared repertoire used in practice. Such a repertoire includes "routines, words, tools, ways of doing things, stories, gestures, symbols, genres, actions, or concepts that the community has produced or adopted in the course of its existence and which have become part of its practice" (Wenger 1998: 83). Communities of practice are, then, containers of practice characterised by mutual engagement, joint enterprises, and a shared repertoire.

Equipped with such an understanding of community as a "well-identifiable social 'thing'" connoted by detectable boundaries and specifiable characteristics (Nicolini 2013: 19), Wenger also addresses how communities relate to and interact with each other as well as how they can be facilitated. He stresses that communities establish relations by different sorts of boundary practices. Communities might engage and share so-called "boundary objects", that is, objects used in more than one community, although these do not agree on the meaning of the object. A forest in which conservationists, joggers and loggers meet might be such a boundary object, as might the coffee machine in an office building where different communities of an organisation converge.

Another form of interaction is through 'multiple participation' and 'brokering'. People usually participate in more than one community, yet only brokers are able to make connections between communities. Brokering involves the translation of knowledge from one community to the other and the aligning of perspectives. If a broker brings in new knowledge or objects to the community, then they need to be assimilated into it. It may become a natural part of the community's repertoire, or it may be rejected. Wenger also elaborates ways by which communities can be built and learning facilitated to the benefit of an organisation. Particularly in his later works, he lays out how targeted provision of resources and opportunity might improve dialogue and communication in order to facilitate learning. In the words of Wenger and Snyder (2000: 140), "communities of practice can drive strategy, generate new lines of business, solve problems, promote the spread of best practices, develop people's professional skills, and help companies to recruit and retain talent".

Given that CPA elaborates practice-theoretical viewpoints on core concepts of IR, such as learning, identity and community, CPA provides a rich repertoire for studying international practice. In IR, Adler has spearheaded the translation of Wenger's concept. In his 2005 book, he suggests that CPA can provide “a unifying and comprehensive way of understanding the role of transnational communities in International Relations” (Adler 2005: 3). He consequently invites us to reinterpret received notions of community in IR, including ‘security communities’, which “practice peaceful change” (Adler 2005: 17), ‘epistemic communities’, which engage in knowledge validation and as science-based communities “construct the practices, identities, and interests of modern rulers” (Adler 2005: 17), ‘critical communities’, which propose alternative knowledge, ‘global public policy networks’ as well as ‘transnational advocacy networks’. All of these are communities “because of what they do” (Adler 2005: 17).

For Adler, the main advantage of such an interpretation lies in the potential dialogue between normative and analytical communitarian approaches, as well in CPA’s productive responses to IR’s core ontological puzzles. According to him (2005: 14 f.), CPA offers an understanding of community that goes beyond IR’s norm-oriented approaches. The learning process that CPA describes not only involves the acquisition of knowledge to perform a distinct activity, but also moral commitments and evaluative standards of excellence, which imply ethics or a set of values. CPA moreover offers a dynamic concept, which is able to project the agency as well as the structural side of practice.

“Communities of practice cut across state-boundaries and mediate between states, individuals, and human agency, on one hand, and social structures and systems, on the other” (Adler 2005: 15). In his later work co-authored with Vincent Pouliot, CPA becomes a cornerstone of his proposal for IPT. Citing Wenger at length, Adler and Pouliot propose that the general ideas of practice theory can be turned into “concrete and workable theoretical meaning in the concept of communities of practice. [...] Practices develop, diffuse, and become institutionalized in such collectives” (Adler and Pouliot 2011a: 18). They suggest that communities are an intelligible focal point for IR research, since core ontological dimensions intersect. As they argue:

> The community of practice concept encompasses not only the conscious and discursive dimensions, and the actual doing of social change, but also the social space where structure and agency overlap and where knowledge, power, and community intersect. Communities of practice are intersubjective social structures that constitute the normative and epistemic ground for action, but they also are agents, made up of real people, who – working via network channels, across national borders, across organisational divides, and in the halls of government – affect political, economic, and social events. (Adler and Pouliot 2011a: 18–19)

With the plea to turn communities of practice into a focal point of IR research, Adler opened up a rich practice-theoretical agenda. How CPA can be used to shed light on core questions of IR is demonstrated in Adler's work on security communities and a range of studies further developing this work. In two articles, one co-authored with Patricia Greve, he substantiates how security communities can be re-interpreted as communities of practice (Adler 2008; Adler and Greve 2009). Adler and Greve describe a security community as a distinct mechanism of security governance; if it is at work, "power does not trigger balancing behaviour" (Adler and Greve 2009: 70), instead alliances and alignments "are rooted in mutual trust and collective identity" (Adler and Greve 2009: 71).

Drawing on CPA, Adler (2008; Adler and Greve 2009) suggests that security communities are characterised by a repertoire of at least six distinct practices: the practice of self-restraint, the practice of directing common enterprises, projects and partnerships, cooperative security practice, diplomacy as the normal practice, a disposition of spreading the community outward through socialisation mechanisms and teaching, and more specific practices of military planning, of confidence building, and of policy coordination. This provides a profound reinterpretation, and directs the study of security communities from understandings of identity as beliefs, expectations or perceptions to ones based in practice. The concept is therefore suitable for investigating processes of enlargement (such as NATO enlargement, see Adler 2008), as well as studying the geographical spread and extension of practices, such as democratic ones.

As shown in other works, such a reinterpretation also allows for integrating insights from securitisation theory into security community theory. Shared practices of turning an issue into a threat (securitisation) and shared securitisations can be seen as forming a core part of the repertoire of a security community (Bueger 2013b; Bueger and Stockbruegger 2012). Niklas Bremberg (2015) demonstrated how shared securitisation practices coupled with cooperative tools such as the institutionalisation of multilateral venues, transgovernmental networks or joint crisis management infrastructures, provide an understanding of how security communities spread their practices and hence grow at their boundaries.

If CPA has principally been used to advance the notion of security community so far, applications of Wenger's framework go far beyond this. This particularly concerns research on regional organisations, such as the European Union, as well as in the field of international law.

Heavily influenced by Adler's work on security communities of practice within European Union studies, CPA has particularly been employed in investigating how common European structures emerge in the field of foreign and security policy. In a series of studies, Frederica Bicchi investigated how European bodies evolve by forming communities of practice. Using CPA as a framework to study the communication and knowledge production of diplomats in Europe's new External Action Service, Bicchi (2011) asks whether a community is emerging, or investigates the performance of Europe by diplomats in the Jerusalem area (2016). Zwolski (2016) investigates how early warning systems lead to the emergence of a European community of practice. Nina Graeger (2016) demonstrates how CPA can be fruitfully used to explore the collaboration between regional organisations by studying the relations between the EU and NATO. Maren Hofius (2016) investigated how EU diplomats both span as well as draw the boundary of a European community of practice, while Matthew Davies (2016) has shown how a distinct style of diplomacy has started to emerge in an ASEAN community of practice.

In the field of international law, CPA was introduced by Jutta Brunnée and Stephen J Toope (2010, 2011). They argue for understanding international law as emerging from and embedded in a legal community of practice that is composed of shared understandings, criteria of legality and a practice of legality. This community creates legal obligation. Following their work, others have investigated the emergence of a community of human rights practice (Orange 2016), as well as a community of fact finding (Heaven 2017).

CPA has also been introduced as a productive tool outside the study of international law and bureaucratic regional organisations. Michael Christensen (2017) argues that international democracy assistance activities can be seen as being organised in emerging transnational communities of practice. Bueger (2013a) analyses Somali piracy as a community of practice, arguing that CPA provides a fuller understanding of the phenomenon in contrast to prevalent conceptualisations of piracy as interaction between rational criminal individuals. Michael Kenney (2017) demonstrates how CPA's account of learning can provide an understanding of the adaptation of terrorist and transnational crime organisations.

Using communities of practice as a focal point and studying world politics as a collection of these focal points promises further interesting insights.[7] CPA provides a rich analytical vocabulary, however existing studies have not made full use of the diverse concepts. Potential further studies will have to make better use of the concept of legitimate peripheral participation and study the manifold socialisation processes in international practices; CPA's rich set of terms also provides entry points for researching the interaction between communities of practices; finally, drawing on CPA might also produce policy recommendations on how communities can be facilitated.

CPA has been subject to considerable criticism, however. Notably, the stronger version as elaborated in Wenger's more recent work and as adopted by Adler raises concerns for the applicability of CPA in an IR context. A first line of criticism concerns whether CPA can be meaningfully applied to the transnational collectives IR is concerned with. Wenger's concept of communities primarily has organisation-based communities in mind, and one of the core criteria of a community is an intense everyday form of engagement of the members. A community in this sense involves a limited number of people, who are to some extent geographically bound. While diplomats in a distinct capital can be said to form such a community, for instance, it is questionable if a collective such as Western diplomats could be studied within the same frameworks.

Adler suggests that "Wenger [...] has dealt mainly with domestic or national communities of practice. There is no reason, however, why we should not be able to identify transnational or even global communities of practice" (Adler 2005: 15). This not only raises the question of whether there might be a difference between a small local and a large transnational group (Roberts 2006: 630), it also remains unclear how communities are nested in each other, how smaller and larger communities relate, and how communities relate to a context that they are part of. Brown and Duguid (2001), for instance, suggest that the concept of communities of practice should only refer to smaller local groups characterised by an intense level of engagement, while they prefer to speak of "networks of practice" (Brown and Duguid 2001: 205) to refer to larger and looser constellations of practice.

A second major line of critique, emphasised by Fox (2000), Mork et al. (2010), Marshall and Rollinson (2004), and Contu and Willmott (2003) concerns the silence of CPA towards questions of power and hierarchy. This relates to the character of hierarchies and policing mechanisms within communities of practice. As Marshall and Rollinson (2004: 74) remark, in CPA the negotiation of meaning can be easily misinterpreted as "excessively quiescent and consensual". However, such negotiations might be characterised by disagreements and controversies, some of which might largely be settled by power mechanisms.

Considerations of power are also important in addressing the issue of the change of practice within a community (Mork et al. 2010; Fox 2000). Since communities naturalise practices and objects, they not only learn, but also forget, and might be resistant to outside change due to powerful predispositions being held (Mork et al. 2000; Mutch 2003). CPA has, moreover, neglected the question of the distribution of power between communities of practice and the role of any external context in it. While Wenger has appropriated the question of boundary relations between communities, the way power effects impact this relation has not been conceptualised or studied so far.

The most fundamental critique, however, concerns the use of the concept of community and juxtaposing it with practice. As Nicolini points out at length, combining the two terms is risky. "[C]ommunity is a term with a long, and somewhat troublesome meaning" (Nicolini 2013: 88), and it is often its romanticised image that has "come to represent social scientists' idealised form of sociality" (Nicolini 2013: 89). Such emphasis easily slips from practice to community. This is fraught with risks: "once we couple the notion of practice with a 'stronger', more entrenched notion, such as community, the former tends to lose its main processural, social temporary, and conflictual character" (Nicolini 2013: 92)

A key advantage of Adler's proposal to centre IPT on CPA is its ability to easily build bridges to constructivist works in IR. However, this also represents an inherent danger that core ideas of practice theory become lost, including the idea that collectives are formed in and through practices and not by like-mindedness or shared beliefs or ideas. CPA therefore opens productive avenues, but relying on communities of practice as the focal point puts the analyst at constant risk of falling into a "static and ahistorical view of practice, one in which perpetuation prevails over change, and the associations between humans overshadow the inherent materiality of all practices" (Nicolini 2013: 94).

3.4 Theodore Schatzki's Ontology of Practices

In the spectrum of practice approaches, Theodore Schatzki's account is most philosophically grounded. He received acclaim in social philosophy for his book *Social Practices*, in which he suggests a Wittgensteinian approach for a better understanding of social phenomena and human activity (Schatzki 1996). From the outset, Schatzki's core claim has been that individuals, their actions, and thoughts cannot be understood separately from the social practices in which they are situated. Schatzki's practice approach builds upon a specific view of human action derived from the work of Wittgenstein (and Heidegger). Inspired by these thinkers, he emphasises the relationship between human action and social order, and understands humans as neither serial rational decision makers nor as cultural/rule/habitus dopes, leading him to focus instead on the conditions of "action intelligibility" (Nicolini 2013: 163).

As the lead editor of the volume *Practice Turn* (Schatzki et al. 2001), he has become a well-known practice theorist in various disciplines, and set the research agenda by stressing the need to overcome single action. In *Practice Turn* he submits that "practices are arrays of human activity" and suggests that "practice accounts are joined in the belief that such phenomena as knowledge, meaning, human activity, science, power, language, social institutions, and historical transformation occur within and are aspects or components of the *field of practices*" (Schatzki 2001: 2, emphasis in original).

Schatzki defines practices "as temporally unfolding and spatially dispersed nexus of doings and sayings" (Schatzki 1996: 89), a definition that has substantially influenced the practice debate in IR and elsewhere. This understanding stresses the close link between doing and saying, and therefore gives equal importance to bodily actions and speech acts. For Schatzki (2002: 72), the point of the qualifiers 'open, temporally unfolding' is that "fresh actions are continually perpetuating" and extending practices temporally. In his "primer on practices" Schatzki (2012: 13), summarises what for him is the essence of practice theory and highlights how a practice is an "organised constellation of different people's activities". However, it would be misleading to reduce Schatzki's sophisticated approach to issues of definition. His major aim, in particular in his later book (Schatzki 2002), is to conceptualise the notion of practices in relation to social order and change. This makes his account promising for IR scholars working on related questions with regards to international politics. Moreover, his focus on the "mesh of practices and orders" as the "site where social life takes place" (Schatzki 2002: 123) develops a complex structural notion comparable to terms such as 'assemblage' or 'actor-network'. Finally, his suggestion of a social ontology centred on practices opens further avenues in IR theory, moving the debate closer to philosophical discussions on the role of (human) agency, the normativity of practice, and the constitution of social life and change.

In Wittgenstein's understanding of practices as language-games, different elements are closely connected. These include background knowledge, practical understandings, routinisation, and situated learning. Following Wittgenstein, practices are understood as patterns of activity; these patterns include action, equipment, sites of activity and are never precisely and finely demarcated (Stern 2003: 195). Schatzki (2002: 71) departs from Wittgensteinian thought, however, arguing that a practice is a bundle of activities; in other words, it is an ***organised*** nexus of actions. Accordingly, any practice embraces two overall dimensions: activity and organisation. Schatzki's complete account is centred on the question of how practices are organised. He distinguishes between 'dispersed' and 'integrative' practices. While ***dispersed*** practices are basic units and refer to examples such as describing, explaining, and evaluating, ***integrative*** practices are "the more complex practices found in and constitutive of particular domains of social life" such as cooking or farming practices (Schatzki 1996: 98).

Understanding practices as sets of doings and sayings means not foregoing one (bodily action) or the other (language) when analysing practices. For Schatzki, doings and sayings are composed of increasingly social wholes that he describes as tasks and projects. That is, a practice almost always constitutes further actions in the context in which they are performed. The set of actions that composes a practice is broader than its doings and sayings alone. Writing a research paper on practice theory, for instance, is a project, which involves many different tasks of doings and sayings (reading, writing, discussing the argument with others, concentrating for a period), but is also embedded in other projects (participating at conferences, getting published, convincing others to read the text). Doings, sayings, tasks and projects hang together in accordance with a characteristic and meaningful organisation. They constitute integral and meaningful 'blocks', described as practices.

For Schatzki (2002: 77) practices are, more specifically, organised bundles of human activities linked through a collection of 'practical understandings', 'rules', 'teleo-affective structures', and 'general understandings'. Together, they form the organisation of practices. Each of these concepts is further discussed below.

Firstly, 'practical understandings' are certain abilities that pertain to the actions constituting a practice. Practical understanding refers to the knowing that derives from being competent within a practice. Following Wittgenstein, knowing manifests itself as being able to proceed unhampered in an activity. To say that two sets of doings and sayings are linked by the same practical understanding means that they express the same understanding of what is going on, making the action of one person intelligible to another when both members are competent within that practice (Nicolini 2013: 165). Mutual intelligibility refers to Wittgenstein's notion of regularity in action in the sense of family resemblance, as participants can disagree within a practice while still understanding each other. For Schatzki (2002: 78–79), practical understanding resembles the concept of habitus, in that it is a skill or capacity that underlies activity.

Secondly, rules are another way by which practices are kept together. For Schatzki (2002: 79), rules are "explicit formulations, principles, precepts, and instructions that enjoin, direct or remonstrate people to perform specific actions". To say that rules link doings and sayings is to say that people, in carrying out these doings and sayings, take account of and adhere to the same rules. This notion implies that rules as programmes of action are not tacit or implicit formulas, but rather formulations interjected into social life for the purpose of orienting and determining the course of activity, typically by those with the authority to enforce them (Schatzki 2002: 80).

Thirdly, the link between the doings and sayings of a practice is also provided through a teleo-affective structure. Schatzki (2002: 80) defines it as "a range of normativised and hierarchically ordered ends, projects, and tasks, to varying degrees allied with normativised emotions and even moods". It emphasises that all practices unfold according to a specific direction and 'oughtness' or 'how they should be carried out'. This concept follows the thinking of Heidegger, who saw purposiveness as one of the most basic conditions of being human (Nicolini 2013: 166). Thus, a practice always exhibits a set of ends that participants should or may pursue; a range of projects that they should or may carry out for the sake of these ends; and a selection of tasks that they should or may perform for the sake of these projects (Schatzki 2002: 80). The teleo-affective structure therefore emphasises the normativity of practice.

Teleo-affective structures also involve a set of emotions and moods that connote ends and project affectively, for instance, a researcher feels happy once her paper is accepted for publication. This internal structure and affective colouring of a practice is part of the learning process by which individuals turn into participants within a language-game. However, as Nicolini (2013: 166–167) explains, this learning process implies a strong normative flavour that gives the impression that the structure of practice is what guides action. This is, however, not the case, as activity is always governed by practical intelligibility – "the teleo-affective structure only contributes by shaping what it makes sense to do". The teleo-affective structure is upheld in a distributed manner by all participants, whereby it is learned and perpetuated through the socialisation of novices within the practice. It also points to normative controversy as "the teleoaffective structure is indefinitely complex" (Schatzki 2002: 83), since participants will never totally agree on which ends, projects, tasks, and emotions are obligatory or acceptable in a practice.

Fourthly, the activities of a practice hang together through a set of general understandings. They are reflexive understandings of the overall project in which people are involved, and which contribute to practical intelligibility and hence action (Nicolini 2013: 167). The general understanding of the project gives the practice its identity, both discursively and practically.

In sum, a practice is a temporally evolving, open-ended set of doings and sayings linked by practical understandings, rules, teleo-affective structure, and general understandings. For Schatzki (2002: 87), it is important that the organisation of a practice describes the practice's frontiers, as it clarifies, on the one hand, that a doing or saying belongs to a given practice if it expresses components of that practice's organisation; on the other hand, this delineation of boundaries entails that practices can overlap, and that a particular doing might belong to two or more practices.

Following this conceptual vocabulary, Schatzki (2002) develops his complex 'site ontology' by describing step by step how practices establish arrangements and social orders by emphasising dimensions of relationality, meanings, identity, and objects. He draws on metaphors such as 'mesh', 'shifting', 'multiple', and 'interweaving' to avoid structuralist notions. He criticises, for instance, Bourdieu for drawing the site of the social as an array of homologous bounded realms of activity, meaning, and arrangement into "large-scale united parcels" (Schatzki 2002: 152). Finally, for Schatzki (2002: 240), practice organisations are never static, as the understandings, rules, and teleo-affective structures that organise integrative practices frequently change in what is described as "reorganisation" and "recomposition".

Schatzki develops his account with reference to two guiding historical cases: the medicinal herb business of a Shaker village in the 1850s, and contemporary day trading on the Nasdaq Stock Market. In doing so, Schatzki uses the relative simplicity of Shaker life to illustrate basic features of his site ontology, for instance when he describes the crucially practical understandings of medicinal herb practices as "grinding, macerating, drying, storing, mixing, labelling, feeding, and printing labels" (Schatzki 2002: 78–79).

The case of stock market trading practices is used to think about agency and change. Although the way Schatzki integrates the material dimension of practice resembles approaches such as actor-network theory, he reserves the notion of practice and agency to humans, and hence argues for working with two terms, practice and material arrangements. The notion of human agency, therefore, remains important. As Schatzki (2002: 209) states: "An actor is not, however, its embedding arrangements: A trader is not his computer, workstation, fellow traders, and managers, just as the day trading office is not the firm, the market-making industry, and the Nasdaq market."

Moreover, "traders can act without their computers and fellows, just as the office can carry on in the absence of other offices (though it cannot in the absence of the Nasdaq market)". Schatzki (2002: 209) therefore develops a notion of agency as an "effect" of embedding arrangements. While agency requires certain general types of embedding networks (e.g. physical things) to act on, components of embedding arrangements can also lead to human action that Schatzki (2002: 209) regards as causal.

Furthermore, embedding networks can also prefigure agency. For example, without their computers it is difficult for traders to follow market activity, though it is still easy for them to bemoan repair delays. As the example shows, Schatzki puts emphasis on agency as the remaining capacity of human action; similarly, he recognises the interwoven character of practices in complex arrangements, which transforms the space for agency in its traditional sense. Finally, Schatzki does not equate agency with change. For him, constant doing must not be equated with change, as many human and non-human doings maintain the practice-order mesh.

Schatzki's site theory – despite some empirical illustrations – is less empirically informed than other approaches. It therefore does not lend itself easily as a framework for empirical research. IR scholars have used his work to both support theoretical arguments and describe empirical phenomena around international practices.

Cornelia Navari (2010), for instance, draws on Schatzki to identify and discuss the concept of practice that has been developed in the English school of IR. Following Navari (2010: 613), the English school concept of a practice has many parallels to that of Schatzki, since it is a purposive goal-oriented conception. Although most English school theorists "may not even know Schatzki's name", Navari (2010: 616) argues that Schatzki's notion of practice most resembles the English school in its aims and structure, and is therefore a valuable aid to understanding that conception. For Navari (2010: 615), the English school agrees in the assumption that practice is not a private idea, but instead "a commitment to communal standards is required for one to talk meaningfully of a practice".

Navari (2010: 616) finds the analytical distinction between dispersed and integrative practices particularly helpful. She makes use of his suggestion of the requisite elements of a practice, thereby giving the concept its empirical grounding. Navari discusses an English school study by Keens-Soper (1978) to illustrate how Schatzki's practice account might be used. Keens-Soper (1978) shows how the balance of power emerged as a new practice. The basis is a historical reconstruction of the changing political order in Europe starting with a letter written in 1458 by Pope Pius II to Mohammed II, the conqueror of Constantinople, and ending with the Treaty of Utrecht that ended the War of the Spanish Succession. As Navari (2010: 619) argues, the new practice of balance of power inscribed in the treaty conforms with all the requirements of a practice as understood by Schatzki: a clear understanding of how to prompt and respond to balances of power had emerged; it had a rule or standard – to counter those with hegemonic ambition, and the practice had a teleo-affective structure, namely the goal of protecting liberty. For Navari, there are various links between Schatzki and the English school; for instance, she suggests that Hedley Bull's concept of an 'institution' is almost identical to Schatzki's conception of practice (Navari 2010: 620).

Another example of a translation of Schatzkian vocabulary in IR is Janice Bially-Mattern's (2011) sketch of "a practice theory of emotion for IR". Bially-Mattern (2011: 64) describes emotions as practices that are distinct to other forms of action, being conceptually and analytically irreducible to more elementary, constitutive forces. She thereby argues against simplifying the phenomenon and assuming emotion as a product of either/or types of causal forces in terms of explanation. The claim that practice rests on a unique ontology, however, can be interpreted differently. She criticises Adler and Pouliot (2011a, b, c) for taking a position "that practice is 'suspended' between structure and agency, materiality and sociality", which implies that "practice is not possible without all four components of social life" (Bially-Mattern 2011: 70–71).

Bially-Mattern (2011: 72, 75) follows Schatzki by arguing that "agency is a result of practice rather than its source", and that "practice is a component of social life in its own right". She uses these insights to develop her conceptualisation of taking emotion as an expressive social practice. That is, emotional ways of being become socially intelligible as bodies competently perform the techniques that bring them into being. Competent performances are things that people *do,* and they are learned through social engagements (Bially-Mattern 2011: 77). Fear, for instance, is an emotion a human being learns to experience, understand, and recognise on many levels (biological, cultural); emotions are therefore "not *just* doings; they are competent ones". Thus, emotion is not understood as an internal, subjective experience, but rather as an external, intersubjective one. As practices, emotions are as much public as they are private. "They happen, as it were, across levels of analysis" (Bially-Mattern 2011: 79).

In sum, Bially-Mattern's notion of emotional practices suggests understanding them as socially meaningful, competent bodily performances that simultaneously constitute and express one's experience of being, generate human social order, and create the agency that transforms it. For her, the major promise of a Schatzki-inspired practice perspective is that "it encourages theories and methods for IR research that embrace, rather than assume away, the complexity of emotion" (Bially-Mattern 2011: 81). As Bially-Mattern (2011: 84) summarises, "the key to analysing emotional practices in world politics is to focus on the competent performances that, in the moment of their enactment, express how the 'doer' is experiencing her own existence as a being in the human world". Whereas emotions are often treated as an issue of impact in IR, Bially-Mattern (and Schatzki) demonstrate that it is more interesting to address how emotional practices matter in world politics.

Schatzki's sophisticated practice account is primarily useful in theoretical terms by providing practice-oriented scholars with guidance on the organisation and complex arrangement of practices as bundles of activities. Many IR scholars use Schatzki's conceptual work to explain the difference and added value of a practice-oriented perspective in specific issue areas such as EU diplomacy (Bicchi and Bremberg 2016), or global environmental change (Spaargaren 2011). In the latter, Schatzki's account is regarded as particularly helpful in bridging the divide between agency, structure, and technology, in that he provides conceptual language that emphasises the symmetry and relatedness of the three concepts (Spaargaren 2011: 817). His definition of practice also conceptualises difficult issues such as the normativity of practice by integrating the element of teleo-affective structures.

To some degree, Schatzki develops a middle ground between the more structuralist, human-focused approaches of Giddens and Bourdieu and the more radical posthuman versions of practice theory developed, for instance, in actor-network theory. Schatzki is, however, first and foremost a social philosopher who translates Wittgensteinian and Heideggerian philosophy into a practice ontology that considers contemporary debates on agency, materiality, and the distinction between society and nature.

For Schatzki, his practice account also has implications for empirical research as he attempts to translate it into organisational research (Schatzki 2005). Following him (2005: 476), one central task in comprehending an organisation is identifying the actions that compose it. A second key task is identifying practice-arrangement bundle(s) in which these actions take part as well as discovering where these bundles cohere or compete. A final task is identifying other nets of practice-arrangement bundles to which the net composing the organisation is closely tied. Although he also makes concrete methodological suggestions such as the requirement of 'participant observation', which involves "watching participants' activities, interacting with them (e.g. asking questions), and – at least ideally – attempting to learn their practices" (Schatzki 2005: 476), the major value of Schatzki's account lies in its high potential to sensitise further theorisation and conceptualisation in vocabularies from other disciplines.

Although Schatzki's ambitious site theory provides powerful methodological tools with which to sensitise empirical observation and theorisation, these are so prescriptive and imprecise, that "they risk hampering, instead of facilitating, the work of empirical social researchers", as put by Nicolini (2013: 179). For him (2013: 179), Schatzki's sophisticated theoretical outline, which considers all the permutations of practice (the four basic mechanisms) is problematic, because "exploring how practices are linked together is an empirical, not a theoretical, question".

Schatzki's attempt to develop a complete architecture of conceptualising practice stands in opposition to less prescriptive approaches such as actor-network theory. A more general problem of practice approaches, which are primarily based on philosophical traditions, is that they do not translate easily into empirical research agendas, and how they can inform the study of international practices therefore remains questionable. This might be why practice turn scholars in IR have principally been interested in sociology, social theory, and to a lesser extent philosophy.

Notes

1. This, obviously implies that we pay less attention to other Foucauldian discussions, such as on the concept of biopower.
2. A task and focus that demonstrates resemblances between Foucault and pragmatists such as Dewey (see Barnett 2015; Koopman 2013; Vanderveen 2010 and Rabinow 2011).
3. For a discussion of these two diverging interpretations of governmentality, see, among others, Walters (2012: 93–109) or Death (2013).
4. Other studies include Merlingen (2003) and Jaeger (2008, 2010).
5. See Fougner (2008), Porter (2012), Davis, Kingsbury and Engle Merry (2012a), or the contributions in Broome and Quirk (2015).
6. See, for instance, Friedrichs and Kratochwil (2009) or Lebow (2007), who use the term without pointing to its origins or further elaborating on it.
7. Besides the works discussed above, other articles using or referring to CPA in contexts related to IR include Wilson (2006) on development policy, Gilson (2009) on NGO networks, Lachmann (2011) on the Alliance of Civilizations, O'Toole and Talbot (2010) on learning in the Australian Army, and Roberts (2010) on Humanitarianism.

CHAPTER 4

Approaches in International Practice Theory II

This chapter continues our review of the main IPT approaches. We discuss three of them; the focus on narratives, actor-network theory and pragmatic sociology. In contrast to the approaches discussed so far, these are examples of groups of authors who have developed a common vocabulary, rather than being clearly focussed on the body of work of a distinct theorist. Moreover, in IR discussions, narrative approaches and actor-network theory have not always been included in the body of practice theoretical thought, although, as we demonstrate, and as is widely acknowledged in other disciplinary contexts, they are an essential part of it. Pragmatic sociology is one of the younger approaches, having only reached the IPT discussion quite recently. As in the prior chapter, our objective is not exegesis, but to provide a concise introduction to the conceptual vocabulary and strategies for the study of practice outlined in the approaches, and to explore their respective advantages and disadvantages.

4.1 Narratives and Storytelling

The concept of narrative has experienced a renaissance across the social sciences, and the practice theoretical discussion is no exception. Narratives are conceptualised in a specific way; if in textualism it tends to become a synonym for 'discourse', 'collective myths', or 'ideology', others relate it to strategic action and conceive narratives in terms of frames, arguments or scripts. The concept should be understood as an intermediary term,

C. Bueger, F. Gadinger, *International Practice Theory*,
https://doi.org/10.1007/978-3-319-73350-0_4

which avoids substantialist notions, however. Practice theorists adopt a processual understanding of narrative and emphasise that narratives or ‘stories’ function as the social bond, or ‘glue’ that gives practices stability over time and space (cf. de Certeau 1984: 70; Rouse 1996: 27).

Narratives, in this sense, are a form of configuration device by which actors make sense of the world and order it in a specific way. They order a heterogeneous world into more-or-less coherent configurations. As Jerome Bruner (1991: 4) remarked, “we organise our experiences and our memory of human happenings mainly in the form of narrative – stories, excuses, myths, reasons for doing and not doing, and so on”.

Narrative approaches therefore assume that “human beings are inherently storytellers who have a natural capacity to recognise the coherence and fidelity of stories they tell and experience” (Fisher 1987: 24). However, storytelling is never an isolated action; stories are part of practices and imply joint activities. Storytelling is a social practice used by people to understand each other and build the social bonds of collective identity. For Barbara Czarniawska (2004: 3) the “enacted narrative” is “the most basic form of social life”. Her notion of the ‘enacted narrative’ points to the performative dimension of narration: narratives are required to be acted out and hence always relate to practical activities.

In practice research, narratives are a tool to analyse controversies as ‘battles’ between different narratives, which are employed by actors in their deliberative practices to make sense of a problem (Fischer 2003). In organisation studies, narratives are used to understand power struggles as practices of successful or failed storytelling (Czarniawska 1997). Narrative is constitutive of action in organisations insofar “that stories shape the organisational landscape as individuals and organisations become actors in their own stories” (Fenton and Langley 2011: 1186). Narrative is, therefore, a mode of knowing and enacting in the world that reminds us that language is not a purely technical repertoire we use in communication to make rational arguments. The splitting of the real from the fictional, or the myth from the logos, is an understanding that holds sway in both natural and social sciences. However, our everyday language makes it obvious that the boundaries are blurred. It is not a coincidence that the consideration of current political events (e.g. the Brexit vote, Donald Trump’s electoral victory, Erdogan’s rise) is often interpreted through the prism of novels (Shakespeare), television series (*House of Cards*), and films (*The Great Dictator*).

In IR, the concept of narrative is principally related to practices of collective storytelling describing the emergence of larger community building and identity construction in the tradition of *Imagined Communities* (Anderson 1991). Some examples include the process of European integration (Eder 2009), narratives of redemption in the Israeli Negev (Galai 2017), and historical foreign policy changes (Barnett 1999). Narrative approaches move practice theory closer to the research agenda of cultural and literature studies by reconsidering identity, legitimacy, and collective sense-making. They are a way of giving meaning to practices, of producing social bonds and identity through collective storytelling, and of providing actors with a sense of direction to coordinate their activities.

Three core ideas provide the foundations of narrative approaches: narration has to be understood as an interplay between storytelling actors (*homo narrans*) and audiences; narratives entail power relations; and narratives organise the stream of polyphony (Gadinger et al. 2014a).

Firstly, narrative approaches conceptualise actors as "storytelling animals" (MacIntyre 1984: 216) or as *homo narrans* (Koschorke 2012). Such a conceptualisation of actors is closely related to the model of *homo ludens*, which projects actors as players (Huizinga 1949), and the understanding of creative actors in pragmatism (Joas 1996; Boltanski 2011). Narration requires agency in two ways: on the one hand, narrative involves human beings as characters or actors in the unfolding of a plot, that is, actors have a distinct role in a story (Polkinghorne 1988: 19–20). They can, for instance, be the heroes in a story. On the other hand, narratives require the voice of a narrator. This means that a narrative is never neutral, and that narrative constructions of the world are attempts to make sense of reality (Patterson and Monroe 1998: 316). Storytelling is subjective, and linked to practical judgments of selective interpretation, personal experiences, and sequencing of events (cf. Somers 1994: 616). Narratives are therefore configurations and attempts at collective sense-making. We are never the sole authors of our own narratives.

Storytelling is embedded in cultural practices of everyday life, and involves an audience. As Czarniawska (2004: 5) argues, "in every conversation a positioning takes place which is accepted, rejected or improved upon by the partners in the conversation". In other words, when narrative is the "main device for making sense of social action" (Czarniawska 2004: 11), it is also a political device that generates legitimacy and mutual agreements. Narratives provide a glue for practices, but they are not static and therefore change over time. Searching for a common understanding through narrative is a fragile process of retelling stories; narratives therefore need to be seen as conditional and joint achievements.

Should they lose their credibility and thus their legitimising function, narrators and their audiences adjust stories. Hendrik Wagenaar (2011: 212) describes this process as follows: "[t]he audience will judge the story's coherence, plausibility and acceptability. If it fails on any of these counts, it will suggest adjustments or suggest a different story altogether". Storytelling therefore depends on the craft of producing a narrative that is both aimed towards the future and resonates with a wider audience.

To provide an example: the plausibility of U.S. presidential candidate Donald J. Trump's ability to 'make America great again' once in office was never the point of the narrative, particularly because no coherent definition could ever capture what this 'greatness' actually was. Instead, inciting collective emotion was the central goal of Trump's campaigning narrative, a ploy that successfully appealed to a significant electorate. Thus, the power of storytelling follows criteria other than the logic of a superior argument. Although Trump's dubious moral convictions and the explicit blurring of the line between fact and fiction may have shocked many people, truth is not necessarily key to the power of storytelling activities. Despite this makeshift construction and temporality of narrative, all groups, communities, or collectives – be it families, organisations, peoples, or nations – depend on collectively shared stories as social bonds. A continuous and active retelling of stories is important for legitimacy and social order. Shared stories, however, can unite and divide, especially in politics.

Secondly, storytelling is always about power. Narratives are organised in particular configurations, or 'plots'. These plots are rooted in a range of practical choices of actors: strategic purposes, moral judgments, aesthetic preferences, or claims of power and authority. This means there is always a close connection between the moral meaning of a story and its plot as well as its ending. Stories are seldom told just for fun; there is an underlying purpose to them (Wagenaar 2011: 214).

To argue that narratives are always part of power relations does not imply that this refers to the material capacities of actors. Rather, storytelling is embedded in cultural practices of communication and related to distinct opportunities of articulation (Gadinger et al. 2014a: 10–12). Not everyone can tell stories at any time. The practice-theoretical understanding of narration involves closely scrutinising the rhetorical devices and narrative techniques used, such as negotiating, governing or disputing. 'Successful' storytelling, which reaches wider audiences, implies the dramaturgical involvement of powerful metaphors, figures of identification and, often, 'tricks'. Maarten Hajer (2009: 40) argues that the right mixture between narrative, conflict, and drama determines whether policy facts have news value and reach a wider audience: "[n]o representation without dramatisation".

Stories also function as "affective triggers insofar as emotions and narrative are deeply intertwined" (Mayer 2014: 7). The dimension of power is crucial when a narrative is configured and sequenced in a beginning, a middle, and an end, also known as emplotment. It is emplotment that "gives significance to independent instances, not their chronological or categorical order" and "translates events into episodes" (Somers 1994: 616). Once a plot has been established, the association of events with actors is likely. These associations occur through narrative configuration, where the cause becomes the initiator, the solution turns into the redeemer and both invoke solidarity or even imitation in a different manner. In processes of conflict resolution, nation-building, and the memorisation of past experiences of violence, for instance, the question of how narratives are configured and how knowledge is selectively appropriated is primarily one of claims to power and authority.

Selecting the beginning of a story is already an intrinsically power-imbued action, because it determines which information disappears and which events are kept alive (Koschorke 2012: 62). In international politics, different types of stories are dominant. Stone (2002: 138–145) argues that in policy issues, two types of stories are most relevant: the story of decline, in several variations (e.g. *change is only an illusion*); and the story of helplessness and control, in several variations (e.g. *blame the victim*). In IR, Paul Sheeran (2007) similarly argues that international politics can be understood through the mode of narrative by referring to key works in world literature that provide typical stories: the romances of heroes and villains, the romantic struggles for a utopian society, and the tragedies of power politics.

Thirdly, storytelling is relational, and narratives tend to overlap. A narrated world is a non-linear stream of multiple narratives, most suitably described as 'polyphony'. Narration is a collaborative and unpredictable practice in which narrators and audiences come to a shared understanding. There is more than one narrative told at any single point in time. Narratives are always both telling/presentation and told/presented; that is, they involve time and sequence.

Narration can be understood as a dialogical communicative process involving the dynamic interaction of two temporal strands, the present and the past (Kreiswirth 2000: 303). Such a bivalent understanding of narrative as a contingent stream of reception and transmission points to a "powerful third entity" between narrator and audience that are organised in distinct practices of communication (Koschorke 2012: 87). The UK riots in 2011, for example, provide an apt case illustrating what polyphony means in political discourse. To make sense of this puzzling event and its violence, both the British government and protesters used the powerful metaphor of a 'broken society', albeit in completely different ways. Whereas the government used it to legitimise a law and order narrative by claiming that criminal youth had broken a societal contract, the protestors (unsuccessfully) mobilised a narrative of moral blame for the Conservative-led government, which had, according to them, reinforced inequalities and structural racism in society (Gadinger et al. 2014b).

The fluid re-arrangement of connected parts and elements in narrative configuration brings the concept close to the notion of 'translation', as developed in actor-network theory (ANT), or by Luc Boltanski, discussed below. Similar to ANT, narrative approaches put emphasis on polyphony and the capacity of narratives to translate heterogeneous elements into single, uniform collectives with joint objectives. Narration can also fail, however. Inconsistent or unmanageable translation may hinder the coordination of multiple voices from becoming a collective sense-making narrative.

In IPT, the concept of narrative is closely related to the work of Iver Neumann (2002, 2005, 2007, 2012). His approach has been notably developed by using diplomacy as the core empirical case. Neumann attempts to re-combine the study of meaning in discourse analysis with the study of practice to gain a better understanding of 'culture'. However, here the term 'culture' is understood not as a fixed entity or as causal variable, but as a circuit of practice, discourse, and stories (Neumann 2002: 637). For Neumann, stories or narratives are of key importance due to their intermediary function in this cultural circuit, and the power relations they establish. As he argues in referring to narrative sociologist Margaret Somers, people are guided to act in certain ways on the basis of "the projections, expectations, and memories derived from a multiple but ultimately limited repertoire of available social, public, and cultural narratives" (2002: 637). For him, "the social fact that actions are ordered in a particular way and not another may be conceptualised as a story that instructs specific people in specific contexts" (Neumann 2002: 637). In this 'instruction', however, lies the duality of narratives: stories can reproduce practices, constrain them and block forces of renewal, or they may produce new practices, "open a field for them", and thereby can lead to social change (Neumann 2002: 635, 637).

Equipped with this conceptualisation of 'narration in practice', Neumann illustrates how diplomacy works in the field, and that "to be a diplomat" (Neumann 2005) involves juggling different and often contradicting scripts rooted in deeper cultural narratives of Western diplomacy. The bureaucratic script, for instance, guides diplomatic work in established routines such as text-producing practices; yet the heroic story that Neumann calls the "script of the deed" (Neumann 2005: 73), requires the diplomat to rove around the world as a trouble-shooter and to gather new intelligence information. Finally, the self-effacing role as mediator completes diplomats' difficult task of balancing the tensions in the Western narration of diplomacy and the performing of practices 'at home' and 'abroad'. Diplomats cannot reconcile the polyphony of different scripts; they can only learn to juggle them in practice.

In a detailed analysis of speechwriting as a diplomatic practice that draws on the case of the Norwegian Ministry of Foreign Affairs, Neumann (2007) shows another aspect of narration: the coordination of different voices to preserve the legitimacy of a collective. Neumann recognises that speeches are attempts of the ministry to speak with one voice. Speeches, then, are less the result of a sort of tug of war; rather they emerge in a process "in which different points of view and emphases are patched together in a manner that everyone can live with" (Neumann 2007: 192). The practice of speechwriting therefore hinders innovative moves by repeating existing practices and ideas. In other words, the "focus of diplomacy is maintenance, not change" (Neumann 2012: 16). Neumann (2012: 171) concludes that diplomats are moulded to serve the needs of power; however, most of the time they are influenced indirectly by discourse and not by direct orders from superiors. Diplomats are caught in reproductive stories; they "monitor and govern their own practices by drawing on the stories that discourse holds out" (Neumann 2012: 171). Neumann clearly underlines how a focus on narratives and stories can provide promising avenues for the study of international practices.

There is a large body of other studies in IPT that translate the narrative dimension of practices into conceptual and empirical work. Bueger (2013a) draws on the concept of narrative to investigate the justification and persistency of Somali piracy. Linking the concept of narrative to the community of practice approach, he argues that Somali pirates are organised by a 'grand narrative' that projects piracy as a quasi-state practice of the protection of sovereignty against foreign intruders. As Bueger (2013a: 1812) argues, the pirate's "coastguard narrative" has two core functions: firstly, it provides coherence to the Somali piracy practice across time and space and stabilises the identity of the community as coastguards. Secondly, the narrative has strategic value, rendering piracy more effective and attempting to produce legitimacy and recognition for piracy as a practice that has socio-political objectives. Such a perspective on piracy as a narrative-driven practice provides a major alternative to theories that conceptualise pirates as economic, rationally calculating individuals, as well as to studies that focus primarily on the root causes of the phenomenon. Paying attention to narrative here reveals how actors justify and organise their practices by positioning themselves.

In the case of US foreign policy, Richard Devetak (2009) provides a different version of the narrative approach and shows how the construction of events in global politics, such as September 11, is intrinsically tied to narratives. In the absence of storytelling, there would be no meaningful event. September 11 did not speak for itself, and is interpreted in many different ways. Devetak (2009: 804–808) identifies five narratives that emerged after the event. These respectively describe September 11 as a trauma, as a world-changing event, as an act of terrorism, as an act of war, or as an act of evil. Each of these interpretations creates different worlds through collective storytelling.

Indeed, as Devetak (2009: 803) argues, events do not exist independently or outside of narratives. This means that events do not precede narrative, but instead are articulated and moulded through them. In this process of enactment, narratives draw on prior moral and political scripts, and predispose policy responses and practices. As a result, the dominant narration of September 11 as an act of (or a new kind of) war provides different strategic choices and legitimises new rules and practices, such as targeting states for harbouring terrorists or doubting the relevance of the Geneva conventions (Devetak 2009: 809). This approach links directly to literature studies. By using Don DeLillo's novel *White Noise*, in which an 'airborne toxic event' is told collectively, he is able to successfully show how similar patterns of narrative practices produce the fictional and real, i.e. the literary and political world.

Studying the war on terror, Lee Jarvis and Jack Holland (2014) use the concept of narrative to explain the political conditions around the death of Osama bin Laden. They argue that the narration of these events was characterised, firstly, by considerable discursive continuity with the war on terrorism discourse of George W. Bush, and, secondly, by a gradual removal or 'forgetting' of bin Laden and the circumstances of his death. The latter construction of forgetting is particularly interesting in terms of narrative. This took place via a "stylistic shift towards 'cleaner' language and metaphorical description", and "through an increasing focus on the consequences – rather than fact and details – of his death for the US and its constituent publics" (Jarvis and Holland 2014: 2). Each of these narrative dynamics contributed to the legitimisation of his killing. Furthermore, the case shows the importance of narrative remembrance and forgetting alike for the conduct and justification of liberal violence.

Ronald Krebs (2015a, b) introduced the concept of narrative in foreign policy analysis and security studies by writing a new description of US foreign policy during the Cold War. For him (2015a: 810), explanations of US policy are narrowly focused on the dominant, but rather static narrative of national security in terms of a *Cold War consensus.* That is, changes in foreign policy are determined by military defeats (Vietnam trauma) while the stabilisation of a dominant narrative follows military triumph (Cuban Missile Crisis). In a detailed narrative reconstruction, Krebs (2015a: 811) submits the opposite, contending that "the disheartening Korean War facilitated the Cold War narrative's rise to dominance, whereas the triumph of the Cuban Missile Crisis made possible that narrative's breakdown before the upheaval of Vietnam". Krebs's broader analysis (2015b) can be understood as a suggestion to overcome the narrow focus on either strategic actors in foreign policy or on structuralist explanations of systemic constraints.

This implies reconsidering much of the received wisdom in international politics, and taking a closer look at narrative changes in foreign policy by considering the narrating skills of political figures such as John F. Kennedy. The role of myths in international politics is therefore closely related to narrative studies, and remains a rather unexplored issue in IR. A recent edited volume (Bliesemann de Guevara 2016) rebuts the common notion of myths as fictions and shows the ideological, naturalising, and depoliticising effects of myths as well as their constitutive, enabling, and legitimatising functions in international politics. Prime examples are the 'graveyard of empire' in Afghanistan, which guides Western thinking in intervention issues (Kühn 2016), and the myth of civil society participation as a legitimising tool in global governance (Dany and Freistein 2016).

Research on transitional justice is another field in which narrative approaches have been developed. Susanne Buckley-Zistel (2014: 144), for instance, notes that the past can never be (re)visited, but only grasped from the purview of today. It is therefore important to look at the construction of knowledge about this past. She argues that people use narratives as a strategy to endow events and experiences in their lives with meaning in order to come to terms with them. Studying the case of truth commissions in South Africa, Buckley-Zistel (2014: 149–154) illustrates how the stories of victims or witnesses of past crimes are embedded into an institutional framework. This framework defines the causal emplotment, selective appropriation, and sequencing of the story, and therefore determines the structure that forms thinking and enunciation. Consequently, she argues, "reconciliation became the term that endowed narratives with meaning in order to foster nation-building in the deeply divided society" (Buckley-Zistel 2014: 155).

Other studies around issues of transitional justice explain processes of conflict transformation and memory politics through concepts of narrative and practice. Mneesha Gellman (2017) demonstrates how ethnic minority groups use strategic narratives in countries including Turkey and Mexico to mobilise memories of violence in order to shame states into cooperating with claims for cultural rights protections.

In the case of Israel and debates about 'New History', Lisa Strömbom (2012) shows that narratives of war can be reversed through the introduction of narratives of thick recognition, which generally play a major role in processes of conflict resolution. Accordingly, Joelle Cruz (2014) explains, with a stronger emphasis on practices, how traumatic memories reconstruct present-day organising practices using a case study of a group of market women (called *susu*) who guarantee food security in the post-conflict context of Liberia. By using an ethnographic approach, Cruz (2014: 453–458) effectively demonstrates how traumatic memories engender and sustain the three organising practices of idealisation, amplification, and contraction.

These studies show how narratives make past experiences understandable and create conditions for future action and organising practices. Narrative approaches here show how various forms of action in which the past and the present are linked are socially negotiated through narrative practices. More generally, the concept of narrative provides a promising methodological entry-point to analyse the negotiation of identity by considering different plots, which are commonly used to make sense in post-conflict scenarios (Khoury 2017).

Narrative approaches foreground the importance of meaning-making and symbolic representation for the study of practices. Narratives not only provide stability for practices, but are also powerful devices for making sense, for justifying political actions, and providing instruction in concrete situations. Storytelling has an ordering effect on practices in everyday life;

a plausible story creates order in a shifting, unpredictable and incoherent environment (Wagenaar 2011: 216). The growing relevance of narrative analysis in practice research is "rooted in its ability to serve as a tool for describing events and developments without presuming to voice a historical truth" (Shenhav 2006: 246). During situations of crisis (e.g. the global financial crisis, the EU migration crisis, and urban protests) a change of practice occurs in conjunction with a reconfiguration of dominating narratives. Narrative approaches also build bridges to other cultural approaches, notably discourse analysis.

The incorporation of practice theory into narrative analysis and vice versa builds a bridge between the practice turn and the linguistic turn in constructivist thinking (Faizullaev and Cornut 2017). The analysis of rhetorical devices and narrative practices, including the use of metaphors, forces of imagination and other rhetorical tricks (e.g. Hülsse 2006; Marks 2011; Oppermann and Spencer 2016) become more relevant than in other IPT approaches. This also includes visual narratives such as films, documentaries, photos, and images as carriers of meaning in political storytelling (e.g. Gadinger et al. 2016).

Critics have raised doubts as to whether narrative approaches are consistent with the family of practice theories (Frost and Lechner 2016b: 300). This broadening can also be criticised for its focus on discourse and structure, in particular when narrative is conceptualised in terms of metastructures such as collective myths or grand narratives. A new dualism of narrative and practice can arise, thereby contradicting the core ideas of practice theory. Narrative approaches, moreover, foreground the linguistic dimension of practice. They focus on sayings rather than doings, and hence tend to downplay the material dimensions of practices, including the importance of bodies and objects. Furthermore, a focus on the fluid process of narration carries the risk of blurring narrative and practice into one fuzzy concept. The narrative approach, however, adds an important dimension to the study of practice, and more directly than others, links the study of practice to recent work in cultural studies.

4.2 Actor-Network Theory

What has become known as actor-network theory, or ANT for short, is an approach to the study of practice developed primarily in science and technology studies. Its best-known protagonists are sociologists of science and technology such as Bruno Latour, Michel Callon, Karin Knorr Cetina,

Annemarie Mol or John Law. ANT has not necessarily been received as a practice theoretical approach in IR.[1] This might be related to the lack of formal declarations of intent to focus on practice theory by ANT protagonists, in the relative hesitation of ANT to give the term 'practice' equal prominence as other practice theorists do, or in the often strange and exotic vocabulary of ANT, which tends to cloud the obvious linkages to other practice approaches and its membership in the practice theory family.

Indeed, in many ways ANT is the black sheep of this family. ANT pushes some of the ideas of practice theory the furthest: it focusses on the study of associations and relations by which the world is assembled and becomes ordered, it stresses contingency and fluidity, invents new terms and concepts, and aims at a thoroughly symmetrical position between the social and the material. However, as commentators in IR and elsewhere have argued, it appears strange *not* to think about ANT as a theory of practice. Social theorists, therefore, usually include ANT in their discussions of practice theory; this move is also significant for IPT.

Like other perspectives, ANT was invented in different places at the same time. For John Law (2009: 142–146) ANT formed at the intersection of studies of technology, field work in laboratories and theoretical discussions in French sociology on Michel Serres' semiotics, Gilles Deleuze's relationalism, and the work of Foucault. The first generation of ANT consisted of studies of scientific laboratories or of technological inventions, as the interest of scholars in what scientists actually do when they go about their work led to ethnomethodological studies of academic practices in laboratories. Latour and Woolgar's (1979) *Laboratory Life*, which reported on the work in the Californian Salk laboratory, and Latour's (1987) *Science in Action* were the most influential.

These studies presented thick descriptions of the kind of activities that scientists perform in laboratories, how they speak and act and thereby create objects, fabricate facts and establish certainty for their knowledge. They showed what kind of social and material infrastructure is required to stabilise facts and other entities, and how it becomes possible for them to travel beyond the laboratory. Latour describes these early studies as attempts to visit the "construction sites" (Latour 2005: 88) in which innovation, new knowledge and new entities were manufactured. As he outlines, through ANT "we went backstage; we learned about the skills of practitioners; we saw innovations come into being; we felt how risky it was; and we witnessed the puzzling merger of human activities and non-human activities" (Latour 2005: 90).

Studies on technological interventions, by contrast, were interested in when and how the invention of new technologies succeeds or fails. These studies demonstrated the complex web of material and social relations that make technological inventions. Classical studies include Michel Callon's (1986b) study of the failure to establish the electric vehicle as a main transport device in France, as well as his investigation of the cultivation of scallops at St. Brieu Bay (Callon 1986a), Law's (1987) study of the Portuguese maritime empire, Law and Callon's (1992) publication on airplane technology, Latour's (1988) work on the success of Louis Pasteur in eliminating anthrax, or his study of a transportation technology in *Aramis, or the Love of Technology* (Latour 1996).

Part of ANT's expansion since the 1990s consisted of considerably broadening the empirical focus. Studies went 'beyond science' and started to address various subject matters, including different kinds of organisations and technologies (Law 1994; Czarniawska 2008), health practices (Mol 2002), financial markets (Callon 1998; MacKenzie et al. 2007), or law-making (Latour 2010). Political entities such as 'the state' also became objects of ANT focus (Passoth and Rowland 2010).

Venturing into such domains also brought ANT much closer to IR concerns. Throughout the 2010s ANT has gained considerable traction in IR, with studies addressing different phenomena, ranging from international organisations, to airports, failed states, or climate change. Although the actor-network *theory* label suggests otherwise, ANT – similar to practice theory in general, as explored in Chap. 6 – should not be understood as a 'theory' in the conventional sense. In Law's (2009: 147) understanding, ANT is primarily "a toolkit for telling interesting stories" about relationality and how one can interfere in these relations. For Mol (2010b: 281) ANT "is a loose assemblage of related, shifting, sometimes clashing, notions, sensitivities and concerns". As these descriptions highlight, ANT is a relatively broad conglomerate of empirical studies. The easiest way of grasping what ANT involves is to investigate a number of core ideas and concepts.

At the heart of ANT is a strong version of relationalism. ANT studies how different 'actants' – that is, anything that acts or has the capacity to do so – are related to each other, the practical work that is required to make and maintain these relations, how actants become powerful by holding multiple relations together, and how these relations are challenged and changed over time. Phenomena such as agency, objects, knowledge, power, or concepts are hence understood as effects of relations.

The concept of actant is crucial here. Rather than postulating that only humans can create and maintain relations, ANT also ascribes such capacities to non-humans, that is, objects, machines, or animals. The intention is to treat humans and non-humans, as well as the respective domains of 'culture' and 'nature', in the same manner, without having a separate vocabulary for each of them. If other practice approaches argue that non-humans, or 'the material', play a key role in practices, in ANT this idea is pushed further, and the material and the social are treated on equal terms.

Due to its emphasis on relations and the practical work that goes into making and maintaining them, ANT has also been described as an extended version of semiotics, as "material semiotics" (Law 2009). In semiotic thinking, words acquire their meaning relationally, through their similarities and differences to other words. Words form part of a network of words. ANT extends such an understanding from language to the rest of the world. Mol (2010a: 247) gives the telling example of 'fish': "the word 'fish' is not a label that points with an arrow to the swimming creature itself. Instead, it achieves sense through its contrast with 'meat', its association with 'gills' or 'scales' and its evocation of 'water' " (Mol 2010a: 257).

In ANT, this understanding is generalised. "It is not simply the term, but the very phenomenon of 'fish' that is taken to exist thanks to its relations. A fish depends on, is constituted by, the water it swims in, the plankton or little fish that it eats, the right temperature and pH, and so on" (Mol 2010a: 257). ANT, then, involves studying the makeup of relational networks in which phenomena such as fish, technologies or concepts are given content and form through relations.

The core intent of ANT is consequently to describe and understand the formation of such networks and the practical work required to make them durable and stable. Most studies provide thick narratives of how relations are woven and maintained, and how different actants become associated with each other. Many of the concepts that ANT uses are from everyday language or taken from the empirical situations in which they have been found. Over the course of these empirical studies, however, a range of distinct concepts has also been developed. It is useful to know them; although ANT implies keeping conceptual vocabulary parsimonious due to the priority given to the empirical, these concepts provide useful conceptual starting points for writing an ANT analysis. The concepts of 'translation', 'blackbox', 'obligatory passage point', and 'laboratory' are especially useful for the concerns of IPT.

The concept of translation is perhaps the most generic concept developed in ANT studies. Introduced by Callon (1986a, b), it addresses the way in which actants become related. Initially, it refers to nothing more than the relation between two or more actants. For Callon (1986a: 197), "to translate is to create convergences and homologies out of particularities." Through translation, actants become interested in working together and develop shared objectives. In this process, the identity of the actants changes as they take on new roles. This notion of changing identities through translation foregrounds a major difference between ANT and conventional network theory, which assumes that actors have a stable identity before they enter the network and that these remain constant. For ANT, actors are not quite the same from situation to situation, as they transform in the process of translation (Gad and Bruun Jensen 2009). They are transformed in their movement between practices; actants are found in different yet related versions, and networks develop through actors' transformational interactions (Gad and Bruun Jensen 2009).

The concept of a blackbox, coined by Latour in his *Science in Action* (1987), describes a situation in which a new entity emerges and the relations and controversies that were required to bring it about have been forgotten or are hidden. What was required for the entity to be built, all the hard work and the conflicts that had to be won, are no longer visible. Think about any machine we use in our everyday life. One hardly questions how these work, or why they work the way they do. We use a smart phone, a car or computer, but if we don't pursue a career as an engineer, we have very little knowledge about why they function as they do.

Latour discusses the example of an overhead projector. Usually, the projector is a "point in a sequence of actions" (Latour 1994: 36), for instance, a lecture. In such situations, the technology mediates. The overhead projector processes an input – a small slide – into an output – a large projection on the wall. It is "a silent and mute intermediary, taken for granted, completely determined by its function" (Latour 1994: 36). But what happens if the projector breaks down? We become aware of its existence. In the event of such a crisis, "the repairmen swarm around, adjusting this lens, tightening that bulb, we remember that the projector is made of several parts, each with its role and function" (Latour 1994: 36). Watching the repairmen at work makes us aware not only of the parts that make the projector function, but also the sequence of human actions required to allow it to do so. Latour's story of the failing overhead projector is a classic case of a blackbox and how it is made visible. In ANT's generalised symmetry, processes of blackboxing and unboxing do not only refer to technologies, but to any phenomenon or entity. A scientific fact can be understood as a black box, as can a concept, a routine, or an institution.

The equally influential concepts of obligatory passage points and spokespersonship were coined by Callon (1986a) in his seminal study of the fishermen of St. Brieu. Both are concepts of power, and grasp the concentration of relations and the emergence of nodal points in webs of associations. The terms refer to a situation in which an actant has achieved a central position and can exert control over the network. The concept of 'obligatory passage points' points to a network in which one actant has become influential to the degree that the network cannot be enacted or transformed in a meaningful way without taking that entity into consideration. Relations have to pass through the element both to enact the network, as well as to transform it.

Obligatory passage points therefore mediate the relations in an actor-network and often define roles or scripts of action for others associated in it. If networks become stabilised and well ordered, this often leads not only to one actant exerting internal control, but also representing the whole of the network towards others. In this scenario, one actant becomes the 'spokesperson' for the network. In ANT logic, such a spokesperson could be, for instance, a non-human entity to which the whole of the network has been delegated. While non-human spokespersonship tends to provide more durable networks (Law 2009: 148), a spokesperson in principle may also be a human, as is the case in Latour's (1988) story of Pasteur speaking in the name of anthrax.

The results of early ethnomethodological work on scientific laboratories led ANT researchers (Rouse 1987, Latour 1987) to generalise 'laboratory' as a concept that stands for a site in which many relations are made and hold together. In this sense, the concept refers to a distinct locale in which different actants work together to process inputs into outputs. For Rouse (1987), a laboratory could be seen as a general model of power. In them, "systems of objects are constructed under known circumstances and isolated from other influences so that they can be manipulated and kept track of" (Rouse 1987: 101).

Latour (1987) coined the notion of 'centres of calculation' to speak about laboratories. For him, such centres were sites "where information is being created, collected, assembled, transcribed, transported to, simplified and juxtaposed in a single location, where everything that is relevant can be seen" (Law 2003: 8). In such centres, traces can be explored which stand, in a single place, for a whole set of events and processes distributed through time and space. These become a centre as the result of an asymmetrical configuration of a structure and the flows that move along it. The efforts of all elements become directed by, and indeed belong to the centre, "which comes to stand for and articulate them all" (Law 2003: 8). The translation of the concept of laboratory in such generic models of powerful locales spurred some criticism. For instance, Guggenheim (2012) criticises the proliferating use of the term, warns about conceptual overstretch, and suggests that the concept should be restricted to actual science laboratories. In response to such criticism, Latour (2005) proposed the notion of ***oligopticon*** to refer to sites that have extraordinary capacities to create and maintain relations. He points to bureaucratic units or military command and control centres as instances that perform such functions. Indeed, state capitals or international organisations can also be interpreted as such.

With these concepts, ANT studies have developed a rich vocabulary. The concepts display a degree of 'emptiness', however. While they imply a certain ontological stance, they require empirical research to bring them to life, and can hardly be said to constitute a theory independent from empirical material.

In IR, William Walters (2002) was perhaps the first to draw attention to the ANT perspective. Arguing that we should pay more attention to the material of politics, he drew on Latourian insights to show how a bureaucratic form is a vital actant in European integration. Since then, ANT studies have gained significant traction, on one side as a consequence of the interest in IR for practices and the material, but also because many ANT scholars have increasingly branched out beyond the narrow focus on science and technology and started to study international phenomena.

Lidskog and Sundqvist (2002) were among the first to demonstrate the analytical power of ANT in the analysis of global governance, and in particular providing a new conceptualisation of the link between science and politics. Studying the Convention on Long-Range Transboundary Air Pollution (LRTAP), they illustrate how one of the most effective global environmental regimes during the Cold War was jointly co-produced by scientists and politicians. Lidskog and Sundqvist argue, in a nutshell, that environmental science provided a neutral ground for political cooperation between Cold War adversaries. As they put it, the "politicians' search for neutral – politically uncontroversial – issues to cooperate on was an important explanatory factor with regard to the scientific character of the regime"

(Lidskog and Sundqvist 2002: 89). Scientific knowledge has continued to shape the evolution of the LRTAP regime in the following years. Drawing on ANT, Lidskog and Sundqvist describe in particular how, in the 1990s, scientists became crucial in translating the interests of states into the expanding LRTAP regime, enabling them to cooperate in a far reaching agreement to cut emissions.

In Bueger and Gadinger (2007), we argued in favour of understanding the discipline of international relations as a web of relations and associations, which makes it the task of a sociology of IR to disentangle these relations. Bueger and Villumsen (2007) used ANT concepts to understand how the 'fact' of the democratic peace was manufactured and translated into foreign policy doctrine. Maximilian Mayer (2012) developed ANT concepts to show that the securitisation of climate change relies on different material artefacts, while Peer Schouten (2014: 23) drew on the case of Amsterdam airport to show how security actants "perform security by enrolling, assembling and translating heterogeneous elements into stable assemblages that can be presented as definitive security solutions or threats".

In an attempt to show the relevance of numerical indices, current peer review practices and their effects, Tony Porter (2012) linked ANT to international political economy. For Porter, humans and objects, in his case indices, form transnational networks that can considerably alter the conduct of states. Criticising the lack of attention to the agency of objects in IR, he reveals, for instance, how World Bank indicators have blackboxing effects. Porter's strategy follows classic ANT studies in that he starts by outlining core concepts of ANT and then proceeds in essentially providing a thick empirical narrative of the formation of transnational networks.

Bueger and Bethke (2014) give us an example of how ANT can be employed to study the career of a concept. Investigating how different actors become associated by the concept of failed states, they show how different actants struggle to establish spokespersonship and obligatory passage points, though none of them fully succeeds. In consequence, the notion of failed states has not become fully blackboxed. While the concept successfully relates security and development actors to each other, the network remains heterogeneous, with no single actor controlling it. These examples forcefully document that the applications of ANT's vocabulary in IR are manifold. In contrast to other IPT approaches, ANT foregrounds attention to detail, and often produces microscopic types of analysis. It is especially useful if one is interested in emerging phenomenon, and wants to put more emphasis on the role of the material in shaping the international.

ANT has not been without criticism, however. In the first instance, this concerns ANT studies' style of analysis – they are often obsessed with inventing new terms. As a result, the language employed can be opaque and lead to rather quirky concepts and terms. The open-ended character and multi-vocality of the narratives developed and the experimentation with different literary styles tends to simultaneously fascinate and alienate many readers. Indeed, at times, it makes ANT studies very difficult to access. The second core critique is levelled at the generalised symmetry of ANT and its attempt to treat humans and non-humans in the same terms. This is not solely an ontological problem, and raises questions of whether non-humans can have intentionality (Schatzki 2002). The anti-humanist stance also leads to ethical *problematiques*, for instance whether it is appropriate to treat humans like objects; whether in a world of actants anyone can still be held accountable for their actions. Finally, the degree of contingency of the world that ANT studies assume also questions the status of historical processes and development at a larger scale. The fluid, relational worlds that ANT describes and its micro-orientation appears to leave little room for history and social stability over time (Nexon and Pouliot 2013). Consequently, larger forces of power and global inequalities, such as class or gender, are hardly conceptualised, or even mentioned in ANT (Winner 1993; Hornborg 2013).

4.3 Pragmatic Sociology and the Work of Luc Boltanski

The pragmatic sociology of Luc Boltanski is a slightly less-established approach in IPT. This is somewhat surprising, given the popularity of Bourdieu's praxeology and the fact that Boltanski presents one of the most prolific critiques of it. Boltanski is one of the main protagonists of a broader counter-movement to the dominance of Bourdieu in French sociology. This movement, sometimes referred to as a 'pragmatic turn', also includes other sociologists such as Laurent Thévenot, Ève Chiapello, Michel de Certeau, and Bruno Latour. Although many of these scholars do not formally claim to be practice theorists, they are effectively doing practice theory.

Boltanski's main focus lies in overcoming dualisms such as the individual and society or agency and structure. He draws inspiration from American pragmatism by focusing on action, situations and 'critical capacities' and rejects methodological individualism. In contrast to rationalist actor-models, he understands 'action' in its broadest sense; it takes place within a multiplicity of orders, in a combination of common worlds, and in hybrid relations between subjects and objects, humans and non-humans (Dodier 1993). To describe this world, Boltanski develops a vocabulary of conventions, coordination, capacities and practices of justification and critique as the main driving forces of social life. He also speaks about translations, relations or associations akin to the ANT vocabulary. Boltanski is, therefore, less interested in the reproduction and stability of practices than the Bourdieusian tradition. Instead, he is fascinated by the fragility, uncertainty and disorder of the social, and how actors are nevertheless able to coordinate their lives. This is characterised by a stream of 'critical moments' and 'tests' they experience in everyday life shared with others in human coexistence.

The objective of Boltanski's pragmatic sociology is not to improve Bourdieu's social theory, although he frequently criticises it and accuses the notions of habitus and field of implying structural determinism (Boltanski 2011: 18–22). His main contribution to the practice turn lies, rather, in the innovative combination of ethnomethodology in the tradition of Harold Garfinkel and pragmatist action theory as laid out, in particular, by John Dewey. In contrast to wider debates on social theory (Bénatouïl 1999; Blokker 2011), IR has yet to recognise recent pragmatist theorising as part of practice theory (Kratochwil 2011: 38). Pragmatists in IR (Friedrichs and Kratochwil 2009; Hellmann 2009; Schmidt 2014) have emphasised the potential of pragmatist thought to develop new research methodologies. However, IR is preoccupied with classical pragmatism, that is, the work of Dewey, James, Mead, and Peirce. In consequence, pragmatism is mainly understood as a philosophical programme, rather than a sociological or empirical one.

Boltanski's pragmatic sociology has the potential for IR scholars to translate pragmatism into an empirical approach to studying practices. This interest in contested normative orders and the moral judgments of actors in the interpretation of situations builds a bridge to norm-oriented theorising in IR, such as Wiener's theory of norm contestation (Wiener 2008). Relying on the notion of 'controversies', Boltanski demonstrates how pragmatism's micro-analytical interests in actions, contingency and creativity can be combined with a macro-structural consideration of normative orders and moral principles – termed as 'orders of worth' or regimes of justification (Boltanski and Thévenot 2006). From such a perspective, in practices micro-(situations) and macro-perspectives (orders of worth) play together when actors attempt to cope with conflicts in everyday life.

In order to understand Boltanski's pragmatic sociology, it is easiest to reflect on some of its core methodological premises, which allow us to navigate through Boltanski's heterogeneous, multi-world approach and manifold concepts.

Firstly, pragmatic sociology stays true to the ethnomethodological dictum of 'following the actors' (Boltanski and Thévenot 2006: 11–12; Latour 2005: 23–25). This implies rejecting a division between 'ordinary actors' and 'professional analysts', or, at least, attempting to minimise the distance between objective and participant observation. For pragmatic sociologists, "social practices cannot be understood from an objective standpoint alone, because they are internally related to the interpretations and self-images of their participants that can only be grasped if one takes their perspective as fundamental" (Celikates 2006: 21).

According to Boltanski, the imperative to 'follow the actors', sometimes misunderstood as simple participant observation, firstly means that actors, thanks to their critical capacities and reflective competences, possess relevant knowledge about the world; therefore an adequate theory of practice can only be developed in a joint enterprise that integrates their interpretations of the world as the main elements in theoretical construction. He therefore rejects the privileged position of social scientists as objective analysts in a static, predictable world, and seeks to inspire the analyst to phenomenologically "return to things themselves" (Boltanski 2011: 24). While this symmetrical position has been criticised by some IR scholars (e.g. Sending 2015) working in the tradition of Bourdieu and Foucault by claiming a loss of scientific autonomy, for Boltanski the opposite is true. He sees it as a way to renew the possibility of a critical sociology by "focusing on the critical capacities of ordinary actors and by taking as the subject of empirical research those situations, abounding in ordinary life, in which actors put into play these capacities, especially in the course of disputes" (Boltanski 2013: 44). Boltanski is aware that such a symmetrical position cannot take the totality of these effects of actors' actions into account. Nevertheless, the focus on analysing situations as the "social world in the process of being made" provides a framework that makes action "itself visible" (Boltanski 2011: 44).

Secondly, pragmatic sociology aims to foreground the importance of actions. Boltanski (2011: 60) understands practice as a "certain register of action". Practices form in a continuous stream of acts and have "neither a definite beginning nor a definite end" (Franke and Weber 2012: 675). To conceive of practice as made up of sequences of acts means understanding situations as open spaces between routines that perform established practices and crises that create new practices (Franke and Weber 2012: 675–677). Agency is, therefore, considered in a more substantial manner, and in pragmatic sociology, actors are "active, not passive" and "frankly critical" (Boltanski 2011: 26). Following this reinterpretation of the concept of action as creative and critical also leads to refraining from stable and fixed understandings of actors.

The term 'actant', developed in ANT to emphasise the lack of definite clarity regarding who or what acts when we speak about action, is also used by Boltanski (2012: 178). He uses it to interpret competences of action that come in different variants and combine the worlds of individuals, groups, collectives or institutions. This understanding underlines the radical uncertainty and "unease" in courses of action "that threatens social arrangements and hence the fragility of reality" (Boltanski 2011: 54).

'Situation' is one of Boltanski's principle concepts, yet situations are not understood simply as an enabling or constraining context of action. In situations, action occurs and relatively undefined goals and means are formulated, modified and reformulated (Joas 1996: 154–161). Human action is therefore deeply implicated in situations or controversies that are always in need of interpretation by the actants involved (Blokker 2011: 252).

The pragmatist notion of 'test', borrowed from Latour (1988), is one of Boltanski's key concepts and sheds light on how actors resolve uncertainty expressed in controversies. Tests in a general sense "refer to the way reality is shaped" (Bogusz 2014: 135). Such ambiguous moments (*situations troubles*), during which feelings of awkwardness and anxiety arise in involved participants (Boltanski and Thévenot 2006: 226), call for clarification and justification: what is the situation at hand, who is involved, and who is allowed to articulate claims? The imperative of justification and the uncertainty of the situation can be much stronger than the rationalist premise of justification as mere rhetorical action by powerful actors.

Thirdly, Boltanski's pragmatic actor model replaces Bourdieusian power struggles of positioning in fields with the practical competences, critical capacities and an "ordinary sense of justice" that actors mobilise in their daily struggles to reach agreements (Boltanski 2011: 27–29). This does not imply that, from a pragmatic point of view, the world is projected to be harmonious. Instead, in complex societies, life tends to be trapped in various sorts of disputes and controversies about what is going wrong and what needs to be done. In such situations, the person "who realises that something does not work rarely remains silent" (Boltanski and Thévenot 1999: 360). Individuals who are involved in such situations are subjected to an imperative of justification, that is, actors prove their competence in these moments of conflict and use higher normative principles ('orders of worth') to defend their cause by justification and critique.

The justification and critique produced by actors in situations are not random or without reason (Celikates 2006: 31). Instead, arguments have to follow rules of acceptability that are based on these different orders of worth, and which need to claim a contribution to a common good in society (such as the *volonté generale* in the civic world, or profit in the world of the market). While the term 'orders of worth' remains vaguely defined, it intends to grasp those central grammars which provide legitimate social bonds in democratic societies and which are culturally embedded as regimes of justification. Thus, orders of worth provide "repertoires of evaluation consisting of moral narratives and objects that enable tests of worth" (Hanrieder 2016: 391).

The relation to a shared order of worth, culturally understood as contributing to the common good, makes it easier to accept a defeat in a 'test' situation. The notion of practice refers to the practical and reflexive competences of actors in which these different forms of justifications are employed, and actors deal with a plurality of potential orders of worth in particular situations (Guggenheim and Potthast 2011: 160–161). A key feature of such tests is their inherent character of contention (Boltanski and Thévenot 2006: 133), as disagreeing actors are often uncertain as regards the worth of people in the situation at hand. Effectively, this means that actors consciously decide when it is either most appropriate to engage in justification – or opening one's eyes – or when it is best to not distract oneself by unproductive struggles – or closing one's eyes (Boltanski and Thévenot 2006: 232–236).

In summary, the pragmatic sociology of Boltanski is the IPT approach that most particularly emphasises the normative and moral dimensions of practice. However, it is important to note that Boltanski is not interested in developing a normative theory of justice. Instead, his objective is to unmask belief in universalism, to unveil pathologies in emerging orders of justification – such as the 'new spirit of capitalism' (Boltanski and Chiapello 2007) – and to strengthen the role of critique by taking the critical capacities of knowledgeable actors who invoke justice in the world seriously (Boltanski 2012: 28). What makes his approach a genuinely practice-oriented one is that the analytical separation between micro (situation) and macro (orders) is permanently transcended through a focus on changing practices of justification and critique. Justification becomes a social practice founded on an intersubjectively and normatively based process of ordering.

In IPT, Boltanski-inspired pragmatic sociology is increasingly used to understand controversies about policy issues that are shaped by a plurality and contradiction of normative orders, and to shed light on the social dynamics of political judgments in international politics (e.g. Kornprobst 2014). If one interprets, for instance, the case of U.S. foreign policy from the perspective of pragmatic sociology, the 'war on terror' transforms from a hegemonic discourse to a fragile justificatory narrative that needs to be tested by critical actors in everyday legitimacy struggles. The 2004 debate over torture and abuse at the Abu Ghraib prison in Iraq can be reconstructed as a controversy between politicians, military personal, journalists, NGOs, and ordinary citizens. These actors not only employ different orders of justifications of international law, human rights or military necessity, but also resources such as expertise, statistics, or visual representations to support their legitimacy claims (Gadinger 2016).

By taking a micro-oriented view on the Senate Armed Services Committee's public hearings, it can be demonstrated that disputing actors use distinct, and in the case of Senator Dayton and General Myers/ Secretary Rumsfeld, incommensurable principles of equivalence based on different orders of worth (Gadinger 2016: 199–200). In other words, actors employ different moral judgement criteria in definitions about the good, the just, or the morally right thing to do, which includes distinct culturally rooted grammars of legitimate behaviour.

It is a typical 'reality test', in that actors disagree on the reality as it is ("[i]t's a misunderstanding of the situation" in the words of Rumsfeld). In doing so, actors use different measurement instruments, proofs, and objects established in each order of worth. Statistics are used to strengthen legitimacy claims by justifying actors when, for instance, a total of "seven bad apples" in Abu Ghraib was compared to the number of American troops in order to relativise the scandal as an "isolated incident".

Meanwhile, critical actors use investigation reports as external expertise, such as the International Committee of the Red Cross report on systematic abuse in U.S. prisons, to strengthen their moral claims. While critics' main general argument was that the war on terror undermined core democratic principles and contradicted the objective of defending the national security of the United States in the long term, justifications by members of the Bush administration were primarily based on rationalist and technocratic orders of worth by using short-term objectives (state of emergency, 'we are at war') and historical comparisons of earlier war experiences. In this moment, the normative contestation cannot be resolved as different rationalities in modern democratic governance are revealed. The moral concern of the actors who criticise the breach of the torture norm and the undermining of civil liberties as the more significant common good contradicts the overall emphasis on national security measures, meaning that democratic and legal standards need to be downplayed during wartime to guarantee the safety of 'our troops'.

Finally, the analysis of the public hearings shows the moral standards and shared values within the practice 'official investigation'. Although the repetitive, routinised statements of nearly all senators who honour the merits of the US military could be interpreted as empty phrases, they reveal the practical understanding and implicit rule of safeguarding the US military as a credible institution that has long guaranteed national security. While this tendency of the established practice can be criticised as support of further militarisation, it sheds light on the criteria of how to follow the rules as political actors, which, in this case, implies narrow limits in formulating critique. While it is acceptable to sentence 'seven bad apples' in the military at the lower level, it seems to be unacceptable to risk the general credibility of the institution by bringing top-level decision-makers such as former defence minister Donald Rumsfeld to court (Gadinger 2016: 201).

The United Nations (UN) is another site of legitimacy struggles where practices of justification can be studied. Holger Niemann (2015) argues that the UN Security Council is narrowly interpreted in terms of great power politics, which neglects its role as a site of social interaction. The Council's legitimacy heavily relies on practices of justification and critique by involving actors. That is, a pragmatic view shifts from "legitimacy as a quality *of* the Council to legitimacy as a claiming of moral rightness *in* the Council" (Niemann 2015: 1). Following Boltanski, even the veto, the Council's most distinctive feature, is not a simple tool of genuine power politics, but rather can be understood as a 'test' between competing legitimacy claims based on a plurality of moral standards. The veto is public, and needs to follow the imperative of justification. Using the case of the 2011/2012 vetoes on Syria, Niemann shows that the veto marks a crucial moment for pragmatic analysis as legitimacy claims are mutually tested, and different orders of worth such as 'appropriate means', 'rule-following', and 'responsibility' are translated into practical reasoning. The different references to responsibility exemplarily show the "normative weight of being a responsible member of the international community constructively cooperating with other UN members" (Niemann 2015: 21).

While such a study is not blind to power, its main emphasis is on a pragmatic notion of legitimacy as an unexplored dimension that analytically grasps the simultaneity of moral dissent and consensus as part of social ordering in a powerful organization. Analysing such practices of justification helps to understand the dynamics of legitimacy claims in an organisation that is caught between diplomatic conventions of politeness and the high politics of war and peace.

Tine Hanrieder (2016) similarly adopts Boltanski's sociology to analyse different moral conceptions of health as a highly valued, but essentially contested issue in global politics. By using the framework of orders of worth, she identifies four main conceptions based on a different idea of health as a common good (survival, fairness, production, and spirit), which therefore provide different criteria for distinguishing a virtuous sacrifice from a selfish pleasure. Hanrieder's pragmatic view enables, on the one hand, an understanding of the ambiguous and contested character of political controversies on health issues. On the other hand, it changes the notion of political identity in terms of self/other narratives in IR scholarship by emphasising the plurality of orders of worth as moral narratives that connect visions of universal humankind to ideas about moral worth and deficiency.

Another source of inspiration for practice-oriented research in IR, particularly in IPE and critical governance research, is Boltanski and Chiapello's (2007) major work on the 'new spirit of capitalism'. In this research, they identify and investigate an emerging order of justification based on managerial capitalism. Matthew Eagleton-Pierce (2014), for instance, explains the early genesis of the policy notion of governance in relation to ideological changes in a 'new spirit of capitalism'. For Eagleton-Pierce (2014: 6), the emergence of governance, such as the formulation of a 'governance agenda' by the World Bank from the 1980s, can be understood in light of a relationship between political crises, social critique, and justificatory arguments around security and fairness claims that form part of an ideological spirit. The new spirit of capitalism therefore provides a flexible vocabulary for politicians to legitimise neoliberal policy changes.

As Christian Scheper (2015) shows in the case of corporate governance discourses, there is a strong recourse to human rights awareness as being perceived in terms of 'good' business. However, Scheper demonstrates that this shift towards a concept of corporate responsibility for human rights represents the capacity of capitalism to absorb fundamental criticism and incorporate the very values that formed the ground for critique.

Vando Borghi (2011) draws on the "new spirit of capitalism" – a term by which Boltanski and Chiapello (2007) identified an emerging order of justification based on managerial capitalism – to describe current transformations in European welfare capitalism. According to Borghi (2011: 323), the two pillars of EU welfare capitalism that serve as crucial institutional guidelines – employability and activation – have emerged as devices for a paradoxical torsion in a process of individualisation. This leads to a growing shifting and weakening of the meaning of 'public'; it is in turn being increasingly replaced by devices and models of social regulation based on direct and horizontal interaction between individuals in a network of coordination that goes beyond any institutional mediation, and is therefore at great risk of de-politicisation (Borghi 2011: 334).

In a similar line of argumentation, Frank Gadinger and Taylan Yildiz (2012) argue that attempts to solve the European financial crisis in the late 2000s indicate shifts in institutional politics to network capitalist regimes of justification. In their reading, the financial crisis represents a moral discourse that involves an irreducible plurality of normative principles. By using the framework of orders of worth, they identify different forms of test in the arena of the European Parliament. In the parliament, actors compete in claiming legitimacy but avoid using any 'existential test' in the form of radical critique. Project-based orders of justification and rhetorical patterns of New Public Management become visible in the parliamentary justifications and critiques. In these justifications, the financial crisis is transformed from a policy issue and a deeper crisis of identity to a management problem.

Finally, Søren Jagd (2011) demonstrates that pragmatic sociology is suitable for empirical studies that shed light on the co-existence of competing rationalities and institutional logics in organisations. He argues that the framework can be used through both a synchronic perspective to describe co-existing orders of worth in particular organisations, as well as a diachronic perspective to focus on 'justification work' by studying the processes of critique, justifications, testing, or compromising performed by actors (Jagd 2011: 348). The links to practice-oriented IR research on international organisations (e.g. Barnett and Finnemore 2004; Best 2012) are quite obvious.

As Paul Blokker and Andrea Brigenthi (2011: 283–284) rightly argue, one of the promises of pragmatic sociology is to challenge monistic assumptions of political order that downplay the plurality of legitimations used by actors. Instead, politics is understood as an interplay of different forms of justification, distribution, constitution, and defiance. Contingency, uncertainty, conflict and the lack of both closure and completion of politics is emphasised. In pragmatic sociology, the "social world does not appear as a place of domination suffered passively and unconsciously but more like a space intersected by a multitude of disputes, critiques, disagreements and attempts to produce local agreements" (Jagd 2011: 345–346).

Contestedness, ambiguity, and contradictions that arise between multitudes of legitimate claims in situations of conflict become visible in empirical studies drawing on pragmatic sociology. More generally, pragmatic sociology provides us, as Anders Blok (2013: 495) rightly notes, with an original theoretical matrix for "registering the grammars of moral evaluation, as actors search for the common good in everyday situations of conflict and coordination". Compromises can always be reached, however, although they are not immediately apparent in logics of action or the personal disposition of actors.

Compromises and agreements are always fragile and provide only a minimal notion of stability in social life. The reproductive understanding of practice in Bourdieu's work is therefore substituted by the creative effort for actors to adapt, modify and arrange their practices of justification and critique in relation to the situation of conflict. For pragmatists, there is a high degree of uncertainty that makes social reproduction and stable order nearly impossible. Sebastian Schindler and Tobias Wille (2015), for instance, recently criticised Pouliot's pioneering Bourdieusian work on diplomatic practices in NATO-Russia relations (2010b) for its strong emphasis on the stabilising habitus, ultimately underestimating moments of uncertainty such as the period after the Cold War.

Such debates are exemplary discussions between 'critical' and 'pragmatic' scholars. The pragmatic view on practice marks a clear shift away from the world of practice theorists focused on power and regularity, such as Bourdieu. This world is perceived by pragmatic scholars as an unlivable world, since it seems to be entirely governed by power and the reproduction of stable hierarchies and classes. However, as Peter Wagner (1999: 349) rightly remarks, the world of Boltanski is "an equally unlivable world, since it appeared as if people were constantly engaged in justice and that they were always in action". Indeed, while pragmatic sociology rediscovers the critical capacities of actors, it tends to underestimate the restricting nature of power structures and institutions (Honneth 2010: 382). The pertinent question, therefore, becomes whether situations can really be conceptualised as an open space in which people interact free from 'fields of power' and are driven primarily by their critical and creative capabilities. The notion of compromise happening in action remains vague in conceptual terms, and needs further clarification.

Pragmatic sociologists are currently broadening their conceptual apparatus from justification to other modes of action, such as love or violence (Boltanski 2012; Thévenot 2007). Until now, Thévenot's promising research programme as part of the 'convention school', which generally analyses economic, social, and political conventions that regulate uncertain coordination (e.g. Thévenot 2007), has remained overlooked in IR research. This can be seen as further engagement with a general social theory of conflicts. However, this ambitious scope does not make it easier for IR scholars to translate this vocabulary into the research agenda of IPT. The adoption of pragmatic sociology to study legitimacy struggles and their "practices of legitimation" (Reus-Smit 2007) thus seems to be the most promising path.

Boltanski's approach provides a valuable tool for analysing political controversies, as it gives us a detailed account of the regimes of justification employed by actors and their normative backgrounds. This does not mean that practice theorists are tricked by the 'cheap talk' of powerful actors. On the contrary, the embeddedness of normative principles in practices unveils the hypocrisy of moral claims and how they obscure relations of power and domination.

Boltanski's suggestion (2011: 103–110) to interpret legitimacy struggles in different kinds of 'tests' could be helpful, in analytical terms, to differentiate between stabilising practices and forms of critique as triggers of a renewal of social orders. The deep trench between pragmatic sociology and Bourdieu's praxeology should not be overstated. As Anna Leander (2011) suggests, the problems raised by pragmatic sociology against Bourdieu's promise could be used as a basis for a non-structuralist reading of Bourdieu, and to broaden empirical use of Bourdieusian concepts in IR. Moreover, while Boltanski's major work on the concept of justification resembles Latour's aversion to structuralism, he has more recently attempted to reconcile his pragmatic approach with Bourdieu's critical project by taking into account issues of resource inequalities, institutions, and complex forms of domination (Gadinger 2016: 189). As a matter of fact, he now describes his work as a 'sociology of emancipation' (Boltanski 2011).

Finally, pragmatic sociology should not be seen as a dogmatic research programme, as Boltanski is more driven by new empirical research topics than a thorough refinement of his conceptual vocabulary. Nevertheless, his work still provides an inspiring source for practice-oriented research. Whereas his recent book *Mysteries and Conspiracies* (2014) explores the practices of reality construction and its implications for sociological inquiry by analysing influential spy novels, detective stories, and conspiracy theories in our society, he has also started a new research project on consumption and value appreciation in capitalism (Boltanski and Esquerre 2017) that expands on his earlier work on the 'new spirit of capitalism'. Both studies bear relevance for IR scholars seeking to tackle questions related to global surveillance in critical security studies and the survival of global capitalism in international political economy.

Note

1. Nexon and Pouliot (2013), for instance, suggest that ANT is an "approach" or a "framework" distinct from relational theories and practice theory, although they suggest that the three share many resemblances and intentions.

CHAPTER 5

Conceptual Challenges of International Practice Theory

The seven approaches of IPT discussed in the preceding chapters represent clusters of scholars, vocabularies, ideas, empirical studies and questions. Our introduction to the core approaches has shown that each of them has their own advantages, as well as certain weaknesses. In this chapter, we consider how the approaches relate to one another, and how their relationships spur exciting new questions for future research.

To explore these relations, we focus on a set of challenges. By challenges, we mean issues that are contentious, present dilemmas or paradoxes, and IPT scholars take different positions on. The approaches outlined address these challenges via different routes. These differences must be appreciated as creative tensions; rather than playing the approaches against each other – suggesting that one is right and the other is wrong – or proposing that one has to choose between them, we argue that the contradictions or even antagonisms amongst them provide fruitful heuristics for advancing the IPT project. Reflecting on these challenges provides us not only with a range of interesting puzzles, but also with an outline of some of the main issues on the IPT agenda.

The challenges we discuss below are major ontological puzzles, and as such not necessarily genuine to practice theory, but of wider relevance in the social sciences. However, practice theory addresses each of these challenges, and this interplay is what we like to explore.

We begin with a discussion of the tension between an understanding of practice as a social regularity and as a fluid entity. This leads us to the question

C. Bueger, F. Gadinger, *International Practice Theory*,
https://doi.org/10.1007/978-3-319-73350-0_5

in how far IPT can make statements on the contingency and change of practical configurations. Next, we address the question of how to conceptualise the scale and size of practice. This is largely a question of (ontological) prioritisation that is nonetheless fundamental for a discipline that is primarily concerned with the international and the global. We continue with a reflection on different standpoints towards three core dimensions; that is, how to think about the normativity of practice, how the material dimension of practices (bodies, technology, artefacts) is prioritised, and how to conceptualise power and critique.

Our discussion is certainly not exhaustive. Further issues of importance, such as how to link theory and empirics, or what it implies to be reflexive, are discussed in the next chapter, where we consider the methodology of practice. Other concerns, whilst worthy of attention, do not receive substantial treatment here.[1]

5.1 Order and Change

One of the initial motives for developing practice theories was to gain a better understanding of the dynamic interplay between order and change (Neumann 2002; Spiegel 2005a). The reconsideration of agency, change and transformation in the context of practice theories has led to new discussions on ontology driven by a common objective of transcending the dichotomy of agency and structure (Spiegel 2005b: 11, 25). By locating the site of the social in practices, rather than individuality/agency *or* sociality/structure, practice theories have a different understanding of social order. They understand forms of social and political order as temporal processes, in which order is continuously produced and reproduced by practices. Orders and structures, in practice theoretical terms, are largely formed by routinisation, which implies their temporality. Routinised social practices occur in a sequence of time; "social order is thus basically social reproduction" (Reckwitz 2002: 255). It is therefore more meaningful to refer to the verb 'ordering', than the noun 'order'. Contrary to the logic of the vocabulary of agency and structure, order and change need to be understood as part of one continuous stream of practice, and not as opposites.

Practices are repetitive patterns, but they are also permanently displacing and shifting. Though they are dispersed, dynamic and continuously rearranging in ceaseless movement, they are also reproducing, organised and structured clusters. This morphing constellation forces practice theorists to be particularly aware of the continuous tension between the dynamic, continuously changing character of practice on the one side, and the identification of stable, regulated patterns, routines and reproduction on the other. Practices, as Rouse (2006: 599) phrases it, can "range from ephemeral doings to stable long-term patterns of activity".

This tension caused by the dual nature of practices defies easy solutions. It requires attention to the interaction between both the emergent, innovative *and* the repetitive, reproducing sides of practice. This leads to one of the most disputed questions posed by practice theories scholars: how can the dual quality of practices between reproduction and renewal be conceptualised? Can practice theory serve both analytical purposes and explain continuity as well as change? The practice approaches discussed all take stances on this question, providing differing suggestions of how to adequately grapple with the interplay of order and change. One should not expect an inevitable conceptual 'solution', however. A closer look at how practice approaches conceive of practical reconfigurations and transformations is needed.

To some degree, a fault line runs through IPT with regards to this question. On one side of this divide are theorists such as Bourdieu, Foucault and Wenger, and on the other relationalist and pragmatist scholars such as Boltanski or Latour. The former theorists are interested in larger formations of domination and historical processes; they tend to focus on regularity and risk to be read as underplaying the potential for transformation. For Bourdieu, repetition and reproduction is the norm; shifts are therefore considered rare and require a revolutionary event. Actor network theorists or pragmatic sociologists emphasise processes and relations and take almost the opposite position, claiming that stability, rather than change, requires explanation. The world is seen to be constantly emerging and shifting; practices are taken as inherently innovative, experimental and erratic. As a result, for these theorists, any context of action is a situation of uncertainty.

This divide is also reflected in the bewildering array of structural metaphors that have been proposed,[2] many of which are (intentionally or unintentionally) under-theorised. Bourdieu's notion of the field is certainly the most developed concept. Drawing on it assumes that a distinct structure exists over time, driven by a unique doxa and distribution of resources. Such an understanding of structure is useful if one is interested in the distribution of power among different agents and their relative positionality (e.g. Williams 2012). Drawing on the field concept is to assume that a fairly homogeneous structure with boundary and identity practices can be identified. The logic of this structure then becomes an object of study. In contrast to other concepts in practice theory, Bourdieu's structural metaphor is the most coherent. Significant similarities, in this sense, can be found in the community metaphor most prominently in Wenger's notion of 'communities of practice'. Here, the assumption is that practice is organised in community structures. Such communities are grasped as having a stable core (or 'repertoire' in Wenger's words) and relying on a significant amount of identity and boundary work by which the community distinguishes itself from others.

The other side of the spectrum of structural metaphors is occupied by notions that draw on the pragmatist obsession with contingency, fluctuation and situations. Examples include the Latourian notion of 'actor-networks', Schatzki's 'bundles and meshes', Foucault's 'apparatuses', but also the Deleuzian concept of the 'rhizomatic assemblage' (Acuto and Curtis 2013). These are almost chaotic notions of structure and order, centering on multiplicity, overlap, complexity, incoherence and contradictions between structural elements. As Marcus and Saka (2006: 102) phrase it, such conceptualisations are employed "with a certain tension, balancing, and tentativeness where the contradictions between the ephemeral and the structural, and between the structural and the unstably heterogeneous create almost a nervous condition for analytic reason."

The advantage of such metaphors is their genuine openness to the various possibilities of orderliness. They should not be understood as anti-structural notions, yet they foreground the ephemeral and stress that weight has to be put on empirical, situation-specific research in order to understand how ordered (or disordered) the world is. The price to be paid for such notions is, firstly, that it becomes almost impossible to lay out grand histories of panoramic scale and the power dynamics they entail. Secondly, employing such notions creates inherent contradictions for the presentation of academic research, given that academic research only becomes intelligible if phrased in relatively coherent narratives.

What are the implications for theorising change? In IR, change has been conceptualised by realists as the outcome of revolutionary wars and the redistribution of capabilities they imply, while constructivists have made the argument that change is caused by the rise of norms, or the work of experts, entrepreneurs and other actors.[3]

On a conceptual level, most practice theorists agree with constructivists that change arises through agency. However, as Latour (2005: 51) rightfully suggests, how to conceptualise agency could be "the most difficult problem there is in philosophy", especially if one, in contrast to the majority of constructivists, does not want to restrict the concept to humans and wants to avoid subscribing to methodological individualism.

Practice theories have been described as starting with the idea that the "world is filled not, in the first instance, with facts and observations, but with agency" (Pickering 1995: 6). The world, then, is "continually doing things" (Pickering 1995: 6). When social order is realised through a continuous stream of practices, agency plays the role of the central motor of that steady current. For Schatzki (2002: 234) agency is "the chief dynamo of social becoming". As discussed further below, for many practice theorists, notably actor network theory, 'doings' are also carried out by nonhumans. One may, therefore, also speak about 'material agency'.

Considering material agency does not assume that objects, things or artefacts act intentionally. It implies that forces of change may also be triggered by material elements (Pickering 1995: 17–18). In the study of practice, it often becomes difficult to decide who or what are the main driving forces of change. No cultural element in the interweaving relationship between the human and the material world is immune to change in emergent transformations of practices (Pickering 1995: 206–207).

For Schatzki (2002: 234), constant doing must not be equated with change. He distinguishes between minor adjustments and major ruptures in practice; a minor adjustment refers to the principle of indexicality (Nullmeier and Pritzlaff 2009) and the fact that any new situation requires adjusting and re-arranging the practice within it. Indexicality indicates the embeddedness of meaning in practical action, and emphasises that any form of social order arises from the situative circumstances of their use. From a practice theory perspective, "all expressions and actions are indexical" (Nicolini 2013: 138). Practice theorists who are principally interested in maintenance work in everyday life focus on activities in which practices are perpetuated and reordered minimally; they regard these gradual mutations in the wave of doings as the main driving forces of social change.

In contrast, a major rupture refers to those moments in which practices fully break down. This can be because of their failure, the rise of a newly emergent practice, the invention of a new object, or a new encounter between practices.

As Adler and Pouliot (2011a: 18–19) argue, there are different general frameworks that are useful in analysing how practice generates transformations in social life. They differentiate between the option of focusing on a practice's lifecycle, which refers to a genealogy and historical evolution of a practice over time and space, and the option of analysing the interplay and shifting relations between practices. Practice theorists following the second option are interested in the "permanent state of connectivity and tension inside a constellation of practices that fuels transformation" (Adler and Pouliot 2011a: 27).

The change of diplomatic practices in Pouliot's studies of NATO and its relationship to Russia is a good case study for the first option in analysing the dynamic historicity and contingent processes of transformations in security communities (Pouliot 2010a, b). The Bourdieusian-inspired studies in the field of European security are good examples of political transformations that emerge from tensions between different sets of practices in diplomacy, security expertise and technology innovation (Berling 2012; Adler-Nissen 2014). Finally, it can also make sense to combine both approaches and grasp the recursivity of practice in producing its own transformation.

The role of change remains a major challenge in practice theories. To make matters more complicated, rich and explicit conceptual discussions on these difficult issues are quite rare – Schatzki (2002: 189–264) is one of the few exceptions. For some approaches, change is a variation stemming from unexpected confusion and events in the reproduction process, while for others, change is constitutive of practice itself. As Reckwitz (2004b: 51) correctly points out, there is, however, no theoretical reason that practice theorists should be forced to accept either the reproductive or the erratic character of practice as the norm. He suggests that this issue needs to be turned into the analytical question of which practices, and corresponding conditions, take on an erratic or a reproductive nature. In other words, the attempt to find a universalist answer to the 'nature' of practices as either stable or ephemeral is fundamentally misleading (Schäfer 2013: 43). In this context, Rouse (2006: 507) argues compellingly from a philosophical point of view that "there is of course good reason to think that different social practices might vary in their stability over time, such that the extent to which social practices sustain a relatively stable background for individual action would be a strictly empirical question, admitting of no useful general philosophical treatment apart from characterising some of the considerations that might generate continuity or change".

The question of whether a practice is an ephemeral phenomenon or established in long-term patterns is primarily an empirical one. Understanding when and how practices transform under which conditions, consequently remains one of the main challenge for future studies in IPT.

A number of authors have proposed models to enable such empirical studies. Reasoning that too much attention has been given to the indexical and habitual side of practice, Ted Hopf (2017) argues for the importance of identifying those situations in which we would expect change to occur. Starting out from the pragmatist model that problematic situations trigger reflexivity and deliberate thought, he proposes a taxonomy of eight such situations.[4] For Hopf, we are to expect to see reflexivity at work in situations that are characterised by meaningful difference and the availability of plausible alternatives to proceed in practice, for instance. As he argues,

> for change to occur, there must be a discursive fit between a set of novel ideas and the already-existing, mostly taken-for-granted, set of ideas that informs the daily life-world of average people. [...] Too little difference will go unnoticed as it is easily assimilable to prevailing beliefs and taken-for-granted common sense. However, too much difference, understood as either unintelligible or excessively counter-normative, will also be ineffective. (Hopf 2017: 11)

While Hopf's taxonomy is a useful starting point for research, his commitment to a binary of two modes of action, action as habit driven routine on the one side, and action as reflexive and deliberate choice remains problematic. Rather than transcending the divide, his proposal risks perpetuating it.

Other useful proposals can particularly be identified in organisation studies, in which change has been one of the major research problems for decades. Here, practice theorists have developed a number of useful suggestions that provide inspiration for IPT. Yanow and Tsoukas (2009), for instance, make a similar move to Hopf, arguing for distinguishing between situations. However, instead of perpetuating the binary mode of habit/routine vs. thought/change, they offer a description starting out with the concept of reflective practice. They grasp moments of change through the notion of 'surprise' and proceed to differentiate between the temporality of surprise. As they suggest, surprise is often linked to the material and the artefacts that a practice is part of; the material talks back and does not allow one to proceed. On this basis, they distinguish between routine activity and three forms of interrupted activity through surprise and disturbances: 'malfunction' that can be addressed immediately, 'mild temporary breakdown' that requires deliberate attention to the task, and 'persistent breakdown' that requires reflective planning and the consideration of alternative actions.

Other organisation scholars make the opposite move, and argue in favour of empirically investigating the work required to stabilise a new practice or to prevent the total breakdown of a practice. Gherardi and Perrotta (2010), for instance, demonstrate how three modes of work stabilise a practice: firstly, 'limitation' implies that a new practice is deliberatively limited to the context and situations to which it would be appropriate, secondly, the categories of the new practices are defined and controversies black boxed through 'rhetorical closure', and finally, the practice is 'anchored in technology'.

Another example is the thick ethnographic study of a historical selection practice by Lok and de Rond (2013). They argue for turning the focus to 'maintenance work' and questioning why change does *not* occur. How can a practice be fixed and kept going and a total breakdown prevented? Investigating a range of cases of practice breakdowns, they develop a model of maintenance work that distinguishes between two basic forms of breakdown and link them to three modes of maintenance work (normalisation, negotiation and custodial work). Minor breakdowns require 'containment work', while major breakdowns, in their case the outcome of an accumulation of minor events, require 'restoration work'.

As these examples demonstrate, the challenge of change and orderliness can be turned into a productive starting point for practice-driven research. The above models provide useful categorical systems to facilitate research. One needs to be aware of the relativity of the distinctions made in these models, however, as what constitutes a minor or a major breakdown, or a breakdown at all, is often a matter of positionality, that is, a matter of from where one investigates practices, as well as what breadth or scale of practices in space and time one investigates. While from the perspective of a participant in an event, such as the failure of an everyday technology, might be a major breakdown, this is not necessarily the case if one zooms out of situations and into history. It is to the question of scale and size that we turn next.

5.2 Scale and Size

The majority of IR scholarship is interested in formations which appear large in scope. Whether it is international order, the international system, 'global' politics, regimes, international organisation, regional integration, state behaviour, or professions such as diplomacy and law, these are phenomena that appear large and 'macro' in scale. In contrast, IPT is often interpreted as a move of going 'micro'. As Ty Solomon and Brent Steele (2017) have argued, the turn to practices is triggered by the disappointment over the focus on global structures and systems and the failures of 'grand theory' to provide an account of global life. In that regard, the discussion in IR clearly differs from those social science disciplines which, for decades, have been heavily influenced by the micro-focus of symbolic interactionism and ethnomethodology. Within organisation studies, or science and technology studies, for instance, practice theory was initially introduced to re-work the assumptions of existing micro studies, but with a growing dissatisfaction over a localist focus, the tendency is to increasingly zoom out and go macro.

IR will certainly benefit from 'going micro' further by paying more attention to face-to-face interactions, routines and the situations and contexts that action is embedded in. However, this should not imply losing sight of the larger configurations, institutions and structures the discipline has focused on for decades. In its stead, practice theory is an invitation to rethink the consequences of working at a distinct scale, and what is implied by concepts of institutions and structures. Practice theory has developed different approaches to the issue, yet the problem of scale, or perhaps better, scaling, will remain a matter of debate and will demand new creative answers. IPT, given its empirical focus and disciplinary history, is particularly well positioned to provide interesting insights for the larger inter-disciplinary debate on practices.

One of the benefits of practice theories is that they do not take constructions of scale for granted. The intention of practice theory is to keep ontology 'flat' and re-conceptualise the ideas behind constructions of scale. Distinctions such as micro (face-to-face interactions, and what people do and say), meso (routines), macro (institutions), local (situations), regional (contexts), or global (universals), are not to be taken as natural categories. Indeed, there is no thing such as micro, macro, local or global; they are not naturally given. They are constructs of social scientists who adopt different strategies to try to make them so. Practice theory therefore aims at allowing "the transcendence of the division between such levels, such as that we are able to understand practice as taking place simultaneously both locally and globally, being both unique and culturally shared, 'here and now' as well as historically constituted and path-dependent" (Miettinen et al. 2009: 1310). The argument is that all social phenomena whether large or small, micro or macro have the same basic ingredients. How, then, does one transcend scale and work within a flat ontology?

One answer from practice theory is that the concept of practice is open in scale. To study practice does not prescribe a scale in time or space. Therefore, it is equally appropriate to study a seemingly large scale, such as Foucault's studies of modernity, or histories of practices of war, as it would be meaningful to study practices with a different zoom on a distinct policy, let's say NATO's military doctrine, or an everyday interaction, such as guarding a military camp. Using the concept of practice does not suggest a distinct level of aggregation. As Frank Nullmeier and Tanja Pritzlaff (2009: 10) have argued, this is not least because the borders of one practice with another are undetermined. Practices are often nested in one another; their inter-relation is complex.

The range of structural metaphors we have already introduced are specific attempts to study the linkages between practices. Notions such as 'fields', 'communities', 'bundles', 'actor-networks', 'apparatuses', or 'assemblages' are means of grasping how practices intersect and how these play out in multiple places, how they are situated and remain shared across situations.

Think about the practice of playing professional football. Football is played around the world every day. There are numerous different leagues; for example, the German Bundesliga is not quite the same as the English Premier League, or Spain's La Liga. A match in FC Barcelona's 100,000-seat Nou Camp stadium, famous for its fan culture and atmosphere, is a very different experience to a game in the smallest Premier League stadium, AFC Bournemouth's 12,000-capacity Dean Curt. Obviously, each match plays out differently. There have also been significant changes over time, as the sport has become more physically demanding, sophisticated new tactics have been developed, as well as new footwear or analytical technology. Despite all these differences, however, the game played is the same, as is what the practice assembles, ranging from boots to jerseys, pitches and goals, to the 22 players on the field. We know that it is a football game when we see it. To understand the practice of football there is no need to argue for a macro or micro dimension.

There are other consequences, the first being that we do not necessarily have to study each and every football game ever played, or every stadium around the world, to understand the practice. The study of practice does not necessarily entail studying the complexity of practice in its entirety. As argued by Schatzki (2005), it is often meaningful to develop overviews of fields of practice; this does not necessarily or always require tracking and registering "the potentially labyrinthine complexity" (Schatzki 2005: 477). In many cases, it is desirable and feasible to provide overviews referring not to the details of practice, but to larger formations. For Schatzki, such overviews operate on a higher plane of abstraction, "in the sense of extraction from a fuller reality" (Schatzki 2005: 477). Analysts might well prefer to describe phenomena on a broader, more abstract scale, rather than starting from a detailed description of situations.

The second consequence is to consider how research can benefit from exploring the interlinkages between sites. Though we might limit our research to the differences between football games in England and Spain, it would certainly be useful to study sites other than the game itself, and investigate what happens in locker rooms, training camps, club offices or the headquarters of football associations. Anthropologists have described such a perspective as 'multi-sited' (Marcus 1995).[5] The concern becomes to research "the logics of association and connection among sites" on the basis of "chains, paths, threads, conjunctions, or juxtapositions of locations" (Marcus 1995: 105).

An important proposal on how to think about the linkages between sites has been made by Karin Knorr Cetina (2005, Knorr Cetina and Bruegger 2002) who argues for the prevalence of what she calls "complex global microstructures". Knorr Cetina's starting point is to introduce a new understanding of what it means to be present in a situation, or 'response presence'. This form of presence is not based on physical locality or visual recognition by others as assumed in classical understandings of face-to-face situations. Instead, participants encounter each other through mediated forms of modern communication technology. They react to each other on screen, despite being in distant locations, which creates global microstructures through this interaction. Knorr Cetina and Bruegger (2002) use this conceptual vocabulary to understand how the global financial markets are produced on screens in connected locations. Knorr Cetina (2005) demonstrates how the same concepts can also shed light on global terrorist networks and the coordination of their actions. This is one productive proposal for how one can grasp the relationship between sites in a flat ontology without introducing overarching macro dimensions.

Distinctions of scale, such as micro-macro or local-global distinctions are dependent on statements. They are the outcome of descriptions by social scientists and others who introduce them and categorise phenomena in them. Another important strategy that practice theorists have adopted is to turn the making of scales and levels into an explicit empirical object of study. Authors including Tsing (2005) and Latour (1988, 2005) have shown how actors combine heterogeneous elements to make the global and the universal. They have foregrounded the work of bureaucrats, scientists and activists in creating scale by framing things as universal and international. The empiricist route of focusing on the making of scale and the emergence of scale hybridity as the main object of study is a promising one.

Not every practice-driven investigation will focus primarily on scale-making, however. Even if this focus is not explicit, it is important to recognise that practice theorists not only challenge traditional understandings of scale, they also introduce their own politics of scale. They construct scale by introducing structural concepts and by situating practice in larger containers. It therefore remains a matter of debate whether, contrary to the rhetoric of flat ontology, the containers and structural concepts *de facto* imply the introduction of meso or macro categories.

It is also noteworthy, as Nicolini (2017a) notes, that not all practice theorists embrace flat ontologies. This particularly relates to Bourdieusian approaches, which insist that there are macro-phenomena outside of practices, such as social classes or the state. One of the reasons for their insistence on macro structures is related to the question of power. Indeed, as we discuss further below (5.5), flat ontologies can be on shaky ground when it comes to approaching 'power'.

In any case, while it will be important for IR to go more micro, this does not imply embracing a romantic localism and restricting IPT to the study of face-to-face situations. In its stead, analysing how the micro is nested in the macro, how different situations are interwoven and how scale is made and grand historical categories are created will remain a major task for IPT in the future. It is a challenge that is linked to all the others, to the question of change, as discussed above, but also the questions of power, or theory and generalisation discussed later in this book (Chap. 6). Paying attention to scale is an important objective, not least as through its experience in the study of large constellations, IR scholarship can make significant contributions to the inter-disciplinary debate.

5.3 Normativity and Accountability

Practices are normative. They include evaluations and value judgments, such as whether a practice has been performed well, or they might suggest ought-to rules of how one should behave in a distinct situation. The widely received notion of practices as 'competent performances' that Adler and Pouliot proposed in reference to Barnes (2001), for instance, implies a strong normative dimension. As they argue, "the structured dimension of practice stems not only from repetition, but also, and in fact primarily, from groups of individuals' tendency to interpret their performance along similar standards", which can be "done correctly or incorrectly" (Adler and Pouliot 2011c: 7–8). This implies that normative evaluation is a fundamental aspect of practice, as its (in)competence is never inherent, but rather attributed in and through social relations appraisable in public by an audience.

The importance of the normative and evaluative dimension of practice remains a contentious issue, however. Developing the normativity of practice is, furthermore, an important driver of further exploring the links between IPT and other approaches in IR theory. The relation between practices and norms, and how to study them, is a shared concern of practice scholars and norm researchers. In IR, normativity is usually related to constructivist norm research. Such studies investigate how norms structure behaviour, how actors are socialised, how norms are diffused and translated and under which conditions individuals or collective entities comply with these.

The majority of constructivist norm approaches, however, rely on the concept of *homo sociologicus*. They often start with the assumptions of methodological individualism or tend to assume that norms, values and rules are rather static entities that have a live independent from activities and situations. In such an understanding, actors are mainly norm and rule followers, and their behaviour can be explained as a causal process. As more fully discussed in Chap. 2, such a determinist understanding of rule-following actors has little in common with practice theory.

From the practice theoretical perspective, obeying a rule is a social practice that is rooted in everyday activities, mutual practical understandings and interpretations of the demands of a situation. Such an understanding of rule-following goes back historically to a line of reasoning established in the work of Wittgenstein and Heidegger. Both gave priority to practice, and argued that meaning and language, and hence norms and rules, have to be understood *in use*. Practice theories share Wittgenstein's (2009: § 114) core assumption that "'following a rule' is a practice". Following rules and using language require a reliance on background knowledge, practical understandings, routinisation and situated learning of how to use language or apply a rule in practice. Wittgenstein's assumption clarifies the definition of practices as competent performances. It reminds us, firstly, that terms like competency and correctness are always established within a community and, secondly, that these terms imply a standard against which practice can be judged (Gross Stein 2011: 88).

Practice theories therefore offer conceptual alternatives to the often incoherent positions one finds in constructivist norm research in IR. Such research all too often ignores that rules and norms are always in need of interpretation in distinct situations. To some degree, the practice theoretical reasoning on normativity continues a line of theorising in IR that has developed Wittgensteinian insights, but hardly reached the (constructivist) IR theory core. Notably, the work of Kratochwil (1989) and Hopf (2002) presents projects aimed at understanding the link between norms and practice by emphasising that the interpretation of rules and meanings is grounded in practice. Both authors stress that norms and rules should be understood from below, and that attention needs to be paid to the practical reasoning of actors in situations. As Kratochwil (1989: 61) argued, "actors are not only programmed by rules and norms, but they produce and change by their practice the normative structures by which they are able to act, share meanings, communicate intentions, criticise claims, and justify choices." Hopf (2002: 12) described this departure from more conventional constructivism in similar terms: "[t]he exclusive search for norms and rules necessarily precludes the recovery of everyday practice, but the search for everyday practice necessarily will recover the explicit invocation of norms". The emergence of norms is based on practices and not otherwise. Practice-oriented researchers therefore prefer the term 'normativity', as it emphasises the fluid relationship between norms and practices (e.g. Schatzki 2002: 80; Frega 2014).

Antje Wiener's (2008, 2014) theory of norm contestation represents another attempt to understand norms as a social activity, in which normativity implies a continuous re-enacting of the normative structure of meaning-in-use by a multiplicity of agents. Wiener's work is in line with other critical norm scholars (e.g. Epstein 2012; Niemann and Schillinger 2016), who have begun to focus less on the effects of norms and instead turn their attention to processes, practices, and actions in international politics in which normativity is negotiated, contested, and embedded. Although these researchers tend not to explicitly frame their approaches within the Wittgensteinian tradition, their perspective enquires how and by whom normativity is produced, and therefore resembles the research objectives of practice-oriented scholars.

Given the importance of the Wittgensteinian argumentation for practice theory, it makes sense to briefly elaborate on it. Wittgenstein (2009: § 217, 219) emphasised that obeying a rule is a practice that is not rationally chosen, but is rather done blindly. Human agents do not decide before they act. They are active and engaged beings who use language as a fundamental resource in their interactive relationship with the world. These practical experiences of actions and reactions constitute the background and practical knowledge that enables sense making through everyday activities. For Wittgenstein, "to make sense of why we act, we have to look around us, not within us. The meaning of an act, just as much as the meaning of words, is in fact established in the practical context in which it appears" (Nicolini 2013: 38). Rule following is not a static procedure, therefore; instead, the decision to follow a rule or not is highly dependent on unarticulated background knowledge, and is related to 'situated accomplishments' (Lynch 2001: 131).

As Mervyn Frost and Silviya Lechner (2016a: 343) argue referring to Winch's definition of language-games (Winch 1958: 32), following a rule is knowing when a mistake has been made whilst stating something or performing an action. This understanding implies that when one learns how to participate in a language game, one also learns to follow a rule as an activity that forces one to make distinctions between successful performances and mistakes. Wittgenstein's understanding of rule-following and his notion of practice as language-games are highly relevant for current debates on normativity, and accordingly points to some major issues in IR research. Firstly, learning the 'rules of the game' is a complex social phenomenon that always involves an intersubjective dimension. Secondly, since it is vital to be recognised as a competent player within a community, the relationship between practices and normativity is inherently conflictual. Lastly, mistakes can happen, and practices can fail.

These Wittgensteinian insights are, however, subject to considerable interpretation, and there is significant divergence within practice theory on how the normativity of practice is conceived. To document this variety, we explore a range of proposals, all of which share a methodological starting point: they begin analyses with practices, not norms. Furthermore, theoretical primacy is always reserved for practice, while norms remain subordinate as a fragile, emerging phenomenon. Joseph Rouse, a central advocate for a normativity-based practice theory, first illustrates a way of coping with normativity, which he refers to as regularism. Normativity is then seen as embedded in regularity. According to Rouse (2006: 528), in regularism normativity lies "in a regularity *exhibited* by what practitioners do, rather than in a rule *followed* by them". Such understandings can be identified in those practice theories that emphasise regularity, such as Bourdieu's praxeology.

Rouse finds such an account unconvincing. Drawing on Turner's (1994) critique of such an understanding of practice, he points to the problem that "a finite set of performances exhibits indefinitely many regularities" (Rouse 2006: 529). Various performances can, in principle, be associated with a practice. There are no obvious criteria by which one can judge which performances belong to which practices. To decipher the normativity of a practice, one is then faced with potentially unlimited interpretations of which performances belong to the practice. To reconstruct the normativity of a practice by relying on the regularity of practitioners' performances is therefore inadequate for Rouse (2006: 529).

Rouse (2006) develops an alternative account based on mutual accountability. The term 'accountability', the origins of which lie in ethnomethodology (Garfinkel 1967), emphasises that social activities and practice are orderly and experienced normatively. Following Rouse, human agents never definitively know whether the use of a term or a rule in a situation is right or wrong; they must always arrange mutual accountability in and through practice. In this alternative conception of practices and normativity, "a practice is not a regularity underlying its constituent performances, but a pattern of interaction among them that expresses their mutual normative accountability" (Rouse 2006: 529). Normativity lies, then, in the mutual accountability relations of the constituent actors and elements of a practice. As Rouse (2006: 529–530) makes clear, "a performance belongs to a practice if it is appropriate to hold it accountable as a correct or incorrect performance of that practice. Such holding to account is itself integral to the practice, and can likewise be done correctly or incorrectly". Rouse's conception of practices as actions constituted by the mutual accountability of their competent performances points to the temporality of practices and their normative groundings; practices are themselves contestable.

A similar account has been developed by Alasdair MacIntyre (1984) from the perspective of moral philosophy. For Nicolini (2013: 84), who bases his argument on MacIntyre (1984), this leads to an understanding that performing a practice also implies absorbing "a moral way of being; that is, a model of excellence specific to that practice that determines at once an ethic, a set of values, and the sense of virtues associated with the achievement of the high standard of conduct implicit in the practice". In such an account, practices must involve such standards of excellence, higher normative ends or positive achievements. To participate in common practice requires accepting the authority of distinct normative standards as well as criteria of moral judgments by others.

Another approach foregrounding normativity is the pragmatic sociology of Boltanski. In this approach, different normative ends become visible in practices of justification and critique through the mobilisation of different orders of worth in disputes. Boltanski and Thévenot (2006) argue that during controversies, actors carry out justifications or critiques by explicating their moral groundings, related to different moral grammars of legitimate social bonds. Rouse's philosophical suggestion (2006: 532) that a performance's accountability to norms is dependent upon its ability to inspire an interpretation of it being done for something at stake in both the interaction and its consequences, is answered by Boltanski through his framework of economies of worth. In their practices, actors negotiate using what can be regarded as an acceptable justification or criticism, and test these statements with orders of worth as established moral evaluation schemes while taking into account the criteria of whether it serves the common good in their respective society. Boltanski's approach can therefore deal with the plurality and multiplicity of norms and normative orders as overlapping moral narratives, which is understood as a normal, and not exceptional, part of our everyday practices.

Practice theories offer an alternative conception of normativity in social life. They elaborate on different understandings that show how normativity and activity are mutual constitutive. Following different interpretations of Wittgenstein, normativity is understood as regularised performance, mutual accountability relations, moral ways of being, or negotiated justifications.

If practice theories offer a viable alternative to IR's constructivist positions, the virtues of different notions of normativity will continue to be a matter of debate. So far, this has mainly been a philosophical debate. As such, the contours of the debate on normativity will depend on how these conceptualisations can be translated into research methodology and utilised in actual projects.

A promising recent case in this ongoing debate is the controversy around Adler-Nissen and Pouliot's study of the diplomatic conflicts around the Libya intervention in the U. N. Security Council. While Adler-Nissen and Pouliot (2014) focused on 'power in practice', and principally analysed the 'competent performances' of different political actors without considering normative positions, Jason Ralph and Jess Gifkins (2017) criticised this position of competence and power struggles for ignoring the close linkage between practice theory and normative theory, that is, uncritically accepting pre-reflexive practices such as 'penholding' as markers of competence. Such controversial empirical cases are useful for discussing the normative dimension of practices further, and examining how we can (and should) study it. Moreover, it leads us to the important question of how we can criticise practices as social science researchers (Schindler and Wille 2017), which connects practice theory more strongly to the concerns of normative theory.

Whether it is more promising to separate norms and practices as norm constructivists do, to conceptualise normativity as the fundamental component of practice, or as one element among others, will remain an issue of debate. Further advancing these arguments in the light of empirical studies will be of particular assistance in identifying the commonalities and differences between explanations based on norm constructivism, international political theories, and IPT.

5.4 Bodies and Objects

At the core of practice theory lies a different recognition of the importance of materiality. Bodies and artefacts are important carriers of practice. The argument for the primacy of practice is, in the first instance, based in the claim that practices are bodily activities, involve a range of objects and artefacts and are, therefore, always materially anchored.

For practice theorists, the body is not a mere instrument that the agent must use in order to act. Bodies are a constituent element in performing an action. Routinised actions are themselves bodily performances (Reckwitz 2002: 251). Such a view not only overcomes the dichotomy of mind and body, it also gives a pivotal status to the human body as a core element in explaining and interpreting practices. Practice theories understand human bodies as a locus of agency, affective response and cultural expression as well as a target of power and normalisation (Rouse 2006: 512). 'Skilled bodies' (Schatzki 2001: 3) are the locus of practical knowledge. The "skilled body commands attention in practice theory as the common meeting point of mind and activity and of individual activity and society" (Schatzki 2001: 3).

To carry out a practice as a skilful performance moreover requires the competent handling of objects, things and artefacts that are necessary elements of any practice. Any human activity is part of a material configuration. With this focus, practice theories destabilise the traditional relationship between subjects and objects, and instead emphasise the active engagement of the latter as constituent within practices. The practice theory-based notion of agency as an interweaving force between the human and the non-human world intends to transcend the dichotomy of subjects and objects.

IR, more broadly, has increasingly expressed an interest in bodies and artefacts. Work on bodies has particularly been conducted by feminist scholars, while artefacts were initially a concern in the discussion of the role of science and technology in world politics.[6] More recently, bodies and artefacts are discussed in the discipline under the label of 'new materialism'.[7] What constitutes 'new materialism', other than a shared appreciation for the material dimension of politics, and how it is related to practice theory remains unclear. From our reading, practices theories, in particular ANT, can be understood as part of and as contributing to the rise of such an 'ism'. However, it is important to note, and as should be clear by now, that the practice theoretical project has much wider and distinct concerns. While it emphasises materiality, it does not reduce research to it, and while it includes materiality in its analysis, it makes it part of the study of practice, in which it is one element among others. While most practice theorists agree that the material dimension of practice matters, the precise status one wants to grant the material remains an ongoing area of controversy within practice theory.

In IR, 'the body' has increasingly become a major issue of study, in particular in critical security studies and feminism. This research mainly focuses on bodily representations in discourses and the political effects arising from them, however. This is the case, for instance, when the political use of representations of the violated female body is studied as a narrative to justify military intervention in Afghanistan (Heck and Schlag 2013), or when gender representations are analysed as myths in the aftermath of the financial crisis (Prügl 2012). Studies such as these provide an important link to the concerns of practice theory and the beginning of a dialogue on the importance of the representational dimension of the body.

In anchoring their arguments in materiality, practice theorists provide a much-needed amendment to the representational view. Robert Schmidt (2012: 47), for instance, elaborates on an example of Bourdieu's work to mark the difference that a thoroughly materialist account makes. The example is the olive harvest in the Kabyle community; Bourdieu analyses how harvesting practices are performed by members through bodily movements, gestures and routines. Here, men shake olive trees with a stick to remove the olives from their branches, while women bend over to collect the olives from the ground. For Schmidt (2012: 47), this division of labour is permanently reproduced through practices as evidenced by these performed roles in gender relations. Hierarchies, which are seen as self-evident and natural by the involved members, emerge from working practices. The hierarchies of gender are here performed through bodily activities, such as bending over. This is a good example of practice theoretical accounts that often begin with detailed descriptions of bodily practices to recognise transformations in spheres of working, consumption, family or urban life.

In IPT, Neumann (2012) stresses the importance of such an account when he describes in detail the everyday practices of diplomats in bureaucratic routines or 'wining and dining'. These routines become habitually embodied. The growing debate on Judith Butler's (1993, 1997, 1999) notion of performativity with regards to issues of international politics provides a promising way to link the concept of practice with the human body. By referring to Butler, Caroline Holmqvist (2013) demonstrates that we specifically need to reconsider our understanding of the human and materiality in the context of drone warfare. In contrast to the claim that robotics takes the human experience out of war, she investigates the human-material assemblage as a complex whole, "taking both fleshy and steely bodies into account" (Holmqvist 2013: 535). Understanding bodily movements and how knowledge is inscribed in bodies remains an understudied dimension, and further effort will be required here in IPT.

In contrast, objects and artefacts have received more attention. ANT studies, particularly, have pushed scholars to study the hybrid sphere between the natural and material world. ANT is also one of the sources of the controversy on materiality, however, since ANT studies push the claim of materiality to the extreme. Practice theorists agree that practices always involve objects, things and artefacts in the practices, and that these need to be considered in the analysis of practice. To write, you need a hand, a pen and a paper.

However, they disagree on how objects and materiality engage in practices, and how the status of agency should be re-conceptualised. In the practice of writing, are the pen and paper of equal importance to the hand drawing letters, the brain formulating sentences and the practical repertoire of knowing how to write? It may be best to describe this debate as one between two extremes; at one end of the practice theory spectrum is the notion of materiality in ANT, where things and artefacts fully submit to practices in the same way human beings do. Both worlds gain equal status in the analysis of practices. Humans act, and things do so do. The term 'actant' is the core concept to achieve this symmetry between the material and the social.

At the other end of the extreme are 'agential humanists' (e.g. Schatzki 2002). Here, the argument is in open disagreement with ANT: only humans can carry out practices, since one can only attribute intentionality and affectivity to human action (Nicolini 2013: 169). Such humanist accounts therefore tend to distinguish conceptually between practices – carried by humans – and related material arrangements – composed of the non-human elements. While arguing that practices and material arrangements are always enmeshed, the suggestion is nonetheless that humans and non-humans should be kept separate. Other practice theorists such as Pickering (1995: 21–22) can be located in the middle of this debate. They give intentionality only to human beings, yet stress the mutual forces of human and material agency as 'the mangle of practice'.

As shown in our overview of key practice approaches, the pragmatic sociology of Boltanski comes close to Latour's and Pickering's notion of agency. Situations are interpreted as relations between "person-states and thing-states" often leading to "the monstrosity of composite setups" (Boltanski and Thévenot 2006: 1, 225). Human intentionality does not appear to be given up in Boltanski's account due to the premise of critical and reflexive actors, however. In narrative approaches, which are the origin of the term 'actant' introduced in Greimas's semiotic linguistics, human agency also floats ambiguously in a fluid zone between narrator and narration. It is generally unclear who or what is the main driving force in narrative practices; that is, is it the storytelling actor or the wider process of storytelling? Bourdieu's praxeology and Wenger's communities of practices fall on the opposite side of the divide. For Bourdieu, practices are materially anchored and habitually embodied, yet the strong emphasis on dispositions in habitus is clearly rooted in models of human action and human intentionality. For Wenger, it is primarily humans that learn and interact in communities of practice. Foucault's work is much more difficult to situate in the debate, and depending on one's reading, he can be said to occupy a middle ground.

IPT scholars drawing on these approaches have populated and enriched the world of global politics with all sorts of artefacts. This includes 'paper' that leads a ministry of foreign affairs to fundamentally change its working practices (Dittmer 2016), 'documents' that organise European integration (Walters 2002) to all sorts of 'weapon technology', including 'warheads' (Pouliot 2010a, b), 'drones' (Walters 2014) and security technology such as scanners (Bellanova and Fuster 2013), computers and databases (Amicelle et al. 2015).

In summary, practice theories develop a different understanding of materiality and stress the importance of bodily movements and objects. Practice theories are therefore innovative in the way they challenge conventional dichotomies between understandings of the subject/human and the object/material. The anti-essentialist ideas of ANT, in particular, have found fertile ground in IPT research. While ANT seems to be one of the most promising paths for the IPT programme to transfer new materialism into IR, it should not be understood as a body of theory that can be simply applied to any empirical example in international politics. The promises of ANT should not be overstretched; as Stefan Hirschauer (2004: 74) rightly argues, ANT primarily understands materiality in terms of technical artefacts, and thus neglects the body because of its core differentiation between humans and non-humans. As a result, the body does not fit very well in the vocabulary of ANT. A conceptualisation of the body, which deviates away from understanding it as predetermined or a mere result of practices and moves toward locating it within practices (Hirschauer 2004: 75), remains a major challenge. This also implies rejecting the notion of fixed bodies by analysing bodies as 'multiple' (Mol 2002) in relation to distinct practices. Therefore, the distinction divergent understandings of the material, whether as bodies or as objects, will make is a theme that will require considerable future attention in IPT.

5.5 Power and Critique

Power has not necessarily been one of IPT's principle concerns, nor has it become a focal point of research. However, as Matt Watson (2017: 170) argues, "to fulfil its potential, practice theory needs to be able to speak of power". Power can be considered an implicit challenge for IPT, not least because many of its accounts do not explicate their understanding of power fully. One of the main reasons for the absence of explicit discussions on power is that "practice theory does not tend to focus on power as a separate or distinct property of the social" (Watson 2017: 181). The relational ontology of practice theories implies that human action is always influenced from somewhere, through relations that shape that action, or provide the capacity to act. In that sense, any practice and any relation is always one of power. However, power relations are always the effect of the performances of practice, and cannot be seen as standing outside of the broader constellations of practice. Nicolini (2013: 6) explains this relational logic as follows: "[p]ractices, in fact, literally put people (and things) in place, and they give (or deny) people the power to do things and to think of themselves in certain ways. As a result, practices and their temporal and spatial ordering (i.e. several practices combined in a particular way) produce and reproduce differences and inequalities". Power is an effect of practice, and is produced within it.

Practice approaches agree on the high relevance of relational power dynamics. Yet, the concept of power plays different roles in the spectrum of IPT, and directs scholarship into different directions. This raises the question whether and how approaches allow for other forms of power that do not directly or immediately follow from the relational logic outlined above. This includes forms of power inscribed in institutions, such as the state, or large-scale phenomena such as race, class or markets.

The practice theories of Bourdieu and Foucault are generally recognised as providing effective tools for the analysis of such forms of power through a focus on symbolic struggles, practices of domination, or technologies of government. They are interested in such forms of power because they emphasise the orderliness of practices; power is what stabilises orders. Approaches that argue on the basis of flat ontologies (such as the vocabularies of Boltanski, Schatzki or Latour) struggle with analysing these forms of power, given that their focus on change and contingency makes it more difficult to explain long term stability.

It is fair to say that power is not the major concern of these scholars, though it does play an underlying role. In ANT, power is always one dimension of relations, and the focus is on sites or technologies that have high ordering capacity. Pragmatic sociology aims at revealing inequalities in the interplay of justification and critique (Boltanski 2011: 37). Schatzki (2002: 66) sympathises with a Foucauldian notion of power. He emphasizes the multiplicity of force relations that hold among social particulars, and operate and constitute their own organisation. However, power needs to be addressed through analysing hierarchies and tying authority and disputation to teleoaffective normativity (Schatzki 2002: 267). Narrative approaches, in particular, put strong emphasis on the underlying conditions behind 'successful' storytelling, with all its implications for political authority and the legitimation of power claims. Shared stories can unite and divide, especially in politics, which is always a question of power. In community of practice research power relations are inherent in a community and the distribution of skills and expertise it entails, but also practices of in- and exclusion, which point to conflicts of belonging and entail power relations between different groups and actors.

A second question concerns the role of power analysis in directing scholarly action. For some scholars, an analysis of power is important because it is the basis of critique. Such a position follows the tradition of critical theory and aims at revealing the reproducing mechanisms of power relations and their effects in objective structures. Such a view implies that the researcher should seek external positions to the field from which he can study power relations and formulate a critique of current social and political dynamics. In contrast to this focus on unravelling hidden power relations, other scholars are more driven by the pragmatist's gaze of reconstructing relations and developing creative problem solutions. From this viewpoint, power does not have to be encountered by critique, but is a tool to be used to build better relations and enable better solutions. While Bourdieusian and Foucauldian approaches are often associated with the former position, this does not follow naturally from the concepts. For Pouliot (2016), for instance, Bourdieu's work provides primarily an analytical toolbox, rather than the basis for critique. Also Foucault's work has been read in different ways, and for instance, Vanderveen (2010), emphasizes that Foucault's intention was less critique but the reconstruction of problematic situations. Latour (2004), by contrast, is an outspoken advocate against critique as the objective of scholarship.

As this brief review already demonstrates, power is a major category in IPT, albeit it is often silenced. How power relations can be analysed on the larger scale, and whether the analysis of power should be a main driver of research, is disputed among IPT scholars, however.

IR was long dominated by reductionist understandings of power that narrowed it down to material capabilities. This has changed since Michael Barnett and Robert Duvall (2005) fundamentally re-ordered the debate by providing a taxonomy of power, and demonstrating that too much attention had been paid to Robert Dahl's notion of 'power over'. This form of power, described as "compulsory power", needed to be complemented. Barnett and Duvall suggested broadening the spectrum by proposing three other forms of power: institutional, structural, and productive power. Institutional power is the control actors exercise indirectly over others through diffuse relations of interaction; structural power can be identified in structural relationships such as capital and labour; and productive power is concerned with the production of subjectivities (Barnett and Duvall 2005: 43). The intention of Barnett and Duvall's taxonomy was not to provide a coherent theory of power, but to encourage scholars to recognise power's multiple forms and its polymorphous character. The different forms of power should not be seen as necessarily competing, but rather as different expressions of how power may work in international politics (Barnett and Duvall 2005: 44).

This objective, to focus on the connections and overlaps between different types of power, closely reflects the concerns of practice-oriented scholars. As Sending and Neumann (2011: 235) exemplarily argue, a turn to practices allows us to explore how different forms of power can be at work simultaneously. In their case, they focus on the role and power of expertise in international organisations such as the World Bank. They study how the bank's expertise is embedded in a set of fundamental practices that structures its relations with states and stabilises its authority. Key among these practices is the bank's annual assessment procedure, by which the 'performance' of client countries is evaluated according to a set of criteria. Sending and Neumann (2011: 232) argue that the procedure is an anchoring practice – a bundle of interwoven practices making possible other, more specific ones such as the bank's allocation system that structures negotiations between management and member states over allocation of funds and overall political direction. The assessment procedure is a direct form of compulsory power that comes through allocation of funds, but it also produces indirect forms of productive power. The ratings produced allow country teams to engage with client countries from a position of authority. This authority is not only grounded in the general expert status of the bank, but produced through the specific ratings and scores produced in the assessment exercise (Sending and Neumann 2011: 235–236). This example shows how practice-oriented research can allow for exploring different types of power in their overlapping workings. It is also an example that documents how practice scholars can scale up and investigate how one practice is more important than another, in other words, the relations of power between practices.

A strength of IPT studies is that they embed an analysis of power in concrete empirical cases, and therefore illustrate how diffuse power relations can be observed in current phenomena of international politics. The following examples underline these claims and show how the different notions of power are linked with various understandings of critique. Bourdieusian IPT is centred on the analysis of power. Guzzini (2013), one of the leading theorists on power in IR (e.g. 1993), praises Bourdieu's vocabulary as one of the rare examples that considers different facets of power between the micro- and the macro-level such as government (order), autonomy (freedom), domination (rule), and influence (cause) within a coherent social theory of power and domination. His relational field theory includes other elements, namely power as relational capital, symbolic violence and the role of language in domination, social stratification and the field of power and its relation to the state. For Guzzini, Bourdieu's concepts hence provide a solid bridge between sociological theorising and political theory (Guzzini 2013: 80–85).

Turning to Bourdieusian IPT scholars, it seems that many of them are interested in a sociological analysis of power (e.g. Berling 2012; Adler-Nissen 2014) and less in categories of political theory. Adler-Nissen and Pouliot's (2014) analysis of the negotiations around the international intervention in Libya at the U. N. Security Council is an exemplary case of prioritisation of a sociological analysis of power. They reveal the inner workings of power in the Council between member states by showing how the struggle for competence in everyday performances lead to different claims of authority and distinct hierarchies in the field. However, they shy away from interpreting the political effects of these power struggles and downplay the normativity of practices and their contested nature. This 'neutral' stance of describing power games has been widely criticised (e.g. Gadinger 2016: 194; Ralph and Gifkins 2017), leading to a distancing from the spirit of the critical tradition.

In contrast to Bourdieu-inspired studies, IR scholars working on governance as governmentality in the tradition of Foucault (e.g. Löwenheim 2008; Sending and Neumann 2006) put more emphasis on the concerns of political theory. In these accounts, the analysis of power is considered in terms of a wider social control, and works through subjecting individuals to it and assessing force as a function of their conduct. Sending and Neumann's example of the practices of expertise in the World Bank demonstrates how standards of 'good governance' interact with those who are subject to it. The study of governmentality thus shows "how expert knowledge on governance is part and parcel of global governance" (Guzzini 2012: 24). As Guzzini (2012: 24) argues, such standards are also 'identifiers' since they distinguish between those who are part of the truly civilized world and those who are not, which implies that being at the forefront of implemented indirect liberal rule has become a marker for gaining status as civilized and acceptable to community. The productive power reveals how such technologies and practices of government 'responsibilise' the subjected nations for their own fate and eventually push even those who did not initially want to abide by those standards to comply, which only reinforces the existing mechanism (Guzzini 2012: 24).

The Foucauldian approach investigates impersonal processes, techniques and mechanisms of government such as statistical devices, benchmarks and indices, and is based on a dispersion of power (Guzzini 2012: 24). For Foucault-inspired scholars such as Sending and Neumann (2006), the increasing relevance of NGOs in global civil society is not an example of transfer of power from state to nonstate actors, but rather an expression of a changing logic or rationality of government by which civil society is redefined from being a passive object of government to be acted upon into an entity that is both an object and a subject of government. The study of such practices of governmentality therefore clearly follows a critical perspective of the effects of power for the "neoliberal subject" (Chandler and Reid 2016). It reveals the dynamic facets of the changing logic of government in policy fields such as development, security, and peacebuilding that stabilises the power relations of the liberal order (Neumann and Sending 2010). The critical research agenda is open and considers other types of power, for instance, practices of resilience as flexible forms of governmentality (e.g. Joseph 2016).

What Foucauldian scholarship showcases in particular is the importance of a critical gaze. For these scholars, the analysis of power is an exercise of critique. They rely on a position that argues in favour of studying and criticising practices of domination from the standpoint of the 'professional analyst' who gains privileged knowledge over what is really happening, in contrast to the actors studied. Such critical scholars are sceptical of the pragmatist orientation one finds in Latour and Boltanski that favours a symmetrical position, and reject the split between 'ordinary actors' and the 'professional analyst'. Sending (2015) finds their perspective problematic, "since it makes it all the more likely that academics simply end up reproducing conventional understandings and participants' self-description". For critical scholars, a symmetrical position risks losing the researcher's scientific autonomy.

For Boltanski and Latour the methodological objective of 'following the actors' is not simply about regurgitating ordinary actors' understandings and self-description on situated grounds, however. Instead, the strong emphasis on the interpretive work of observing actors *en situation* renews the possibilities of critical sociology by taking the critical capacities of ordinary actors seriously. Put simply, Boltanski's sociology aims to expand critical theory by "making actors part of it" (Bogusz 2014: 130). Such a perspective aims to become an active 'sociology of emancipation' by treating 'ordinary actors' not as passive judgmental dopes, but rather as "frankly critical" (Boltanski 2011: 26).

The underlying objective in pragmatic sociology is that in examining how ordinary actors make moral judgements and interpret reality, the discrepancies between their "moral expectations" and the actual social world will be exposed. That is, pragmatic sociology establishes an unprecedented 'compromise' between social theory and social critique practiced by non-academics (Nachi 2014: 308). The pragmatic way of criticising practices is therefore rooted in a division of labour between the researcher, who describes and reconstructs the disputes and controversies, and the actors studied, who are sometimes silent in cycles of domination (such as the decline of critique in the new spirit of capitalism, as shown by Boltanski and Chiapello 2007), but often break the power of institutions through critique and the imperative of justification.

A major difference between Bourdieu's praxeology and pragmatic sociology lies, as Médéric Martin-Mazé (2017) argues, in the agonistic facet of practices and the different notions of conflicts as struggles or disputes. Whereas disputes break out every day in countless concrete situations of high uncertainty, actors settle disputes once they have reached a fragile agreement over how to properly test their respective worth. But actors are realists in picking their battles, as they limit themselves to the situations that they know instead of calling into question the larger social contexts in which they are embedded (Martin-Mazé 2017: 216). Struggles, on the contrary, are specific to distinct fields, in which actors tacitly agree on the value of resources in forms of capital that they strive to accumulate, and whose scarcity defines stronger and weaker positions. "Struggles are therefore driven by a complex combination and of dispositional and positional logics. They do not end, but reboot on the rare occasions when challengers manage to topple incumbents" (Martin-Mazé 2017: 216).

This terminological distinction is useful, as it explains the different notions of power in relation to order and change. The never-ending struggles of critical scholars have a higher degree of orderliness and control in more (Bourdieu) or less (Foucault) visible power relations. Disputes (Boltanski) and controversies (Latour) also entail power relations, but they are characterised as situations that provide more opportunities for agency and change and an escape from the reproducing mechanisms of hierarchies and technologies of government.

In ANT studies, the notion of power is even more fluid, as it is never predictable whether relations and translations in an emerging, heterogeneous network of human and non-human actors hold together and develop performative effects. To act collectively and to exercise power, "we depend upon the agency of human and non-human others, an agency which is often truculent, recalcitrant, crafty, and self-interested" (Best and Walters 2013: 333). In short, translational power in ANT studies is a relational concept examining the abilities of actors to create durable relations between previously unconnected entities and represent this very assemblage (Berger and Esguerra 2017: 219). This notion of power prompts the researcher to investigate how actors achieve consolidated yet never-fully-stable relations between different entities, as well as how they make these relations present (Berger and Esguerra 2017: 221).

The analytical potential of other IPT approaches, such as the narrative and community of practice approaches, to analyse power relations requires further elaboration, and indeed they can be developed in different directions. Narrative approaches consider the relation of power and language in quite similar terms to discourse theory. A clash of narratives in political crises, for instance, the Crimean crisis (Faizullaev and Cornut 2017), shows the interconnectedness of both practices and storytelling when fuelled by power claims. The question of how narratives are configured and which knowledge resources are selected in the employment of a story has an impact on authority and power claims. The community of practice approach is often taken to either be indifferent towards power, considering the harmonious assumptions of the community metaphor, or only concerned about power relations within a community, and not the power relations that communities are subjected to.

Recent scholarship has started to address these issues, however. For instance, as Maren Hofius (2016) demonstrates, a focus on the boundaries of communities can be particularly revealing. In her case study, EU field diplomats engage in constant boundary work that establishes insiders and outsiders in relation to the neighbouring state of Ukraine. In this case, power in practice means that the EU diplomats function as 'boundary workers' as they are engaged in both boundary-spanning and boundary-drawing practices on an day-to-day basis, which reveals a more complex understanding of community and identity as an emergent structure of possibilities, and experienced as borderland.

As we see in these examples, IPT studies contribute to the ongoing debate on the relation between different forms of power in international politics. If practice-oriented studies refrain from narrowing power down to a singular form, practice approaches will be able to demonstrate how different forms of power work simultaneously and merge in practice. This will include addressing power relations on larger scales, such as institutions.

Practices provide a useful methodological entry point for the analysis of power. IPT scholars take different positions over why we should be interested in power, however. If, for Foucauldian and Bourdieusian scholarship in particular, the goal is to develop forms of societal critique on the basis of an analysis of power, other versions of IPT do not necessarily share this concern; following the pragmatist gaze, the focus turns to reconstruction.

How these positions can be reconciled will remain an ongoing matter of debate, as will learning more about the empirical workings of power in practice.

5.6 Productive Tensions

One of the means of judging the productivity of a research perspective goes beyond questioning what new insights it provides, to asking what new puzzles it poses. As we have shown in this chapter, IPT provides a rich set of questions for further inquiry, as different approaches provide divergent takes on a number of the core ontological questions at the heart of practice theory. There are significant tensions between these approaches.

Awareness of these tensions is, firstly, important in terms of the kind of ontological baggage and conceptual problems one takes on board if one neatly follows one approach. If understood as a trading zone, drawing on IPT does not necessarily imply a pick-and-choose approach. None of the IPT approaches provide the right or wrong answer to the ontological questions we have addressed. Part of the value of future IPT research will stem from appreciating the tensions between approaches, and turning the ontological questions into explicit research questions. Asking when and how change occurs, how the micro is embedded in the macro and scales are made, how different understandings of normativity lead to different results on the prevalence of norms and the regularity of practice, or how bodies and objects play a role, are questions that will drive the IPT research agenda into innovative and productive directions.

Not every research project will be able to address all of these questions. Nevertheless, issues of change, scale, normativity, materiality, power and critique are major debates providing theoretical direction to empirical research. Much of these debates have so far been carried out in a philosophical language and often in an overly abstract manner and do not give justice to the demands of understanding practice. As we have often alluded to, much will therefore depend on how these conceptual and ontological challenges are translated into actual research projects. Addressing the debates requires methodological and empirical work. Tinkering with methodology is, therefore, the pivotal step, and the issue we turn to next.

Notes

1. This includes the more detailed debates on visuality and the practice of seeing (e.g. Lisle 2017), cognition and the role of the brain in practice (e.g. Turner 2007; Lizardo 2009), knowledge and learning (e.g. Turner 2001; Alkemeyer and Buschmann 2017), or affectivity and feeling (e.g. Reckwitz 2012; Bially Mattern 2011).
2. In addition to those discussed below, metaphors recently introduced include the concept of 'textures of practice' proposed by Silvia Gherardi (2012) , 'practice architectures' proposed by Stephen Kemmis (see Mahon et al. 2017), the concept of 'complexes of practice' developed by Elizabeth Shove (Shove et al. 2012), Karin Knorr Cetina's concept of 'global microstructures' (Knorr Cetina 2005; Knorr Cetina and Bruegger 2002), as well as various recent understandings of discourse and discursive formations (see Schatzki 2017).
3. For an outline of these respective positions, see Gilpin 1981, and the contributions in Ikenberry 2014 for the realist position, for the constructivist discussion see Widmaier et al. (2007), the contributions in Avant et al. (2010), and the reviews in Flockhart (2016) and Hopf (2017).
4. Hopf distinguishes between meaningful difference or novelty, repeated exposures to I, exposures to social margins and liminars, weakly socialised and institutionalised environments, institutionalised differences and novelties, discursively resonant challenges to the status quo, intelligible and plausible alternatives to the status quo, and productive crises.
5. For the relation between multi-sited ethnography and practice theory, see Schmidt and Volbers (2011) and our discussion of the methodological relation between IPT and ethnography in Chap. 6.
6. See the reviews in Mayer et al. (2014) and McCarthy (2017).
7. See Srnicek (2017) as well as the special issue on 'Materialism and World Politics' of *Millennium: Journal of International Studies* 41(3).

CHAPTER 6

Doing Praxiography: Research Strategies, Methods and Techniques

IPT is often understood to primarily seek to clarify concepts, re-orientate theory and argue for a focus on practices. What tends to be forgotten is that the majority of approaches and studies "emerged in close and constant touch with empirical studies and developed from reflecting experiences in empirical research" (Schmidt 2017: 3). The approaches discussed in chapters three and four all derive their concepts and ideas from empirical studies. Diligent and intensive empirical work is crucial for IPT; indeed, as we suggested in Chap. 2, the primacy of the empirical is one of the shared core commitments of practice accounts. As Schmidt (2017: 3) proclaims, "the practice turn also amounts to an empirical turn in sociology and social sciences".

If we agree with Schmidt's diagnosis, in the study of the international, practice turn discussions have often failed to pay sufficient attention to the empirical side of the study of practices. Many studies in IPT include and discuss empirical material; often, however, it is unclear how this empirical material has been gathered, assembled and interpreted. There is therefore little guidance on how to actually undertake and write up practice-theory-driven research. A growing number of reflections on the methodological implications of practice theory have been published recently, in particular in other social science disciplines.[1] However, overall, the debates on methodology, research strategies, methods and techniques required to study practices remain limited. What are the most promising paths to practice? How should we best generate empirical data

C. Bueger, F. Gadinger, *International Practice Theory*,
https://doi.org/10.1007/978-3-319-73350-0_6

about practices? What research strategies follow if one takes practice as the smallest unit of analysis? Which techniques allow for deciphering of practices, and how do they do so?

In this chapter, we set out to address these questions. Our goal is to provide orientation for those interested in undertaking a practice-theory-informed analysis, but also to provide reflections for those who are already studying practices empirically. Our goal is not to prescribe how to do a practice-driven research project. Instead, we offer an exploration of a range of parameters, tools and techniques that provide inspiration for designing and practicing research.

We advance the notion of praxiography as the set of methods and techniques corresponding to practice theory needs. The term praxiography implies that the study of practices has much in common with ethnography (but also other more established procedures, such as those of ethnomethodology and interpretative social science). The common concern is to record, to describe and to reconstruct (*–graphy*); however, the interest lies not in culture (*ethno*), but with practice (*praxis*). If ethnography is usually concerned with people's way of life, praxiography is interested in understanding practices and their configurations.

The chapter starts out with a range of epistemological and methodological considerations. This is to provide a reminder about the specificity of studying practice, but also to elaborate more on the connections between praxiography and other forms of interpretative analysis. We discuss the importance of recognising that 'doing praxiography' should also be understood as a practice, explore the status of 'theory' and generalisations in praxiography, and emphasise the significance of recursive and abductive reasoning. What follows is that "practice theory is not a theoretical project (in the traditional sense), but a methodological orientation supported by a new vocabulary" (Nicolini 2017b: 25).

If this section aims at providing a general sense of orientation and of the modalities of praxiography, the next one addresses research strategy. We take the question of research strategies to be primarily a problem of where to begin empirical research. There are several different plausible starting points for a praxiography, and to some degree they directly follow from an approach's emphasis on certain elements of practice. For instance, field analysis encourages us to study fields, while narrative analysis sets out from the reconstruction of storytelling.

We conclude this section with an outline of five productive starting points for praxiography, while the following section addresses the question of methods and technique. Praxiographers can draw on considerable experience of methods gained through decades of anthropological and social science research. However, many of these methods must be tailored to the particular needs of practice theory. In this section we discuss, firstly, differing techniques of participant observation, field work and action research, and secondly, conversation techniques such as interviews and focus groups, as well as, finally, document and artefact analysis. We provide a short sketch of each of these techniques and how they can be employed in praxiography, and introduce some paradigmatic examples. Together, these techniques provide a rich repertoire for praxiography that can be blended in various ways, depending on the demands and methodicity of the phenomenon studied.

Our final section is concerned with the reporting of research. How does one write about practice? This question has received relatively sparse attention, and is difficult to answer. Writing about practice implies taming the unruliness of practices, and ordering them into a more-or-less coherent narrative. We argue that we should firstly think about writing as a practice that is not exterior to producing knowledge, but a fundamental part of it. In practical terms, we consider writing about practices to be primarily about the problem of intelligibility. How can a narrative about practice be written in a way that makes sense to a distinct audience? We argue that praxiography requires experimentation and creativity, and introduce ideas from ethnography and filmmaking as inspirations.

6.1 Towards Praxiography: Methodology and General Guidelines

Theorising is a practice; undertaking research is a practice. Everything that has been said about practice in general also applies for the practice of theorising about practice, as well as undertaking research driven by practice theory. As sociologists of science have noted, this implies that we may use practice theory to make sense of researchers' practice as well as our own. Indeed, the study of epistemic practices has been a vital object of research in driving practice theory.[2] Undertaking praxiography is then, first and foremost, as Greiffenhagen et al. (2015: 461) phrase it, not to follow "programmatic doctrinal statements of the aims of the social sciences wedded to meta-reflection, critique and inter- and intra-disciplinary jostling and one-upmanship. Rather than using idealised conceptions of social science as decontextualised standards to judge what social scientists do, the focus has [to be] on understanding the scale, range and diversity of the social sciences practical entanglements in social and cultural life".

Consequently, there is no universal standard for how to undertake practice research. As Pouliot (2013: 46) points out with reference to Bourdieu, "the craft of research is, first and foremost, a practice, which rests on various skills developed through actual training and experience. Stylised exposes and abstract standards […] are methodologically useless if not problematic."

Nevertheless, we can draw on the existing repertoire of methodological discourse and practice that provides basic guidance, rules of thumb, tips, tricks and help to avoid basic mistakes. Methodology does not and cannot provide answers to all questions and practical decisions that a researcher will face in the process of carrying out a project, however.

Barbara Czarniawska (2007: 5) starts her book on methodology with the following quote:

> Intense methodological awareness, if engaged in too seriously, can create anxieties that hinder practice, but if taken in small doses it can help to guard against the most obvious errors. (Seale 1999: ix)

As she alludes to in this passage, methodological uncertainties or "troubles" (Greiffenhagen et al. 2015) are a constitutive part of the research process. It is, moreover, important not to push methodological reflexivity too far. Methodological explication should not hinder actual research or halt one's curiosity about a practice. The majority of discussions on methodology and techniques only become meaningful in the conduct of actual research, and when encountering practical problems.

Theories, approaches, concepts, and techniques make sense when they are actually used in a research project, that is, they are enacted in observing, interpreting or writing up. Methodology negotiates between theory and empirical phenomena. For many practice scholars, methodology is therefore crucial, both to address the conceptual challenges discussed in the prior chapter, for reformulating theoretical approaches, and, perhaps most importantly, to write enlightening and critical narratives of empirical phenomena.[3]

What, then, is the status of 'theory' in practice theoretical research? What theory is and what it is not remains quite contentious. The controversy over the 'end' of international relations theory is a quite telling indicator in this regard. Scholars disagree over what theory is, what it is for, and how to gauge the quality of a theory.[4]

By 'theory', we often understand an abstract system of generalisations that is universally valid, independent from time and space. The notion of theory that IPT embraces is quite distinct from such an understanding, however. If practices are ever-moving, shifting and changing entities situated in space and time, how could we consider to formulate a universally valid theory of practice? How can we judge the quality of theory in the absence of an actual practice?

As Schmidt (2017: 5) notes, in practice theory, "the separation of theory and empirical research is deliberately destabilised. Both realms are methodologically re-assessed in their mutual entanglement". While for some the implication is to revoke the notion of 'theory' altogether,[5] for the majority of practice theorists, it is a call for novel understandings of theory.

When practice theorists use the notion of theory, they often refer to it as a collection of 'sensitising concepts'. This notion was coined by the social theorist Herbert Blumer (1954), who contrasted sensitising concepts with "definite concepts" that have defined attributes and clearly point to an empirical object. A sensitising concept, by contrast,

> gives the user a general sense of reference and guidance in approaching empirical instances. Whereas definitive concepts provide prescriptions of what to see, sensitising concepts merely suggest directions along which to look. [...] They lack precise reference and have no benchmarks which allow a clean-cut identification of a specific instance and of its content. Instead, they rest on a general sense of what is relevant. (Blumer 1954: 7)

The IPT approaches we have discussed provide sensitising concepts in this sense. Concepts such as field, community, laboratory, situations and so on, have no direct empirical reference. They provide us guidance and tell us what is relevant. IPT is therefore best understood as "a heuristic device, a sensitising 'framework' for empirical research in the social sciences. It thus opens up a certain way of seeing and analysing social phenomena" (Reckwitz 2002: 257). As Annemarie Mol suggests, we should take the notion of "sensitising" quite literally, implying the use of all our senses. For her,

> a "theory" is something that helps scholars to attune to the world, to see and hear and feel and taste it. Indeed, to appreciate it. [...] A theory is a repository of terms and modes of engaging with the world, a set of contrary methodological reflexes. These help in getting a sense of what is going on, what deserves concern or care, anger or love, or simply attention. [...] A theory helps to tell cases, draw contrasts, articulate silent layers, turn questions upside down, focus on the unexpected, add to one's sensitivities, propose new terms, and shift stories from one context to another. (Mol 2010b: 262)

As Reckwitz and Mol emphasise, practice theorists follow the insight of classical pragmatism, that theory should be understood in functionalist terms, as a toolbox of concepts and sensitivities that allow us to describe, interpret and cope with the world differently. This point is also emphasised by Nicolini (2017b: 24) when he argues that

> the aim of theory is not to provide general laws or explain casual or associative relationships between constructs; rather, it aims to provide a set of discursive resources to produce accounts, overviews and analyses of social affairs that enrich our understanding of them: a social ontology. Put differently, practice theory provides a set of concepts (a theoretical vocabulary) and a conceptual grammar (how to link these concepts in a meaningful way) that allow us to generate descriptions and 'bring worlds into being' in the texts we compose.

If research is a practice, and practice theory a sensitising framework, it is also important to keep in mind that all the main IPT approaches we have introduced do not provide fixed systems of reference, but are open ended and starting points for asking questions. Whether one relies on Bourdieu's, Wenger's or other versions of practice theory, the concrete research project one engages in requires one to adjust, to change and to add to the framework. Practice-theory-driven research does not fill a pre-existing 'gap' in an established body of knowledge (Sandberg and Alveson 2011). It problematises phenomena, adds new perspectives and interpretations, demonstrates how things play out in different contexts, and it enriches. Theorising and researching empirical phenomena are therefore not opposite poles, but part of one recursive thought process. As argued by Schmidt (2017: 5), "theory should be constructed in such a manner that theoretical concepts are continuously irritated and revised by empirical observations. Such a version of theory seeks to ensure that theoretical assumptions [...] are not excluded from being empirically questioned, altered and reconstructed". As Nicolini (2017b: 25) suggests, "practice theory cannot be written first and operationalised later; it can only emerge through engagement with the phenomenon. [...] While debating what practice is can be a useful exercise to refine our vocabulary and sharpen our analytical categories, this is only a means to an end. At some point, one has to engage with practice itself and allow the phenomenon to bite back".

As expressed in these arguments, the overall research logic of praxiography is recursive and abductive (Schwartz-Shea and Yanow 2012: 26–34; Friedrichs and Kratochwil 2009; Thomas 2010). Conducting research implies a constant movement (Bueger and Mireanu 2014); one moves back and forth between theory, methodology and empirical material. In these movements, chains of reference between concepts and the world are built, which culminate in the practice of writing up results and publishing them. These movements imply a constant negotiation of proximity to practice (Bueger and Mireanu 2014). In many ways, practice-driven research involves what Kurowska and Tallis (2013) call "chiasmatic crossings", that is, the co-production of knowledge by collaborations of analysts and the practitioners studied (Down and Hughes 2009). Practitioners and analysts search and find, interpret and reconstruct practices and knowledge, or develop concepts together through conversations.

If practice is a situated phenomenon and theoretical arguments are always tied to a distinct set of practices, does such an understanding imply that researchers should give up on the idea that research can generalise? Generalising and universalising are not quite the same. If praxiographers emphasise the impossibility of the latter – as "there is no universal" (Law 2004: 156) – this does not imply that praxiographic narratives are tied to the local and narrow situational description. Praxiographies 'zoom out' and make 'partial connections' between sites, practices and configurations. They never provide a full explanation or description, but only limited ones. They offer context-specific and situated generalisations in, for instance, exhibiting how practices achieve overarching regularity across time and space.

Halkier, for instance, suggests three concrete strategies for how one can generalise on the basis of praxiographic data. She argues in favour of building Weberian ideal typologies, that is, synthesising "diffuse and discrete empirical phenomena into a unified abstract analytical construct" (Halkier 2011: 790), for 'category zooming' that focusses on one aspect of a set of data in order to allow for case comparisons (Halkier 2011: 792), and for 'positioning' to allow generalisation by linking a distinct knowledge claim to a position within the field (Halkier 2011: 794). Her proposals are examples of how practice-focused research can overcome the dualism of theory and empirics, while refraining from the idea that only universalism can advance arguments of relevance broader than the immediate context of study.[6]

If the notion of practice theory, and IPT in particular, are relatively recent labels, this does not imply that the methodological wheel needs to be re-invented when conducting practice-theory-driven research. Rather, many of the considerations, guidelines and experiences of ethnographic, interpretive and qualitative research are also relevant for practice theory research. With that in mind, the vast body of methodology works on interpretive, qualitative or ethnographic approaches are also useful for practice theory.

As we discuss further in the following sections, some adjustments to the specific concerns of practice theory are required. As already suggested, to mark the way that practice-theory-driven research combines old and new insights, we find the term 'praxiography' useful in speaking about the type of research that practice theory produces (Bueger 2014).[7]

The term was originally coined by Annemarie Mol (2002) to describe a style of ethnographic research primarily concerned with objectual practices. It is helpful in that it clarifies that the reconstruction of practice shares many concerns with ethnography, in particular the idea of thick description. The common concern is to record, describe and to reconstruct *(-graphy)*, but the interest is not in culture (*ethno*), but with practice (*praxis*).

If ethnography is normally focussed on the way of life of a people, praxiography is concerned with understanding of a practice, a phenomenon situated in time and space. Drawing such a link to ethnography clarifies the overall methodological direction that practice-theory-driven research takes: much of what has been written on (reflexive) ethnography is also valid for practice research, and there is a wide spectrum of method mixes available for the study of practice. To speak about praxiography is to avoid narrowing down the methodological discussion to that of traditional ethnography and its field work practices.[8] It is also to open the discussion up to techniques that have not (yet) influenced the ethnographic discourse, or are generally considered to be separate projects. This includes interpretive traditions such as action research, ethnomethodology, discourse analysis, visual analysis or social media analysis, which can offer important techniques for praxiography. Much as contemporary ethnography is not limited to a single method, the same can be said about praxiography; mixing and assembling methods as appropriate to the practice one studies is the general guideline.

In this section, we have outlined a set of general guidelines and orientations: research is a practice and as such erratic and open ended; theory is not fixed, but provides an apparatus of sensitising concepts that become meaningful in use; practice theory research does not seek to fill gaps but to problematise, to add and to enrich; praxiography draws on the principles of recursivity, abduction, mobility, proximity and co-production.

To flesh out the methodological bone, let us discuss how praxiographers have attempted to study practice. The first question to be addressed is where to start; from which points does one initiate research? This is, in essence, a question of research strategy.

6.2 Knowing Where to Start: Basic Research Strategies

A praxiography starts out from a phenomenon, which might be, but is in no way limited to, a traditional one, such as gender, class, economy or security. The initial starting point is to turn this phenomenon into an object of praxiography. Gender becomes a problem of doing gender, class of classification practices, economy of economisation practices, security of securitisation practices, and so on. The next step is to generate praxiographic questions with the help of the conceptual vocabulary and grammar of practice theory. One initiates the process of abduction by identifying sensitising concepts.

Basic research strategies therefore develop more-or-less directly from the theoretical approaches hitherto discussed, and the sensitising concepts they provide. If one then relies, for instance, on a Bourdieusian or Wengerian framework, the initial objective becomes one of reconstructing the practices of a distinct social figuration, that is, either a field of practice or a community of practice. From a Foucaultian framework, the goal becomes to study the problematisation practices that produce and govern an epistemic object. The narrative approach suggests identifying narratives, reconstructing storytelling in situations and studying the effects of the narrative across situations. Drawing on ANT opens up a more contingent spectrum of possibilities, but the majority of studies have been following actants and their activities of weaving and organising a net that produces objects, facts or powerful actors. The pragmatic sociology of Boltanski invites us to zoom in on controversies and their settlement to unravel patterns of justifications across situations and the emergence of new practical orders. These starting points differ considerably, and are direct consequences of the respective sensitising framework.

The methodological consequences of Bourdieu and how his framework can be put into research practice in an international relations context has been spelled out in detail by Pouliot (2013). Acknowledging that Bourdieu provides perhaps the most consistent framework of practice theory, he argues that a three-fold research strategy follows. This consists of reconstructing (a) practices within a field, (b) the practical dispositions of actors, and (c) the positions and struggles between actors within that field. Such an account pays significant attention to objectifying findings, since it works from the assumption that practice is entangled in a range of objective relations (fields). Pouliot points to the importance of multi-method mixes and methodological devices such as 'relational biography' to objectify dispositions. For him, surveys among the actors in fields are also a plausible means of gathering insights into the positions and rivalry within them.

Foucaultian genealogy encourages us to trace problematisations throughout time. The goal becomes identifying those epistemic practices through which a phenomenon was rendered problematic and distinct problem solutions were developed (Koopman 2013). It is an invitation to explore the moments in history where distinct turns were taken and certain understandings of problems became dominant over others, and to trace these practices up to the present. Such problems are not necessarily the grand modern issues, such as sexuality, punishment and madness that Foucault was concerned with. As demonstrated by Bonditti et al. (2014) for security studies and Carol Bacchi (2009, 2012) in policy studies, the approach lends itself to the study of 'smaller' contemporary problems and corresponding policies.

Community of practice research attempts to disentangle the practices that are shared by a community, the elements of meaning that a community uses, or the mechanisms of learning by which one becomes a member of the community. Adler's reading of communities of practice foregrounds the importance of identifying typologies of practices that are relevant for a distinct community. In his research on security communities, for instance, he identifies a set of six practices that characterise a security community (Adler 2008). Others draw on Wenger's idea that communities are constituted by a 'shared repertoire' of meaning, 'joint enterprises' and 'mutual engagement', and investigate each of these elements in detail (Bicchi 2011; Bueger 2013b). Studies of the learning processes by which one becomes a member of a community of practice – what Wenger described as legitimate peripheral participation – have so far not been pursued, but are a reasonable third research strategy following from the framework.

The narrative approach zooms in on situations in which narratives are recounted. The attempt is to reconstruct which narrative devices are being used and how story-telling unfolds, while the invitation is to study the strategies and tactics by which orders become legitimate, actors are capable of proceeding with their actions even in the light of contradictions, and thereby manage to successfully cope with their everyday lives.

Many narrative research strategies investigate how political events are portrayed by a variety of narrators in moments of public controversy. What rhetorical techniques and tricks are used by narrators? Moments of crisis create an imperative for clarification and the search for a collective solution, providing researchers with an excellent analytical opening and methodological entry-point. This is because actors often strategically scramble to make sense of complex social realities. The use of metaphors is, for instance, one of the crucial practices of narration, and studying them is an elucidating strategy for uncovering how actors translate a complex reality into a simplified image. For example, the metaphor of a 'sick patient' requiring immediate treatment was often used by US politicians during the 2008 economic crisis to justify bank bailout schemes and to make sense of a world in crisis. One research strategy in the narrative approach is, therefore, to follow such metaphors, and study how they relate to narrative practices and cultural backgrounds. Additional starting points are the differing plot patterns used in storytelling, such as the various genres of romance, satire, comedy and tragedy – initially outlined by Hayden White (1975: 7–11) – as well as the figuration of actors as story characters (hero, villain, troubleshooter). These plot patterns are means of modelling causality in a culturally compatible manner.

ANT, as a heterogeneous set of studies, does not necessarily lead to a carved-out research strategy, but rather a spectrum of options. The basic tenet here is to rely on a strategy that Nicolini (2013) describes as "zooming in, zooming out". The first step is to study a configuration by zooming in on a distinct element. This can be a certain type of relation, a practice, an object, a concept or a site in which different practices prevail. The second step is then to zoom out to gather an understanding of the effects of the element and the resources the element requires to have this effect. Walters (2002), for instance, studies the bureaucratic form and then asks how this object structures European integration. Bueger and Bethke (2014) zoom in on the concept of 'failed states' and then follow its history and ask what relations between disciplines, policy makers and international organisations it establishes. Schouten (2014) argues for initiating research by investigating controversies over the meaning of security at a distinct site, in this case, an airport. Bueger (2011) argues for studying a distinct site, the UN Peacebuilding Commission, and then traces how the practices at this site structure international peacebuilding. Porter (2012) starts with an investigation of material elements of the practices of peer reviewing in international political economy, and then enquires as to their effects.

Pragmatic sociology takes controversies as starting points, and invites us to study in detail what goes on in these situations. The attempt is to reconstruct how justification and critique clash with each other and produce friction. This requires an ethnomethodological gaze and acknowledgement of the creativity of actors. What do actors mobilise in these situations? How do they invent or re-enact existing orders of meaning?

It also entails asking whether actors form new creative combinations, how they manage or settle controversy, and thereby create new forms of orders.

Every situation in which justification and critique meet each other is a useful analytical entry point for studying the dynamics of social change. The spectrum of such 'critical moments' is potentially wide; in world politics one finds such moments in, for instance, UN Security Council debates. Boltanski and other pragmatic sociologists have demonstrated that practices of justification and critique can be studied through detailed textual analysis of manuals and textbooks. To describe the fundamental change of a 'new spirit of capitalism' Boltanski and Chiapello (2007) used management literature, which directs newcomers on how to become successful managers. As they argue, such texts are revealing analytical material since they are normatively coloured and prescribe how an ideal practitioner in a particular field should perform their occupation (Boltanski and Chiapello 2007: 529). They also provide vital culturally and historically specific insight on how to deal with (global) phenomena such as capitalism. This approach thereby allows for rich comparative analysis of how justifications and legitimacy claims are made across various social boundaries.

As these examples of research strategies document, and as summarised in Table 6.1, there are several plausible access points from which one can begin the recursive process of interpretation and formulation of empirical statements. In principle, we can derive a set of five different starting points from the approaches to initiate a praxiographic project. One can start

Table 6.1 Starting points and sensitizing frameworks

Social space	*Single practice*	*Site*	*Object or artifact*	*Situations*
Field (Bourdieu) Community of Practice (Wenger) Actor-Network (ANT)	Organizing/ Relating (ANT) Storytelling (Narrative) Problematising (Foucault)	Oligopticon/ Laboratory (ANT)	Actant (ANT) Boundary Object (Wenger) Epistemic object (Foucault)	Controversies (Boltanski, ANT) Storytelling (Narrative)

1. from the reconstruction of a figuration, social space, or collective, such as a field, community of practice or actor-network with the goal of describing the relations, struggles, dispositions of that entity;
2. from a single concrete practice, such as a practice of governing or knowledge production, analysis of what acts and statements the practice consists of, and which practical understandings and material elements it contains;
3. from a distinct 'site' that hosts various practices and figurations, such as an international organisation, a mission headquarter or a planning cell; the goal is then to describe the multiplicity inherent in the site and the relations between practices and figurations;
4. from an object or artefact, tracing how these form part of practices in different sites, such as a bureaucratic form or a policy document, or
5. with the study of a problematic situation or controversy as a transformative moment in which old practices are challenged and explicated and new practices are formed, such as a UN Security Council debate, or a crisis moment.

6.3 Praxiographic Methods: Observations, Conversations, and Artefacts

The next question that needs to be asked in designing and planning a praxiography is: what techniques are available to produce data and to reconstruct practices? The choice of methods depends on the demands of the phenomenon one studies, as well as the practicalities of the study, such as resource and time constraints. As already emphasised, praxiographers can draw on a rich spectrum of established techniques, but need to translate them to their particular conceptual needs and ontologies.

In the following section, we provide an outline of four basic techniques that have been used by praxiographers: (1) observing practices, (2) learning practices, (3) talking about practices, and (4) interpreting practices from texts and other artefacts. The first two techniques are often clustered around the notion of 'participant observation', the third usually revolves around different types of 'interviews' or 'focus groups', while the fourth implies different forms of 'text' or 'artefact analysis'. The first techniques (participant observation and interviews) are active modes of co-production, and involve direct encounters with the participants in a practice, while text and artefact analysis is a more passive, desk-based practice. As already suggested, the techniques are anything but exclusive, and the majority of praxiographies will benefit from mixing them. For the purpose of clarity, we discuss them separately, however.

6.3.1 Observing Practices: Participant Observation and Fieldwork

Participant observation is often seen as the 'corresponding method' to practice theory, as it allows for the immediate and unnegotiated recording of practice in real time (Reckwitz 2008; Pouliot 2013; Bueger 2014).

There has been a growing interest in IR in this technique. Much of the discussion draws on ideas imported from anthropology, and in common with that field, much confusion remains in IR as to what should or should not count as participant observation. Should, for instance, attending a parliamentary assembly or a summit of an international organisation count as participant observation? To what extent should participant observation be actual participation in the practices, and to what degree can it be merely passive observation? To mitigate the confusion, we find Czarniawska's (2007) proposal helpful: to reserve the term 'participant observation' to studies in which the researcher has become an actual participant in the practice he or she investigates. For studies that are more inclined towards observation, she suggests the broader term of 'field work' – understanding the term 'field' as referring to a field of practice, and not in the restricted Bourdieusian sense.

While there is a rich body of studies to draw on,[9] the two best-known examples in IR are Neumann's work on Norwegian diplomacy and Michael Barnett's (1997) studies of decision making in the UN General Secretariat. Barnett worked as political officer at the U.S. mission to the United Nations, and provided a detailed account of the bureaucratic processes that played out during the Rwanda peacekeeping disaster of 1994. He later developed his insights further into a general theory of bureaucratic culture of international administrations (Barnett and Finnemore 2004).

Neumann's observations have been published across several studies and are of direct interest since they explicitly link to IPT. Neumann worked in the Norwegian Ministry of Foreign Affairs for three and a half years as a planner and senior advisor. In his two books *At Home with the Diplomats* (2012) and *Diplomatic Sites* (2013), he documents the practices of the 'art' of diplomacy, providing detailed accounts of the life of the diplomat, the kind of work diplomacy implies, and the bureaucratic practices of the ministry. This includes studies of when and how to serve food at ministry meetings (Neumann 2012: 111), how speeches are written for the minister (2012: 63–93), or how diplomatic dinners unfold (2013).

The methodological principle of participant observation can perhaps best be understood through Lave and Wenger's (1991) concept of legitimate peripheral participation. In the research process, the researcher becomes a participant in the practices of his or her role, organisation or profession. Over time, the researcher learns what is needed to perform the practices that are required in the respective setting, how to master and adjust them across different situations, and how to evaluate the performance of others. Neumann, for instance, learned how to write a speech for the foreign minister, and how to behave appropriately at a diplomatic dinner. During this process, the researcher then carefully records his or her own learning experience, and what is required to perform a practice. As Zahle (2012) points out, paying attention to the evaluations of practices in particular can provide key insights in understanding practical knowledge. This can be the evaluations of what she calls "competent assessors", or the reactions to and evaluations of the analyst's activities.

An important version of participant observation is auto-ethnography, which centres on self-observations in the process of learning a certain (set of) practices.[10] From a praxiographic stance, auto-ethnography's core strength is the way it incorporates the body and material dimensions into the analysis through direct experience. Louis Waquant's (2004) study of the habit and practice of boxing is widely received as a paradigmatic auto-ethnographic praxiographic study. By practicing in a gym and participating in amateur tournaments, Waquant elaborated on the bodily and social formation of the habitus by constantly reflecting on his own mental, social and bodily transformations. As Sophie Merit Müller (2016) clarifies in her study of ballet practices, the praxiographic form of auto-ethnography is quite different from others. It is not about the individual subject's experience *per se*, but using the researcher's body as a methodological tool. "The researcher's body is used here as a highly sensate and tuneable instrument for picking up data" (Müller 2016: 707). As Waquant and Müller demonstrate, this particular method is capable of explicating implicit and practical modes of knowledge that are otherwise difficult to access.

Another variant of participant observation are techniques known as 'action research'. Action research is a direct interventionist strategy that centres on participation, rather than observation, implying direct engagement in a field of practice, not only with the intent to learn the practices of the field, but also to make a contribution to, or an intervention in it. Action research has primarily been received as a tool for contributing to transformation and critique, but may also be readily employed as a praxiographic technique. One takes a rather agnostic stance and intervenes in order to experiment with(in) the field of practice; if in auto-ethnography it is the body of the researcher that is the tool of knowledge production, in action research it is the interventionist and knowledge production practice.

Action research, as introduced by Olaf Eikeland and Nicolini (2011: 166), provides a way to avoid starting research from a segregated spectator position, and instead begins from below and within, by being practically immersed in the practice being studied, and by taking the notion of co-production of knowledge between academics and practitioners seriously. As a praxiographic approach, action research has become particularly influential in organisation studies, where the approach implies working in and with an organisation, often a company (Marshall 2011). As Koen Bartels (2012) suggests, action research implies being "immersed in an ongoing situated process [...] with policy actors to generate knowledge by and for acting in problematic situations". In action research, therefore, the practice of knowledge production is moved within the field, and participation and collaboration with practitioners becomes the primary mode of knowledge production.

Participant observation, auto-ethnography and action research are resource-intensive techniques, and require a high degree of commitment and personal investment in which one's identity as a scholar and position in the new role become blurred. It is part of the process that one becomes what one studies. The dual role one performs in learning how to participate, intervene, as well as records is demanding. Over time, the researcher might become naturalised in the practice, a situation wherein one can no longer assess it from the perspective of a stranger. Access can also be problematic, and require a lengthy negotiation process. On occasion, participating may not be possible; for instance, if a previous career trajectory is required: one cannot become a high-ranked soldier or a trained physicist overnight. There may also be ethical or temporal constraints: to study the practices of genocide by participant observation seems unthinkable. If one is interested in historical practices, the practices are already in the past, and one cannot learn them through participation.

Participant observation is, however, only one of the techniques that allow recording practice in real time. There are similar field techniques that might be more promising, particularly as a starting point or in conducting a project with very limited resources. In the following section, we discuss the observation of meetings and the technique of shadowing as possible alternatives.

Observing meetings (often combined with interviews with the participants) is increasingly used as a technique, and is particularly fruitful in an international political setting. The observation of meetings, conferences and summits revolves around the concept of studying situations in which larger groups of actors meet, negotiate and deliberate. This provides an ideal opportunity to understand how different actors engage in joint practices or negotiate their value.

Larger global events such as UN conferences, in particular, are relatively easy to access and have therefore become increasingly studied through direct observation. A range of anthropologists have spearheaded such accounts; Paul E. Little's (1995) observation-based study of the Rio Earth Summit as a ritual is one of the classic studies. Annelise Riles (1998, 2006, 2008) observed UN-sponsored women's rights conferences in order to understand how actors draft legal documents, deploy negotiation techniques such as bracketing, and how these documents are used in further meetings. Noella Gray (2010) studied the negotiation of protected areas through observations at a world conservationist conference, Florian Weisser (2014) observed global climate change conferences to understand practices of exclusion and the performativity of documents, while Joel Wainwright and Theresa Wong (2009) studied global economic governance meetings such as those of the World Trade Organisation or World Bank in order to understand practices of hegemony and resistance in global governance.

Treating these meetings as "spaces within which global norms may be constituted" (Wong and Wainwright 2009: 425), they show how "concrete practices of spatial regulation contribute to producing spaces of resistance" (Wong and Wainwright 2009: 403). Campbell and Brosius (2010) report on a larger research project that studied a global conservationist meeting. They clearly point to the virtues of taking such an approach:

> It is at the physical site of meetings that the interactions, associations, and politics associated with specific policies are performed in front of an audience. Further, because of the audience, meetings are where dissenters often target their resources. Meetings bring together thousands of actors in one space for a short period of time, and thus represent unparalleled opportunities to study not only individual agents and institutions of global environmental governance, but also the networks in which they are embedded. (Campbell and Brosius 2010: 247)

As they suggest, the sheer size and scope of such meetings creates specific demands that cannot easily be met by an individual researcher, however. "It is simply impossible for any single individual to gain a broader analytical perspective on the events unfolding before them as these meetings proceed apace." (Campbell and Brosius 2010: 247). To cope with these constraints, they worked in the realm of what they call "collaborative ethnography" and observed the meeting with a team of 22 researchers.

Event observations might also be conducted in more formalised settings, such as meetings of governance councils or committees of international organisations. Lisa Mcentee-Atalianis (2011, 2013), for instance, worked as an intern at the International Maritime Organisation; access to committee meetings provides the background for her detailed study of the language and identity of the organisation.

Though not widely used in IR to date, shadowing provides a further option. It is another field technique that allows the recording of real time practices, involving the following of actors in their day-to-day lives and recording their activities, encounters and conversations. As Czarniawska (2007: 55–56) points out, "compared to participant observation, shadowing is easier, because it does not require a simultaneous action and observation. [...] [I]t permits one to preserve an attitude of outsideness, whereas participant observation creates many opportunities for 'going native'".

Czarniawska (2007) traces the technique back to a seminal study by Harry F. Wolcott (1973) on school principals. Attempting to investigate 'What do school principals actually do?', Wolcott followed a principal in his day-to-day life for two years. The results of his study were a detailed description of the personality of the actor, his work, the school, the system in which he was embedded, and principalship as a form of human activity (Czarniawska 2007: 32). In another seminal study, Italian sociologist Marianella Sclavi (1989) followed two school students for half a year each to compare different educational experiences and systems.

If these examples show the worth of a prolonged period of shadowing, Czarniawska (2007) in her work on city managers spearheaded an approach that draws on short-term, two-week shadowing with several such individuals. Like participant observation, shadowing is a demanding technique that requires ongoing negotiation of access. In organisational sociology and management studies, shadowing has become an approach widely used to record practice (McDonald 2005). To the best of our knowledge, shadowing has not been used systematically in IPT studies or in IR to date. Initial studies nevertheless showcase the productivity of this technique in the study of politics. Ruth Wodak (2009) shadowed a member of the European Parliament to understand everyday life as a parliamentarian, while in his study of daily life in the British government, R.A.W. Rhodes (2011) shadowed two ministers and three permanent secretaries for five working days each.

Shadowing is conventionally associated with following actors, that is, humans. The technique could just as well imply following objects, technologies and artefacts, however; indeed, many praxiographers have followed non-humans. This includes the study of documents to understand how they are used and how they inform bureaucratic practice and are circulated in and across offices (Walters 2002; Neumann 2007; Freemann and Maybin 2011), specific technologies, such as bush pumps or pipelines and how they are applied and integrated into practice at different sites (De Laet and Mol 2000), or connecting different actors (Barry 2013), and even incorporeal objects such as 'the international financial market' that can be traced across different sites, such as the offices of traders (Knorr Cetina and Bruegger 2002). Following objects is not necessarily easier, however. While access does not have to be negotiated with the object itself, it must be done with its users. Moreover, objects can travel with breath-taking speed, often causing researchers to have to be elsewhere before they have even arrived at one site.

Participant observation, observing meetings and events, as well as shadowing, are all promising techniques for directly observing practice. Though these techniques require that significant efforts are made to gain access to the field, prior fieldwork in IR as well as other disciplines indicate that this access is generally possible, including in sensitive or highly securitised environments. Field access is not, in principle, more difficult in an IR context than in other fields, although an intricate and often sustained negotiation process will always be involved. That said, there will remain situations in which participant or direct observation is impossible, including situations of extreme violence and insecurity, or historical cases.

6.3.2 Talking Practices in Conversations

Researchers therefore need to be creative and invent other forms of praxiographic techniques. The most widely used of these techniques, interviews, is perhaps the most problematic. Interviews are frequently adopted in IR, and the speech subsequently recorded and transcribed is conventionally used as 'evidence' for accounts of how things 'really happened'.

The intent of praxiographers is almost the opposite, however: interviewing implies talking about practices – that is, something other than the practices themselves. Interviews primarily provide *post-hoc* rationalisations by practitioners, and have rightfully been criticised as providing little insight into actual practices (Pugh 2013). For Schmidt (2017: 15) "procedures such as interviewing seem to be inept because they are geared to make interviewees look retrospectively at social practices and tend to address them as if they were the authors or theoreticians of practices they were participating in." Others are more optimistic about the prospects of talking about practices, however, pointing to the reflexive capacities of individuals (Hitchings 2012).

In any case, carefully designed interview strategies are required to make the empirical material gathered in interviews useful for the reconstruction of practices. Conceptually, one must differentiate between participant interviews and expert interviews. In the first type of interview, the objective is to acquire clues about the practical knowledge of someone who is a participant in the practice. In the second instance, the interview is a dialogue with a fellow observer who has expert knowledge about a practice, site or figuration.

Participant interviews not only provide an ideal complement to field work, but can be of value in their own right. A number of interview strategies have been outlined in order to produce empirical material of value for the reconstruction of practices. Pouliot (2013: 49) points to the importance of asking interviewees to recount their actual practices and to treat interviews as practices or performances in their own right. Nicolini (2009) outlines a sophisticated strategy centred on asking the interviewee to provide instructions to a virtual double about how to go about his or her daily life. This "induces the interviewees to produce a highly idealised narrative description of the practice from a particular moral and normative angle" (Nicolini 2009: 204). This narrative therefore allows us to unravel the normative and evaluative dimension of practice. Pugh (2013) develops a related outline of in-depth interviewing that focusses on the emotional stances of practice.

Expert interviews, by contrast, are conducted with individuals that have significant experience with a practice or a setting without necessarily being a part of it. Experts are long-term observers who closely monitor a field of practice, but not strictly part of it. Examples include a war correspondent who has been reporting on conflict for some time, a policy expert who follows a policy issue, or a fellow academic studying the practice from a different angle. Through these experts, we intend to gather interpretations about practices, or to co-interpret practices with someone who is closer to them.

One might also ask this expert to act as observer, in situations where he or she might have access the researcher cannot gain. Using multiple such expert observers enables us to make observations at several places at the same time, and can thereby be a means to investigate how practices are enacted at different sites. Czarniawska (2007), for instance, suggests that a productive type of observation becomes possible by conducting interviews with such expert observers at regular intervals (bi-weekly in her case).

If it is important to conduct interviews decentered from the individual and his attitudes, beliefs and memories, conversations about practices can also be conducted with groups. This technique is known as focus groups. Trowler (2014: 26) gives a range of examples of strategies that can be used: this can be "the real-time discussion of alternative points of view, tensions and conflicts"; "collective discussion of real-life episodes that respondents have shared", "specially created fictional accounts can be offered to groups of respondents for discussion, with prompts", or using "mediating artefacts such as pictures, case notes or documents as catalysts for discussion". Halkier (2010) reports on the use of focus groups in a study of the transformation of cooking practices. As she suggests, in focus groups, knowledge is enacted. She proposes employing a range of established analytical techniques to analyse conversations, namely Goffman-inspired interaction analysis, conversation analysis, discourse psychology and positioning theory.

6.3.3 Reading Practices: Textual and Artefact Analysis

The second major alternative to field work is to draw on textual analysis and attempt to 'read' practices from texts, documents and visual and material artefacts. Textual analysis is of particular importance in the case of historical practices, or when other methods are not viable. A discussion of the different genres of text and the clues they provide about practice is crucial here. As Pouliot (2013: 49) suggests, one must "select particular textual genres that offer a window onto enacted practices". We can distinguish initially between (1) ego-documents, (2) manuals, (3) records of activities and (4) social media data. The most important form of such texts are 'ego-documents' that provide details of activities carried out by individuals. This includes memoirs, personal diaries, or written correspondence. Such documents can be identified, for instance, through archival research. Handbooks and how-to manuals are a second major genre. These describe practices in an idealised way, often through step-by-step guidance. Texts that provide detailed recordings of activities include, for example, court cases, annual reports, diplomatic cables, meeting minutes, recordings or transcripts. Many individuals, organisations or missions furthermore provide detailed public diaries on their social media accounts. Such documents and artefacts are widely used in praxiographies, and have often become the primary empirical material used to reconstruct practices.

Documents require careful reflection of the conditions under which they were produced, as well as how they are used (Prior 2008). One would not, for instance, assume that analysing a recipe book provides us direct access to cooking practices in kitchens around the world, or that a catalogue necessarily grants insight into the world of real-life fashion.

Reckwitz (2008) stresses that visual and material artefacts might also provide us with understandings of practice. Visual artefacts include, for instance, paintings and photographs of everyday scenes. Live streams of meetings or recorded videos, such as the rich repertoire we find on video sharing websites like YouTube, provide indirect observations of practice. CCTV can also be a useful data source. Also a range of recent experiments using video in ethnography point to the potential of visual data for the study of practice (Heath and Hindmarsh 2011).

Also, in the context of the visual or aesthetic turn, scholars in IR have developed visual methodologies that may be productive for praxiography. These point to the interpretive repertoire provided by the arts, visual aesthetics, or film studies. Axel Heck and Gabi Schlag (2013), for instance, adopt the iconological approach by Erwin Panofsky (1970) to demonstrate how a cover of Time magazine, featuring a young Afghan woman whose ears and nose had been cut off, led to visual securitisation and strengthened a justificatory narrative for continuing military intervention. Hansen (2015) draws on the case of hooded prisoners in the U.S. detention centre at Abu Ghraib to demonstrate how images 'make world politics' through practices of circulation and appropriation. Andersen and Möller (2013) analyse photographs as examples of invisible forms of warfare and surveillance being revealed.

Graphic images, such as comics (Shim 2017), cartoons (Hansen 2011), or even children's drawings (Aradau and Hill 2013) have also started to become objects of analysis. Such visual-based studies share the praxiographic intent that images or other visual artefacts should not be interpreted as representations, but as artefacts socially and bodily embedded in practices of showing and seeing. As argued in these discussions, studies on visual artefacts and media also lead researchers to reflect on their own visual practices, and imply a process of 'learning how to see' (Lisle 2017).

Material artefacts can be interpreted, given that they have been made for practical use. Technologies, as well as architecture, buildings or even cities can become a source, and one can reconstruct how they were intended to be used from their design. A classical study is that of Langdon Winner (1980), who shows how bridge design prevented the poor and ethnic minorities of New York from gaining access to Long Island resorts and beaches. Contemporary examples include, for instance, a study by Endres Dany (2011) considering practices of democracy through an in-depth investigation of the building of the Hungarian parliament. In IR, Jenny Edkins (2003) analysed practices of memory in sites such as memorials, museums, and remembrance ceremonies to explore how people commemorate traumatic events of wars and genocides. In this broader sense, the spectrum of artefacts a praxiographer can draw on is wide.

Praxiography differs from other styles of textual analysis by prioritising certain kinds of 'text'. However, this is not the only element that makes praxiography distinct. As Reckwitz pointed out, in analysing such texts, many of the ideas of discourse analysis are relevant. To do so effectively, discourse needs to be understood as a collection of practices of representation that produce the texts one analyses (Reckwitz 2008: 203). The core task of analysing these texts is then to interpret them in light of the practices necessary to produce them, how practical knowledge or means of using these texts are ascribed to them, and what ways of receiving and using these texts are viable. The texts and artefacts are an element of practices, and should not be understood as having meaning outside of these practices. Textual analysis in this sense always understands text as part of a practical configuration, and uses it to deduce practice and larger configurations.

6.3.4 *The Spectrum of Praxiographic Techniques*

Table 6.2 summarises the advantages and disadvantages of the different techniques. It would be a mistake to assume that these praxiographic techniques can be clearly separated from each other. If discussing them separately makes sense for reasons of clarity, anyone who has conducted praxiographic research will recognise that in practice, they meld into one another.

During field work, one will interpret texts and artefacts or encounter interview-type situations. Halkier (2017: 199) rightfully argues that "in data production, participant observation usually includes conversations [...] and many types of interviewing include materials, observations and exercises". As Czarniawska (2007: 54–55) points out: "You cannot say 'Sorry,

Table 6.2 Praxiographic techniques

	Advantages	*Disadvantages*
Fieldwork	Recording of real-time practices	Resource intensive, access problematic,
Participant Observation	Experiencing practical knowledge through learning	Access difficult in highly skilled settings, requires usually prolonged involvement
Auto-ethnography	Bodily experiences	Prolonged commitment
Event Observation	Direct observation of interaction of multiple actors in one place, Access often unproblematic	Cacophony, size and scope, speed are difficult to manage by individual
Shadowing	Direct observation of activities, high mobility	Access requires continuous re-negotiation
Action Research	Participant mode, co-production of knowledge	Loss of academic autonomy, risk of co-optation
Conversations	Co-production of interpretations	Only in-direct observation, lack of material dimension of practices
Participants	Clues on activities and evaluative standards, co-production	Post-hoc rationalisations
Experts	Interpretations of activities and background knowledge, co-interpretation, potentially indirect recorded observations	Second hand interpretations
Focus Groups	Collective knowledge, shared evaluations	Second hand interpretations
Text Analysis	Situations where fieldwork or interviews are not possible, large pool of material	No direct observation, no co-production, interpretative procedures required, selection criteria
Ego-Documents	Clues on the activities and evaluations of individuals	Idealized and incomplete Narratives, difficult to access
Descriptions of Practice	Easily available, inter-subjective descriptions and evaluations of practice	Idealized and incomplete narratives
Visual and Material Artifacts	Indirect observation of practices	Very difficult to interpret

I am not doing a participant observation' when somebody asks you for help with a falling shelf, and neither can you say 'You forgot I am shadowing' when the person you shadow instructs you to stay in the office and not to follow her". How one mixes, blends or prioritises these strategies and techniques not only depends on which set of sensitising concepts one initiates research from, but is also contingent upon the actual (set of) practices one studies and the resources available.

The spectrum of techniques and strategies we have sketched out is far from exhaustive. While we discussed the main methods that praxiographers have developed so far, praxiography is an invitation to be inventive and to develop and experiment with new strategies and techniques. This holds especially true in an IR context, given that many of the phenomena international praxiographers are concerned with are widely dispersed across sites, practices of interest are enacted simultaneously at different places, many of the actors studied have a high degree of mobility, and the circulation of objects and artefacts is fast paced. These are challenges that call for creativity.

As global praxiographers, including those discussed above, have shown, a focus on international practices does not prevent proximity to the actors, direct observations, or detailed empirical reconstruction work. A lack of empirical material is usually not a problem: in the internet age, available sources and documents have multiplied, and interlocutors can be reached via VoIP or email. The question tends to be the opposite: how to limit the empirical material one uses and analyses. Fieldwork can be an important device in this regard, since the actors studied guide the selection procedure, and point out which resources are important and which are not. Being creative also implies going beyond conventional method divides. Schatzki (2012: 26), for instance, invites us to bridge the quantitative-qualitative divide and suggests the potential usefulness of statistics. Quantification can be useful to "provide overviews of the quantifiable features of large classes of phenomena and thereby contribute to the attainment of overviews of social affairs", but only, as he cautions, if used in conjunction with other methods (Schatzki 2012: 26).

6.4 Writing Praxiography

The next challenge concerns how to present the results of a praxiography. At some point, research has to stop, either when one runs out of resources, or (ideally) reaches a point of satiation. "The day when everything said at a meeting is fully understandable is the day to return to one's office – not only for reasons of efficient resource management, but also because complete understanding means 'going native', at which point the attention drops and outsidedness is at peril. When one understands everything, there is nothing left to explain" (Czarniawska 2007: 27). That is when one faces the question of how to write a praxiography.

In ethnography and interpretive policy analysis, a nascent discussion addresses the problem of how to write, which is also relevant for praxiography. Most IPT texts to date have opted for conventional narrative styles to present their research. This traditionally implies discussion of literature, clarification of the contribution of the text, elaboration of theory and presentation of the empirical material in the form of one or two cases. Such a style of presentation does not necessarily lend itself to praxiography, since it does not reflect its core premises of the recursive link between theory and the empirical, nor does it provide adequate engagement with the practices studied.

Just as with theorising and researching, we should understand writing as a practice. This approach has at least two consequences. Firstly, as shown in detail by Engert and Krey (2013), writing in social science should be understood as an epistemic practice in which not only representations of prior academic research are presented, but in which and with which knowledge is actively produced. In other words, the text is a laboratory of social scientists in which they produce facts and other phenomena by making connections between prior texts, the world studied and the readers.

Secondly, and particularly if one takes a strong stance concerning the performativity of practices, writing about practices is much more than reporting results; it is a practice constitutive of the phenomena (the practices) one writes about. In ethnography, it is a well-established proposition that in writing, reality is not represented but transformed, and meaning not found but created (Clifford and Marcus 1986).

Müller (2016: 711, emphasis in original) argues that the goal of praxiographic writing must be "to transgress the boundaries of 'conventional' ways of written representation: instead of striving toward producing exact (and thus "objective") *replica* of social life, [it is to…] try to create informative and expressive *sketches* that capture what the respective research is interested in." As Rouse (1996) points out, the core criteria of academic writing is not so much adequate representation and truth, but intelligibility. An academic narrative has to make sense for and inspire a certain readership. To do so it needs to connect to what they already know and what is familiar to them.

Discussing ethnographic narratives, Schwartz-Shea and Yanow (2009) stress the importance of 'trust' to intelligibility, in that successful writing implies establishing a relation of trust between reader and author. They outline six criteria that contribute to a trustworthy narrative, pointing to different forms of reflexivity. This is, firstly, the level of detail, or 'thickness' of a narrative, which demonstrates that the researcher actually has made significant efforts to understand a practice. Secondly, reflexivity towards the researcher's own position "shows that the researcher understands herself as the means, the instrument through which the research (as well as its reporting) has been produced." (Schwartz-Shea and Yanow 2009: 60). Thirdly, triangulation clarifies that the researcher has made efforts to understand a phenomenon by drawing on as many analytical tools and perspectives possible. Fourthly, an "audit" describes the "changes to the original research design made in response to situational realities" (Schwartz-Shea and Yanow 2009: 81). Fifthly, reflexivity towards negative cases demonstrates that the researcher has considered that things could be otherwise and might play out very differently in other situations. Sixthly, a documented process by which the researcher has verified the narrative produced with the interlocutors it draws upon, for instance in sending them drafts, or discussing the narrative.

Yanow (2009) adds the importance of transparency, that is, a sufficiently detailed description of the research process and choices a researcher has made (e.g. the number of days spent in the field, the choice of individuals to shadow, or the selection of interviewees).

Intelligibility also implies that a text is written in a style that is acceptable to the audience. This is the main reason why the majority of IPT texts have opted for conventional styles, since they aim to reach a wide IR readership, especially those not yet convinced of the value of praxiographic accounts. Nevertheless, one can take advantage of the practice theoretical trading zone, recognising that the potential readership is broad and includes other disciplines. Moreover, there is a clear trend towards a broadening of the ways in which IR studies can be presented, and that different styles are becoming increasingly accepted.

Indeed, there are other ways to achieve intelligibility. As Czarniawska (2008: 14) points out, "literary theory [...] has an old recipe for achieving the goal of being read: to dramatise." She points to heroic stories that centre the narrative on a lead protagonist, fictionalisation, or drawing on styles we find in movie documentaries, such as Sweetwood's *Beerland*, discussed in the opening chapter.

A revealing example from practice theory that draws on the style of a heroic narrative is Hendrik Wagenaar's (2004) study of administrative practice. In the article, Wagenaar draws on an interview with an administrator to develop an account of the creativity of the milieu. He introduces Judy, a 34-year-old lawyer working in the Dutch immigration ministry, and uses her voice to expand central categories and dilemmas of bureaucracy. In the article, we learn a great deal about Judy and what she does, but it remains entirely open, as well as largely irrelevant to the argument, whether Judy is a fictional character or not.

Fictionalisation is a style that has been used in various ways in ethnography as well as science and technology studies. A prime example from practice theory is Bruno Latour's *Aramis or the Love of Technology* (1996). The book presents a study of the failure of a transport technology, written as a detective novel.[11] The plot involves a murder entwined with a love story. Latour asks, 'Who killed Aramis, the transportation technology?', and comes up with the answer that Aramis died because nobody loved it. While this is certainly a unique example in the way it tends towards fiction – Latour speaks about "scientifiction" – there are various degrees to which narratives can be fictionalised.

An experiment in innovative IR writing that has received much attention is Elizabeth Dauphinee's *The Politics of Exile* (2013a). Throughout the book, about experiences of war in Bosnia, Dauphinee attempts to avoid conventional ways of presenting research, and experiments instead with fictionalisation. She provides a narrative of an unnamed protagonist – a professor of international politics in Canada – involving stories of a handful of men and women caught up in the Bosnian war and, later, their exile in Toronto. The narrative centres around one researcher's encounter with a Bosnian Serb named Stojan Sokolovic, but also involves other protagonists such as a young man refusing to go to war, a priest who listens to confessions of war crimes, and a young woman who tries to commit suicide after her partner is killed. These multiple voices and personal stories provide insights into the horrors of the Bosnian war, its aftermath, and how IR scholars familiarise themselves with these events.

Dauphinee vividly illustrates wartime Bosnia, a place that often exists as an abstract notion of a onetime warzone, by exploring different figures, rituals, and practices such as dinners and funerals. In a later reflection, Dauphinee (2013b: 350) explains this form of writing as follows: "trauma and grief must be shown in order to be fractionally intelligible: 'the war' lies in every gesture, in every moment of musculature, in every silence in which the imperative to witness is too exhausting to contemplate too urgent to ignore". Though Dauphinee's work is perhaps the most ambitious in terms of its narrative prose, other IR researchers have engaged in similar experiments in fictionalisation to recount war experiences (e.g. Sylvester 2012; Park-Kang 2014).

As Humphrey and Watson (2009) point out, since the researcher is the core instrument in the research process and the goal is not to obtain 'truth', narratives are invariably contrived to some degree. There is a variation in how far one develops this as a style, however. Humphrey and Watson (2009) discuss four approaches: the *plain* style largely attempts to tell the narrative by following the standard writing models of social sciences, and presents research as a 'case'. The *enhanced* style "uses the presentational techniques of the novelist: descriptive scene setting, use of dialogues, author as character in the narrative; inclusion of emotional responses by authors and subjects, attention to the perspectives and stories of subjects" (Humphrey and Watson 2009: 43). The *semi-fictionalised* style represents a more manipulated version, restructuring the events of several investigations into a single narrative, for instance. This is especially important when one draws on sensitive empirical material that would not be publishable otherwise. The *fictionalised* style combines elements from the second and third style, but goes further in its attempt to construct "an entertaining and edifying narrative [...]. Characters and events may be 'created' out of the material gathered" (Humphrey and Watson 2009: 43).

Documentaries are another source of inspiration. As Rens van Munster and Casper Sylvest (2015: 230) have argued, the genre provides "a particular arrangement that creatively brings into play the boundaries between fiction and fact, entertainment and education, or data and theory." Documentaries give voice to participants and aim at providing immediate experiences. They "assemble first-order representations and data such as speeches, interviews, and media footage and weave them into entertaining and, increasingly, commercially viable second-order interpretations" (van Munster and Sylvest 2015: 230). What one can learn from documentary narrative styles is, primarily, how to construct narratives that include different places and voices and move between these in one story without creating a cacophony. Theoretical or methodological considerations and the author's own voice can then become one of the sites and voices that one moves between.

Theorising and conceptual development do not necessarily have to come first in a narrative; one might tell a story of generalizing, extracting and abstracting, ending with theory. Alternatively, one might want to retain the abductive spirit and jump continuously between theorising and one or several empirical narratives, or employ a 'Russian doll' plotline, with each layer revealing further elements. Neumann's (2007) article on speechwriting in the Norwegian foreign ministry, for instance, places a detailed description of the practice at the centre of the narrative, as he introduces details of each stage of speech production and briefly reflects on them in theoretical terms. He then ends his narrative in discussing the links between his observations and different theoretical accounts.

A common objective of writing praxiography is to avoid the alienation that disciplinarity often produces between academics and the worlds they write about. As Dauphinee (2013b: 349) argues, writing can instead be understood as a "thread of connection" that follows the logic of hope in terms of overcoming political hardship, rather than the truth-seeking form of rational argumentation that dominates the academy. Reflecting on writing as a creative practice that overcomes the dichotomies of truth and fiction as well as academic and literary writing highlights the practical political effects that writing can produce (Edkins 2013).

Experimenting with new techniques to attract a readership and to present the unruly world of practice in a different light is an invitation to learn from literature theory, journalism, and filmmaking. It implies taking risks, which is important, not least in finding or constructing wider audiences beyond the immediate peer group, ideally including the practitioners studied.

While these practitioners might not necessarily agree with our narratives, that is not our primary objective. To write a praxiography is to add a narrative to the field of practice. As Czarniawska puts it, "an observer can never know *better* than an actor; a stranger cannot say *more* about any culture than a native, but observers and strangers can see *different* things than actors and natives can" (Czarniawska 2007: 21, emphasis in original). Identifying what matters, and communicating it to a wide audience: that is the point of doing praxiography.

Notes

1. See, in particular, the contributions in Jonas et al. (2017), and, in the context of German sociology, Kalthoff et al. (2008), and Schäfer et al. (2015).
2. See, in particular, Karin Knorr Cetina's work (e.g. 1981, 2001), but also the thriving discussion on the "social life of methods" in social science, summarised in Greiffenhagen et al. (2015).
3. See, for example, contributions in Jonas et al. (2017).
4. Compare the special issue of the *European Journal of International Relations* on this matter (Wight et al. 2013).
5. See, for instance, Kratochwil (2011) for whom theory and practice are opposite poles and hence the notion of 'practice theory' doesn't make much sense. As Stern (2003: 201–203) argues, much of the debate on the status of theory is related to different interpretations of Wittgenstein.

As he concludes, "perhaps it is the protean character of practice theory, the way in which it holds out the promise of accommodating both the aim of rigorous theory of society, and the desire for a close description of particulars, that has made it both so attractive and so hard to pin down." (Stern 2003: 203).

6. For related discussions on techniques of generalisation, see the discussion on the methodology of case studies, in particular Flyvbjerg (2006), Ruddin (2006) and Thomas (2010).
7. Other scholars prefer the term praxeology to speak about the methodology of practice theory. Given that "-ology" refers to a subject of study or a branch of knowledge, rather than an epistemic activity, we prefer the suffix of "-graphy".
8. Trowler (2014) provides a useful short discussion of the relation between praxiography and ethnography. For the broader discussion on the twists and turns of recent ethnography and its reception in international relations and political science, see the discussions in Kapisezewski et al. (2015), Eckl (2008), Vrasti (2008), Sande Lie (2013), Wedeen (2010), Kuus (2013), De Volo, and Schatz (2004), Stepputat and Larsen (2015), Bueger and Mireanu (2014), and the contributions in Schatz (2009).
9. Summarised, for instance, in Bueger and Mireanu (2014) and Schatz (2009).
10. For the more general (not practice-focussed) debate on auto-ethnography in international relations, see Brigg and Bleiker (2010), Dauphinee (2010), Löwenheim (2010), Doty (2010), Neumann (2010) and Hamati-Ataya (2014).
11. For a discussion of the book's style and underlying methodology see Czarniawska (2008) and Austrin and Farnsworth (2005).

CHAPTER 7

Conclusion: Completing the Practice Turn

If one may meaningfully speak about a 'practice turn', it remains fair to say that it has not yet been completed; more needs to be done to realise the full potential of practice thinking, and while the community of scholars is growing, it remains small. IPT has significantly matured over the years; practice theorising has been around since at least the 1980s in social theory, sociology or anthropology, but the call to 'turn' or 're-turn' to practice has only recently been heard in the study of international relations, particularly when compared to other disciplines. If the 2001 edited volume '*The Practice Turn in Contemporary Theory*' (Schatzki et al. 2001) was a game changer in other disciplines, in IR, the agenda-setting efforts of Emanuel Adler and Vincent Pouliot (2011a, b) brought significant attention to practice theory. Since then, IPT has thrived, and a rich body of literature has been developed.

Research relying on what we have termed the main approaches of IPT forms the heart of that literature. While it was initially Bourdieusian research and the community of practice approach that was associated with turning to practice, today we see a much wider spectrum of approaches being developed. Importantly, the approaches we outline tend not to be followed dogmatically. Instead of exegesis, creative combinations of approaches and their concepts under the general header of practice theory are favoured. The concepts, strategies and ideas of the seven approaches we outlined will continue to form main pillars of IPT in the near future.

C. Bueger, F. Gadinger, *International Practice Theory*,
https://doi.org/10.1007/978-3-319-73350-0_7

It is important to note, however, that there are other practice approaches available to speak to issues of the international. Several of these have already been introduced to the discipline, but did not receive sufficient attention in this book, including the discussion of classical pragmatism and the ways it can be developed as an approach of IPT,[1] adoptions of Wittgenstein's language philosophy (Fierke 2002), the cultural sociology of Ann Swidler (as introduced by Sending and Neumann 2011), assemblage theory that develops insights from the work of Gilles Deleuze and Félix Guattari (Acuto and Curtis 2013), or Karin Knorr Cetina's theory of epistemic practices and infrastructures (Bueger 2015).

Other approaches that have notably influenced the practice debate in other disciplines hold significant potential for IPT as well: activity theory in the tradition of Lev S. Vygotsky, the work of Judith Butler, the symbolic interactionism of Erving Goffman, Harold Garfinkel's programme of ethnomethodology, the normative practice theory of Alasdair MacIntyre, and the social theories of Charles Taylor, Margaret Archer and others. The more recent practice theories of Barbara Czarniawska, Silvia Gherardi, Stephen Kemmis, Davide Nicolini, Andreas Reckwitz, Joseph Rouse, Robert Schmidt, Elizabeth Shove or Stephen Turner, which have significantly influenced our discussion without being outlined as 'approaches', also hold great promise for further development in IR, as do discussions on 'strategy as practice' or 'institutional work'. Integrating this body of work into IPT will provide further important concepts and fresh thinking, and will make IPT an even more heterogeneous field than it already is, as well as a stimulus for increasing the inter-disciplinary exchange of scholars in the trading zone.

That IPT is a heterogenous movement is what we hoped to clarify through the metaphor of a trading zone that includes many participants. While practice theorists share a range of basic commitments, there are tensions and differences between them. Our core argument is that the ontological puzzles that lead to such tensions are productive challenges for pushing IPT forward. We outlined a broad range of challenging issues, including the question of how stable practices are, how to conceptualise change, how the micro and the macro are related, whether flat ontologies successfully transcend scales in world politics, whether norms can be separated out from practices, whether normativity is the vital element of practice or merely one dimension of it, how to integrate non-human elements and conceptualise bodies, and how to relate reflexivity and performing research to theorising. None of these questions are definitively 'solvable'.

There are no grounds upon which we would be able to formulate the right position; rather, looking through a multi-perspective lens and recognising that no single approach provides one-size-fits-all answers is the preferred strategy. Appreciating the tensions within practice theory, clarifying differences and using these creatively will allow to push the debate in promising new directions.

The work on ontological questions will, moreover, continue to be one of the vehicles through which the relation between practice theoretical accounts and other accounts of the international will be discussed. For instance, discussing order and change allows to draw distinctions with the grand theories of IR and their understanding of structures and change, or the debate on normativity provides potential collaboration between norm constructivism, international political theory and IPT. This is an opportunity to convince scholars about the value of IPT and the insights it can provide; for instance, in pointing to those facets of international political life that other perspectives miss. Defining differences vis-à-vis other perspectives should not, however, be undertaken predominantly on philosophical grounds. As we have emphasised throughout this volume, IPT is an empirical project rather than a theoretical one.

Understood in this sense, practice theory provides a methodological orientation for praxiographic research. It is the praxiographies – the actual studies of practices – that make the difference. Compared to elaborating on conceptual vocabularies and their strengths, too little debate has taken place in terms of how to perform praxiographic researching and writing practices. As we argued in Chap. 6, praxiography sets out from the understanding that methods are practices, as is writing about practices. We highlighted the importance of creativity and improvisation in praxiography, as opposed to working with a rigid set of ideal methods. To provide inspiration for studies, we outlined some of the repertoire of praxiographic tools and strategies. Tools and strategies from qualitative research and ethnography, ranging from participant observation and action research to interviews, text, video and architecture analyses can become useful praxiographic methods if translated in an appropriate way. Using this repertoire will produce an increasing amount of interesting and enlightening insights about international life.

In this concluding chapter, we come back to one of the questions raised at the beginning of the book, namely how to think about IPT as a project, and where it is situated in IR. One might contend, given the open idea of a trading zone and the contention that it is the practices that matter, that the question of within which disciplinary structures practices are studied in becomes moot. While we would like to agree, it remains important to consider IPT's position in the "practical configuration of IR" (Bueger and Gadinger 2017), as well as its future path.

As a way of summarising our discussion, we firstly return to the promises with which practice theory was introduced to IR. We briefly evaluate the current situation, starting with a discussion on the question of whether practice theory has already lived up to its promises. Following that, we speculate about the future of IPT by considering three scenarios; the first implying that IPT is becoming an even more heterogeneous trading zone, the second positing that it is being normalised into a paradigm, and the third proposing that it should be understood as a passing fashion, destined to fade away.

7.1 Living Up to Its Promises?

Along with new perspectives, approaches and, particularly, 'turns' come great promises of what these innovations allow us to do, see and say differently. These promises not only provoke calls for evidence of whether the perspective has actually added value, but also in how far the practice turn has already been completed. In this section, we provide a short evaluative review asking whether IPT has already lived up to its promises, and if not, evaluating the prospects that it eventually will.

As argued in the introduction, practice theory comes with several promises:

1. to get closer to the actions, routine and lifeworlds of the practitioners who practice international relations;
2. to produce knowledge that is of relevance beyond the immediate group of peers, and might even address societal concerns, or contribute to crafting better political responses;
3. to avoid and overcome (traditional) intellectual dualisms, such as structure and agency, micro and macro, or the ideational and the material;
4. to develop a perspective that is receptive to change as well as reproduction;
5. to more fully integrate material aspects, ranging from bodily movements to objects and artefacts.

So far, IPT has arguably performed well relative to some of these promises, but less so on others. The verdict remains mixed, and more work will have to go into delivering some of the promises. Clear success appears to have been achieved in promises number three and five, however.

Together with the broader debate on 'new materialism', IPT has led to a new appreciation for the material side of international life. Scholars have become increasingly attuned to a broad host of objects, artefacts and technology, and their role in international practice. Whether it is documents or surveillance technology, the worlds described by IR scholars today are populated by more than just humans. The importance of bodies and their movement has attracted less attention, but is clearly on the agenda.[2] One can plausibly expect that that this trend will continue, that more attention will be paid to the material, and that studies will investigate not only documents or technologies, but will also scrutinise aspects such as architecture or bodily expressions much more closely.

Promise three also represents a success story. The new vocabularies introduced by IPT have the clear intention of avoiding dualisms whilst sketching out a more complex and receptive universe of concepts. The notion of practice in itself is a mediator of structure and agency, as are concepts such as habitus, doxa, field, narrative, communities of practice, justification and translation, to mention just a few. IPT research has clearly shown that research does not have to begin by accepting binaries as given. At the same time, practice theory remains at constant risk of introducing new binaries and dualisms, however. The modern mindset easily creeps in, and temptation exists to form new binaries: practice vs. structure, practice vs. narrative, action vs. practice, doxa vs. habitus, routine vs. reflexive action, or practice theory vs. praxiography are examples of this. Constant reminders of the importance of an anti-dualist stance and the rejection of fixed taxonomies will continue to be necessary. Favouring relationalism and performativity over dualisms and rigid categories is, and remains, one of the core drivers of practice theory.

Promise four, to develop a perspective that is receptive to change, remains, as we saw in Chap. 5, a major challenge that requires ongoing attention, not least in responding to those critics who argue that practice theory can easily slip into statism (Duvall and Chowdhury 2011). The question of change has nonetheless become a focal point of attention. Although there is some risk of falling into a dualism of two modes of practice – as routine and as reflective action – researchers have started to develop convincing answers in terms of how practice theories can conceptualise change (see, in particular, Schindler and Wille 2015; Hopf 2017). The strategies outlined, whether in terms of studying how actors respond to moments of crisis, or how they maintain order in the face of practice breakdowns, have not yet fully translated into empirical research, but we expect that that they will do so in due course.

Promise one, to get closer to the activities, routines and performances of the practitioners of international relations, presents a mixed record. On one hand, there is a clear intention among IPT scholars to seek proximity to practice. There is a turn towards working more empirically, and research driven by ethnographic or in-depth interpretive methods is becoming increasingly widespread. In the study of diplomacy, researchers now seek to speak to the diplomats and participate in their meetings, for instance, while in security studies, researchers shadow security experts or spend time at airports, exposition centers, or military headquarters. The narratives of IPT have, without doubt, become richer and thicker. We now know more about what happens in NATO (Pouliot 2010a, b; Schmitt 2017), at the United Nations Security Council (Pouliot 2016; Ralph and Gifkins 2017) or the European Union (Bremberg and Bicchi 2017).

One the other hand, there is a clear continuation of a trend in which philosophical discussions, conceptual development and abstract reasoning is prioritised. Quality of research is not judged by its capacity to tell us more about a dedicated practice, or how thought provoking, illuminating and thick the empirical narrative is; rather, it is often the philosophical meta-point that counts as a 'contribution'. There remains the risk that such prioritisation will not change in the long run, not least because of disciplinary reward structures. IR, in contrast to anthropology, for example, continues to be a discipline that favours theory and abstraction over intensive empirical work. The 'grand' publications in the discipline are those which outline a 'new' theory or advance an existing one. In these publications, the empirical hardly ever gets beyond the status of mere 'illustration'. Often, empirical narratives, particularly if they do not advance a causal story, are evaluated to present 'policy commentary', or, even worse, to be simply a good 'story' or merely a 'description'. Practice theory will have to challenge this mindset; enriching our understanding of what practitioners 'do', will imply more description and deeper empirical narratives.

Getting beyond current disciplinary evaluations and reward structures, and making the case that any theory's worth depends on careful empirical reconstruction work, will require continued efforts. Foregrounding methods and an understanding of theory as methodological orientation will be a valuable strategy here.

A more negative evaluation can be made in regards to promise two, that of producing knowledge that is of broader relevance, addresses societal concerns and can drive change. IPT scholars have not advanced any strong case or demonstrated how their knowledge actually makes a difference, for example how the study of practice can inform the everyday work of practitioners, or can be of more general societal interest. Similar to other disciplines, IR continues to nurture a disciplinary split between those doing theory (or 'science') and publishing in prestigious journals (that are hardly ever read by anyone outside the immediate discipline), and those commenting on policy and current developments as 'experts' in the media, via working papers or other widely recognised outlets.

One of the promises of practice theory is to rebuild a bridge and produce theory-driven scholarship that can speak to societal concerns, and, indeed, also inform policy formulation. The quality of the praxiographic narratives developed and the way these provide new illuminating re-descriptions of international activities is the core access point for broader relevance and making a difference.[3]

Practice theory, moreover, provides a rich repertoire of strategies of how to intervene in policy processes and how to relate to societal concerns. Three such strategies are outlined in Berling and Bueger (2017): firstly, a strategy of acting as an organic intellectual that directly supports societal (and often marginalised) groups, secondly, developing collective intellectuals that use their academic autonomy as the basis on which to act as experts in societal decision-making processes, and, thirdly, the strategy of intervening in practice through ironic re-descriptions. These are but three of the strategies for intervention that can be derived from practice theoretical thinking; there are doubtless many others.

In our discussion of methodology, we pointed to another possibility, that is, participatory action research. In this strategy, one does not distinguish between knowledge production and intervention, but develops research in concert with practitioners. To live up to the promise of making a difference in the world implies leaving scholarly comfort zones. It is to turn from a spectator mode of analysis towards participation and immersion. Practice theory provides the tools for successful immersion and interventions, and IPT will also benefit from experimenting with ways of how to draw in wider audiences.

In summary, since practice theory was introduced in IR, it has made significant steps towards changing how research is conducted. The practice turn in IR is a success, though not all of the promises associated with turning to practice have been fulfilled. The scorecard remains mixed, and further effort is required.

7.2 Prospects for the Future: Three Scenarios

Given the success of IPT in establishing itself as one of the most important innovations in the discipline of IR, what are its long-term prospects? What will be left after the practice turn is fully completed? What legacy will it leave for the discipline, and beyond? Thinking about these questions is important in at least two regards. Firstly, they are essential questions for informing individual career choices – is it worth investing intellectually and engaging in IPT if one wants to pursue an academic career or make a difference in the world? Secondly, addressing these issues is to give international practice theory a *telos* – a sense of direction in which it is or may be heading. There are at least three plausible long-term scenarios, each of which stresses a different impact that IPT may have: a thriving trading zone, paradigmatisation, and mainstreaming. In the following section, we investigate each scenario in detail, using an earlier discussion (Bueger and Gadinger 2014) as the baseline.

In our first scenario, IPT becomes an ever-growing trading zone in which heterogeneity increases as further concepts and approaches are introduced. Exchanges with various disciplines interested in questions of international relations increase, IPT attracts a growing number of researchers, and practitioners who are interested purely in using the toolboxes and results generated in the zone also start participating. As the trading zone metaphor implies, IPT does not become anything like a settled community of scholars or develops a fixed identity. Instead, it remains a loose network of scholars and practitioners interested in various facets of IPT. Some of the ties within this network become stronger over time, as scholars agree on matters such as the strengths and weaknesses of the different approaches. Other ties necessarily remain looser, particularly as insights on more and more kinds of practices are introduced.

The overall direction in this scenario is the multiplication of connections between different researchers and practitioners and to increase 'trade', that is, communication about practice theory and its challenges, as well as to enable creative, or eclectic combinations of approaches. This does not necessarily imply working towards consensus and agreement; rather, the ongoing concern is to appreciate the controversies over the challenges and the tensions between approaches, as well as to facilitate the conditions under which the accompanying creative power can be harnessed.

Our second scenario follows from the first. As historian of science Ilana Löwy (1992) has shown, trading zones often become stabilised as trade increases. As she argued by drawing on the history of the discipline of immunology, traders are able to establish a common identity, a common language and repertoire of tools. The trading zone starts to grow into what she terms a more stabilised "pidgin zone", or even into a more fully institutionalised "creole zone", membership of which provides the main professional identity.

This leads us to our second scenario, in which IPT grows from a trading zone into a creole zone that provides a common identity. IPT becomes a new paradigm in the discipline, comprised of an established in-group and a periphery, seminal authors, agreed definitions and tools, a common 'thought style' and a set of clearly laid out questions to be addressed. IPT becomes stylised in handbook chapters, and is discussed in IR textbooks as a paradigm alongside realism and constructivism. Someone may then state, with the same conviction that some would have today in claiming to 'be' a constructivist: "I am a practice theorist". Such a scenario would imply that scholars increasingly agree on core concepts and their definition.

This would not be an inherently negative development, since the heterogeneous, and sometimes confusingly plural character of IPT raises the question of how much homogeneity is actually needed for furthering research. Do we need to agree on concepts? If so, do we need concepts other than that of practice? This scenario would also make IPT more accessible, widen participation, and better introduce newcomers to the discussion. It is also a risky scenario, however, given that practice theory might then lose one of its core strengths, namely its adaptability and flexibility across different research situations.

A third scenario, equally worthy of consideration, is that of disappearance or mainstreaming. Academic disciplines are subject to trends, fashions and fads (Bethke and Bueger 2014; Bort and Kieser 2011) as new perspectives, turns, and theorists come and go. At some point in time the discussion (or hype) surrounding a practice turn, practice theory and the concept of practice may fade away. Such a scenario is not unlikely; as Randall Collins (1998) shows in his intellectual history of philosophy, academic disciplines have limited attention spans and are subject to what he calls the "law of small numbers". Over the *longue durée*, intellectual space is usually occupied by no more than three, and a maximum of six theoretical positions. IPT might well fail and fall out of the picture.

Moreover, concepts tend to have distinct lifecycles. Once they have served the purpose of intellectual renewal, many become forgotten. Johan Galtung (1986: 15–17) describes the life of concepts as going through a cycle in which they follow a five-step path: (1) a fresh concept is co-opted from outside for the purpose of organisational renewal; (2) the concept becomes part of texts and manifestos; (3) the concept's meaning is gradually changed to accommodate everyone; (4) the concept has been integrated, and can no longer serve the purpose of renewal; and (5) a new concept comes along and replaces the old one.

The concept of practice, and the entire notion of practice theory, may suffer a similar fate. This scenario allows for an optimistic and a pessimistic reading. From an optimistic standpoint, the decline of practice might lead to the integration of core insights from practice theory into the discipline – a sort of mainstreaming process. As Ulrich Beck and Wolfgang Bonß (1989) argue, the disappearance of a term or insight does not necessarily point to its failure; on the contrary, it can indicate success, as insights might be incorporated into everyday thinking and practice to the degree that they no longer need to be specifically highlighted. This is, quite obviously, difficult to prove, and a pessimistic reading of the same situation would suggest that declining attention or even the disappearance of practice theory would imply its failure; practice theory would have been merely a fad; nothing more.

The above represent three plausible scenarios of how IPT may develop. Using 2014 as a baseline, to what extents can we identify trends and tendencies for these scenarios?

That year, Erik Ringmar (2014: 1) argued that the practice theoretical project "will fail". If by 2015, Adler and Pouliot (2015) were still hesitant, suggesting that "at this stage the jury is still out", by 2017 we can confidently argue that Ringmar was mistaken. A search on Google Scholar provides initial quantitative evidence: over 630 results appear for the term "international practice theory" covering publications between 2010 and 2017.[4]

IPT has grown not only when evaluated quantitatively in terms of publication, but also in substance, with practice theory now being discussed across all subfields of IR, whether it be in international political economy, security studies, peace research, international organisations, or the more specialised fields of study on diplomacy, peacebuilding, European, Asian or African politics. It seems that no area of scholarship has been left untouched by the turn to practices. Also an increasing number of sections and panels at international conferences focus on IPT. With this quantitative and substantial expansion of IPT scholars, which is likely to continue, the field has become more plural and diverse.

If a 2015 review led us to express concern that the debate was being dominated by a discussion of Bourdieu's vocabulary (Bueger and Gadinger 2015), this appears less worrying from the perspective of 2017. Recently introduced approaches, such as ANT, pragmatic sociology and the work of

Boltanski, or the ontology of Schatzki, have become more widely used and moved to the centre of debate. New vocabularies and approaches continue to be added to the debate.[5] With this expansion, the kinds of international practices studied and the empirical basis of IPT have also been enriched. As outlined above, there is, moreover, a visible interest in exploring the relation between IPT and other theorising in IR, particularly within the international political sociology and norm constructivist debate. The relations between IPT and other turns are increasingly observed and discussed, ranging from the visual and aesthetic turn, to new materialism or the affective turn. However, one cannot come to the same conclusion regarding inter-disciplinarity. IR's version of the practice turn appears largely unrecognised in other disciplinary contexts, and remains insular that sense.[6]

Do these observations imply that the first scenario is what we expect to unfold? The IPT debate has certainly become more heterogeneous and more pluralistic; no one approach dominates, and definitions are not settled. Internal clarifications and divergences continue to be explored, and there is an ongoing debate on the particular identity of IPT and what actually constitutes the family resemblance (see, in particular, Kustermans 2016; Frost and Lechner 2016a). IPT has revealed itself able to progress while remaining adaptable as new challenges and empirical constellations arise. In 2014, the first scenario was our preferred option, and in this sense the developments observed are positive. However, one could have envisaged heterogeneity and, in particular, inter-disciplinarity growing even stronger. Indeed, there is plausible evidence that tends towards the logic of the second and third scenarios.

Some trends towards paradigmatisation have become identifiable; for instance, Schatzki's definition of practices as an organised nexus of doings and sayings has become an almost universally adopted standard. Adler and Pouliot's (2011a) practice theoretical manifesto that blends, in particular, approaches of Bourdieu and Wenger has become an authoritative reference point in the debate. By October 2017, their article had been cited over 600 times, according to Google Scholar, which implies that almost all of the publications in IR refer to it in one way or another. It remains by far the most cited article, with the next most popular by another author being Hopf 2010, with 257 citations.[7] While the existence of a common reference point for IPT is not problematic in principle, there is a risk that the way the article frames practice theory becomes taken for granted, with diversity therefore undermined.

One of the core elements of Adler and Pouliot (2011a) was to outline a framework. This proposal can be interpreted as a narrowing down and, indeed, disciplining of IPT. As they rightly argue, this framework bares similarities to our outline of commitments presented here in Chap. 2 (see Adler and Pouliot 2015). It will remain a core conundrum that on the one hand, IPT gains its strength from its open and pluralistic character, while on the other it requires some sort of commonality to drive the project. The solution to this conundrum lies in relational thinking, as IPT is constituted by relations. While the language of commitments is preferable in this regard, the Adler and Pouliot (2011a) article should be evaluated as an anchoring point within IPT, and does not unambiguously point us to paradigmatisation.

Other developments tend more clearly in that direction, however. More recently, David McCourt (2017) published an article in which he claimed that practice theories should be seen as an expression of what he termed "new constructivism". While he rightly pointed out that IPT did not fall from the sky, and as we have frequently emphasised, develops outlines and arguments from earlier constructivist work, subsuming IPT under constructivism, as he proposes, has the sole effect of mainstreaming it (Bueger 2017). As IPT matures and the distinctions with other perspectives become more clearly delineated, boundaries become increasingly defined and reference texts box IPT into certain categories, we are likely to see more such developments.

While IPT looks set to continue engendering thriving trading zones in the near future, all three scenarios remain plausible as the field matures and becomes richer. The first scenario continues to be our preferred one; it reflects the spirit of this book and the direction in which we would like to see IPT develop. This implies a further opening of the debate while continuing to maintain existing connections, thereby strengthening the conversation with other disciplines while clarifying what is specific about the international; it is working towards greater internal consistencies of approaches, while utilising their productive tensions; it is aiming at philosophical sophistication whilst grounding analysis more deeply in empirical material and real-world practice; it is describing international practices in order to revisit and stimulate theorising. "Then", as Reckwitz (2002: 259) comments, "in future the hitherto loose network of praxeological thinking might yield some interesting surprises."

Notes

1. As discussed and developed, in particular, by McCourt (2012), Drieschova (2017), Franke and Weber (2011), Pratt (2016), or Schmidt (2014).
2. Lauren Wilcox's (2017) invitation to build stronger links between practice theory and gender studies is one signal in that direction.
3. Examples of practice theoretical research from science and technology studies, policy studies, or organisation studies document that other audiences can be reached. Mol's (2002) ANT-inspired study of a hospital, for instance, is not only widely read in science and technology studies, but also among practitioners of health. Indeed, the history of the community of practice approach also provides an example; Wenger's approach has become widely used in actual organisational reforms, including in international organisations such as the United Nations. Yanow's work on category-making practices and troubled taxonomies (race/ethnicity) in bureaucracies concerning the inclusion and exclusion of immigrant groups (Yanow et al. 2016) is another instance for practice driven research that had a direct impact on a critical policy debate in the Netherlands and led to a fundamental change of established categories.
4. Data as of 25.10.2017. Related Google Scholar queries, such as "practice theory" + "international relations" produce similar outcomes (656).
5. See our short overview at the beginning of this chapter.
6. That IPT research was included in a recent interdisciplinary edited volume on "Praxeological Political Analysis" (Jonas and Littig 2017) is, however, a promising indicator for the developing exchange with sociology, social theory, and philosophy.
7. Data as of 25.10.2017 referring to the period 2010–2017. Neumann 2002 is listed with 462 citations, while Pouliot 2008 with 436.

Literature

Abrahamsen, Rita, and Michael C. Williams. 2011. Privatization in Practice: Power and Capital in the Field of Global Security. In *International Practices*, ed. Emanuel Adler and Vincent Pouliot, 310–332. Cambridge: Cambridge University Press.

Acuto, Michele, and Simon Curtis, eds. 2013. *Reassembling International Theory: Assemblage Thinking and International Relations*. Basingstoke: Palgrave Macmillan.

Adler, Emanuel. 2005. *Communitarian International Relations: The Epistemic Foundation of International Relations*. London/New York: Routledge.

———. 2008. The Spread of Security Communities: Communities of Practice, Self-Restraint, and NATO's Post-Cold War Transformation. *European Journal of International Relations* 14 (2): 195–230.

Adler, Emanuel, and Patricia Greve. 2009. When Security Community Meets Balance of Power: Overlapping Regional Mechanisms of Security Governance. *Review of International Studies* 35 (S1): 59–84.

Adler, Emanuel, and Vincent Pouliot. 2011a. International Practices. *International Theory* 3 (1): 1–36.

———, eds. 2011b. *International Practices*. Cambridge: Cambridge University Press.

———. 2011c. International Practices: Introduction and Framework. In *International Practices*, ed. Emanuel Adler and Vincent Pouliot, 3–35. Cambridge: Cambridge University Press.

———. 2015. Fulfilling the Promises of Practice Theory in IR. *International Studies Quarterly Online*, 14 December. https://www.isanet.org/Publications/ISQ/Posts/ID/4956/Fulfilling-The-Promises-of-Practice-Theory-in-IR. Accessed 25 Oct 2017.

C. Bueger, F. Gadinger, *International Practice Theory*,
https://doi.org/10.1007/978-3-319-73350-0

Adler-Nissen, Rebecca, ed. 2013a. *Bourdieu in International Relations. Rethinking Key Concepts in IR*. London: Routledge.

———. 2013b. Introduction. In *Bourdieu in International Relations. Rethinking Key Concepts in IR*, ed. Rebecca Adler-Nissen, 1–23. London: Routledge.

———. 2014. Symbolic Power in European Diplomacy: The Struggle Between National Foreign Service and the EU's External Action Service. *Review of International Studies* 40 (4): 657–681.

Adler-Nissen, Rebecca, and Vincent Pouliot. 2014. Power in Practice: Negotiating the International Intervention in Libya. *European Journal of International Relations* 20 (4): 889–911.

Alkemeyer, Thomas, and Nikolaus Buschmann. 2017. Learning in and Across Practices: Enablement as Subjectivation. In *The Nexus of Practices. Connections, Constellations, Practitioners*, ed. Allison Hui, Theodore R. Schatzki, and Elizabeth Shove, 8–23. London: Routledge.

Amicelle, Anthony, Clauda Aradau, and Julien Jeandesboz. 2015. Questioning Security Devices: Performativity, Resistance, Politics. *Security Dialogue* 46 (4): 293–306.

Andersen, Rune S., and Frank Möller. 2013. Engaging the Limits of Visibility: Photography, Security, and Surveillance. *Security Dialogue* 44 (3): 203–221.

Anderson, Benedict. 1991. *Imagined Communities*. London: Verso.

Aradau, Claudia, and Andrew Hill. 2013. The Politics of Drawing: Children, Evidence, and the Darfur Conflict. *International Political Sociology* 7 (4): 368–387.

Ashley, Richard K. 1987. The Geopolitics of Geopolitical Space: Toward a Critical Social Theory of International Politics. *Alternatives: Global, Local, Political* 12 (4): 403–434.

Ashley, Richard K. and R.B.J. Walker, eds. 1990. Speaking the Language of Exile. Dissidence in International Studies. Special Issue in *International Studies Quarterly* 34 (3): 259–268.

Austrin, Terry, and John Farnsworth. 2005. Hybrid Genres: Fieldwork, Detection and the Method of Bruno Latour. *Qualitative Research* 5 (2): 147–165.

Avant, Deborah, Martha Finnemore, and Susan K. Sell. 2010. Who Governs the Globe? In *Who Governs the Globe?* ed. Deborah Avant, Martha Finnemore, and Susan K. Sell, 1–26. Cambridge: Cambridge University Press.

Bacchi, Carol L. 2009. *What's the Problem Represented to Be?* Frenchs Forrest: Pearson.

———. 2012. Why Study Problematizations? Making Politics Visible. *Open Journal of Political Science* 2 (1): 1–8.

Balzaq, Thiery, Tugba Basaran, Didier Bgio, Emmanuel-Pierre Guittet, and Christian Olson. 2010. Security Practices. In *International Studies Encyclopedia Online*, ed. Robert A. Denemark. Blackwell Publishing. http://www.isacompendium.com/. Accessed 16 Oct 2017.

Barnes, Barry. 2001. Practice as Collective Action. In *The Practice Turn in Contemporary Theory*, ed. Theodore Schatzki et al., 17–28. New York: Routledge.

Barnett, Michael N. 1997. The UN Security Council, Indifference, and Genocide in Rwanda. *Cultural Anthropology* 12 (4): 551–578.

Barnett, Michael. 1999. Culture, Strategy, and Foreign Policy Change: Israel's Road to Oslo. *European Journal of International Relations* 5 (1): 5–36.

Barnett, Clive. 2015. On Problematization. Elaborations on a Theme in "Late Foucault". *NonSite* 16, available at http://nonsite.org/article/on-problematization.

Barnett, Michael, and Raymond Duvall. 2005. Power in Global Governance. In *Power in Global Governance*, ed. Michael Barnett and Raymond Duvall, 1–32. Cambridge: Cambridge University Press.

Barnett, Michael N., and Martha Finnemore. 2004. *Rules for the World: International Organizations in Global Politics*. Ithaca: Cornell University Press.

Barry, Andrew. 2013. *Material Politics. Disputes along the Pipeline*. Malden: John Wiley.

Bartels, Koen P.R. 2012. The Actionable Researcher. *Administrative Theory & Praxis* 34 (3): 433–455.

Beck, Ulrich, and Wolfgang Bonß. 1989. Verwissenschaftlichung ohne Aufklärung? Zum Strukturwandel von Sozialwissenschaft und Praxis. In *Weder Sozialtechnologie noch Aufklärung? Analysen zur Verwendung sozialwissenschaftlichen Wissens*, ed. Ulrich Beck and Wolfgang Bonß, 7–45. Frankfurt a. M.: Suhrkamp.

Bellanova, Rocco, and Gloria Gonzáles Fuster. 2013. Politics of Disappearance: Scanners and (Unobserved) Bodies as Mediators of Security Practices. *International Political Sociology* 7 (2): 188–209.

Bénatouïl, Thomas. 1999. The Critical and the Pragmatic Stance in Contemporary French Sociology. *European Journal of Social Theory* 2 (3): 379–396.

Berard, T.J. 2005. Rethinking Practices and Structures. *Philosophy of the Social Sciences* 35 (2): 196–230.

Berger, Tobias, and Alejandro Esguerra. 2017. Conclusion: Power, Relationality and Difference. In *World Politics in Translation*, ed. Tobias Berger and Alejandro Esguerra, 216–231. London/New York: Routledge.

Berling, Trine Villumsen. 2011. Knowledges. In *Bourdieu in International Relations. Rethinking Key Concepts in IR*, ed. Rebecca Adler-Nissen, 59–77. London: Routledge.

———. 2012. Bourdieu, International Relations, and European Security. *Theory and Society* 41 (5): 451–478.

Berling, Trine Villumsen, and Christian Bueger. 2017. Expertise in the Age of Post-Factual Politics: An Outline of Reflexive Strategies. *GeoForum* 84: 332–341.

Bernstein, Richard. 1971. *Praxis and Action: Contemporary Philosophies of Human Activity*. Philadelphia: University of Pennsylvania Press.

Best, Jacqueline. 2012. Ambiguity and Uncertainty in International Organizations: A History of IMF Conditionality. *International Studies Quarterly* 56 (4): 674–688.

Best, Jacqueline, and William Walters. 2013. 'Actor-Network Theory' and International Relationality: Lost (and Found) in Translation. Introduction. *International Political Sociology* 3 (7): 332–334.

Bethke, Felix S., and Christian Bueger. 2014. *Bursts! Theoretical Fashions in the Study of International Organizations – A Bibliometric Analysis*. Presented at the 55th Annual Conference of the International Studies Association, Toronto, March 2014.

Bevir, Mark. 2010. Rethinking Governmentality: Towards Genealogies of Governance. *European Journal of Social Theory* 13 (4): 423–441.

Bially Mattern, Janice. 2011. A Practice Theory of Emotion for International Relations. In *International Practices*, 63–86. Cambridge: Cambridge University Press.

Bicchi, Frederica. 2011. The EU as a Community of Practice: Foreign Policy Communications in the COREU Network. *Journal of European Public Policy* 18 (8): 1115–1132.

Bicchi, Federica, and Niklas Bremberg. 2016. European Diplomatic Practices: Contemporary Challenges and Innovative Approaches. *European Security* 25 (4): 391–406.

Bigo, Didier. 2002. Security and Immigration: Toward a Critique of the Governmentality of Unease. *Alternatives* 27 (1): 63–92.

———. 2005. Globalized In-Security: The Field and the Ban-Opticon. In *Translation, Philosophy and the Colonial Difference: A Multilingual Series of Cultural Theory*, ed. Naoki Sakai and Jon Solomon, 109–157. Hong Kong: Hong Kong University Press.

———. 2011. Pierre Bourdieu and International Relations: Power of Practices, Practices of Power. *International Political Sociology* 5 (3): 225–258.

Bigo, Didier, and Mikael R. Madsen. 2011. Introduction to Symposium "A Different Reading of the International": Pierre Bourdieu and International Studies. *International Political Sociology* 5 (3): 219–224.

Bliesemann de Guevara, Berit, ed. 2016. *Myths and Narrative in International Politics*. London: Palgrave Macmillan.

Blok, Anders. 2013. Pragmatic Sociology as Political Ecology: On the Many Worths of Nature(s). *European Journal of Social Theory* 16 (4): 492–510.

Blokker, Paul. 2011. Pragmatic Sociology: Theoretical Evolvement and Empirical Application. *European Journal of Social Theory* 14 (3): 251–261.

Blokker, Paul, and Andrea Brigenthi. 2011. Politics Between Justification and Defiance. *European Journal of Social Theory* 14 (3): 283–300.

Blumer, Herbert. 1954. What Is Wrong with Social Theory? *American Sociological Review* 19 (1): 3–10.

Bode, Ingvild. 2017. Reflective Practices at the Security Council: Children and Armed Conflict and the Three United Nations. *European Journal of International.* Online First.

Bogusz, Tanja. 2014. Why (not) Pragmatism? In *The Spirit of Luc Boltanski. Essays on the Pragmatic Sociology of Critique*, ed. Simon Susen and Bryan S. Turner, 129–152. London: Anthem Press.

Boltanski, Luc. 2011. *On Critique: A Sociology of Emancipation.* Cambridge: Polity Press.

———. 2012. *Love and Justice as Competences.* Cambridge: Polity Press.

———. 2013. A Journey Through French-Style Critique. In *New Spirits of Capitalism?* ed. Paul du Gay and Glenn Morgan, 43–59. Oxford: Oxford University Press.

———. 2014. *Mysteries and Conspiracies.* Cambridge: Polity Press.

Boltanski, Luc, and Ève Chiapello. 2007. *The New Spirit of Capitalism.* London: Verso.

Boltanski, Luc, and Arnaud Esquerre. 2017. *Enrichissement. Une critique de la merchandise.* Paris: Gallimard.

Boltanski, Luc, and Laurent Thévenot. 1999. The Sociology of Critical Capacity. *European Journal of Social Theory* 2 (3): 359–377.

———. 2006. *On Justification. Economies of Worth.* Princeton: Princeton University Press.

Bonditti, Philippe, Andrew Neal, Sven Opitz, and Chris Zebrowski. 2014. Genealogy. In *Critical Security Methods: New Frameworks for Analysis*, ed. Claudia Aradau, Jef Huysmans, Andrew McNeal, and Nadine Voelckner, 159–214. London: Routledge.

Borghi, Vando. 2011. One-Way Europe? Institutional Guidelines, Emerging Regimes of Justification, and Paradoxical Turns in European Welfare Capitalism. *European Journal of Social Theory* 14 (3): 321–341.

Bort, Suleika, and Alfred Kieser. 2011. Fashion in Organization Theory: An Empirical Analysis of the Diffusion of Theoretical Concepts. *Organization Studies* 32 (5): 655–681.

Bourdieu, Pierre. 1977. *Outline of a Theory of Practice.* Cambridge: Cambridge University Press.

———. 1986. *Distinction: A Social Critique of the Judgment of Taste.* London: Routledge and Kegan Paul.

———. 1990. *The Logic of Practice.* Cambridge: Polity Press.

———. 1996. *The Rules of Art.* Cambridge: Polity Press.

Bourdieu, Pierre, and Loïc Wacquant. 1996. *Reflexive Anthropologie.* Frankfurt a. M.: Suhrkamp.

Bremberg, Niklas. 2015. The European Union as Security Community-Building Institution: Venues, Networks and Co-Operative Security Practices. *JCMS: Journal of Common Market Studies* 53 (3): 674–692.

Bremberg, Niklas, and Federica Bicchi, eds. 2017. *European Diplomacy in Practice*. London: Routledge.

Brigg, Morgan, and Roland Bleiker. 2010. Autoethnographic International Relations: Exploring the Self as a Source of Knowledge. *Review of International Studies* 36 (3): 779–798.

Broome, André and Joel Quirk, ed. 2015. The Politics of Numbers. Special Issue, *Review of International Studies* 41 (5): 813–818.

Brown, John Seely, and Paul Duguid. 2001. Knowledge and Organization: A Social-Practice Perspective. *Organization Science* 12 (2): 198–213.

Bruner, Jerome. 1991. The Narrative Construction of Reality. *Critical Inquiry* 18 (1): 1–21.

Brunnée, Jutta, and Stephen J. Toope. 2010. *Legitimacy and Legality in International Law: An Interactional Account*. Cambridge: Cambridge University Press.

———. 2011. Interactional International Law and the Practice of Legality. In *International Practices*, ed. Emanuel Adler and Vincent Pouliot, 108–136. Cambridge: Cambridge University Press.

Buckley-Zistel, Susanne. 2014. Narrative Truths. On the Construction of the Past in Truth Commissions. In *Transitional Justice Theories*, ed. Susanne Buckley-Zistel, Teresa Koloma Beck, Christian Braun, and Corinna Mieth, 144–162. Milton Park: Routledge.

Bueger, Christian. 2011. The Clash of Practice: Political Controversy and the United Nations Peacebuilding Commission. *Evidence and Policy* 7 (2), Special Issue on the Practice of Policymaking: 171–191.

———. 2013a. Practice, Pirates and Coast Guards: The Grand Narrative of Somali Piracy. *Third World Quarterly* 34 (10): 1811–1827.

———. 2013b. Communities of Security Practice at Work? The Emerging African Maritime Security Regime. *African Security* 6 (3–4): 297–316.

———. 2014. Pathways to Practice. Praxiography and International Politics. *European Political Science Review* 6 (3): 383–406.

———. 2015. Making Things Known: Epistemic Infrastructures, the United Nations and the Translation of Piracy. *International Political Sociology* 9 (1): 1–18.

———. 2016. Security as Practice. In *Routledge Handbook of Security Studies*, ed. Thierry Balzacq and Myriam Dunn Cavelty, 2nd ed., 126–135. London: Routledge.

———. 2017. Let's Count Beyond Three: Understanding the Conceptual and Methodological Terrain of International Practice Theories. *International Studies Quarterly Online*, 3 April. http://www.isanet.org/Publications/ISQ/

Posts/ID/5478/Lets-count-beyond-three-Understanding-the-conceptual-and-methodological-terrain-of-international-practice-theories. Accessed 31 Oct 2017.

Bueger, Christian, and Alena Drieschova. 2017. *Conceptualizing International Practices.* mimeo, Cardiff: Cardiff University.

Bueger, Christian, and Felix Bethke. 2014. Actor-Networking the Failed State – An Enquiry into the Life of Concepts. *Journal of International Relations and Development* 17 (1): 30–60.

Bueger, Christian, and Frank Gadinger. 2007. Reassembling and Dissecting: International Relations Practice from a Science Studies Perspective. *International Studies Perspectives* 8 (1): 90–110.

———. 2014. *International Practice Theory: New Perspectives.* Basingstoke: Palgrave Macmillan.

———. 2015. The Play of International Practice. *International Studies Quarterly* 59 (3): 449–460.

———. 2017. From Community to Practice: International Relations as a Practical Configuration. In *The SAGE Handbook of the History, Philosophy and Sociology of International Relations*, ed. Andreas Gofas, Inanna Hamati-Ataya, and Nicholas Onuf. London: Sage, forthcoming.

Bueger, Christian, and Jan Stockbruegger. 2012. Security Communities, Alliances, and Macrosecuritization: The Practices of Counter-Piracy Governance. In *Maritime Piracy and the Construction of Global Governance*, ed. Michael J. Struett, John D. Carlson, and Mark T. Nance, 171–191. New York: Routledge.

Bueger, Christian, and Manuel Mireanu. 2014. Proximity. In *Critical Security Methods: New Frameworks for Analysis*, ed. Claudia Aradau, Jef Huysmans, Andrew McNeal, and Nadine Voelckner, 118–141. London: Routledge.

Bueger, Christian, and Trine Villumsen. 2007. Beyond the Gap: Relevance, Fields of Practice and the Securitizing Consequences of (Democratic Peace) Research. *Journal of International Relations and Development* 10 (4): 417–448.

Butler, Judith. 1993. *Bodies That Matter: On the Discursive Limits of Sex.* New York: Routledge.

———. 1997. *Excitable Speech: A Politics of the Performative.* New York: Routledge.

———. 1999. *Gender Troubles: Feminism and the Subversion of Identity.* New York: Routledge.

Callon, Michel. 1986a. Some Elements of a Sociology of Translation: Domestication of the Scallops and the Fishermen of St Brieuc Bay. In *Power, Action and Belief. A New Sociology of Knowledge?* ed. John Law, 196–234. London/Boston/Henley: Routledge & Kegan Paul plc.

———. 1986b. The Sociology of an Actor-Network: The Case of the Electric Vehicle. In *Mapping the Dynamics of Science and Technology*, ed. Michel Callon, John Law, and Arie Rip, 19–34. London: Macmillan Press.

———. 1998. *The Laws of the Markets.* Oxford: Blackwell Publishers.

Campbell, Lisa M., and J. Peter Brosius. 2010. Collaborative Event Ethnography: Conservation and Development Trade-Offs at the Fourth World Conservation Congress. *Conservation and Society* 8 (4): 245–255.

Celikates, Robin. 2006. From Critical Social Theory to a Social Theory of Critique: On the Critique of Ideology After the Pragmatic Turn. *Constellations* 13 (1): 21–40.

Chandler, David, and Julian Reid. 2016. *The Neoliberal Subject*. London/New York: Rowman and Littlefield.

Christensen, Michael. 2017. Interpreting the Organizational Practices of North American Democracy Assistance. *International Political Sociology* 11 (2): 148–165.

Clifford, James, and George E. Marcus, eds. 1986. *Writing Culture: The Poetics and Politics of Ethnography*. Berkeley: University of California Press.

Collins, Randall. 1998. *The Sociology of Philosophies: A Global Theory of Intellectual Change*. Belknap: Harvard University Press.

Contu, Alessia, and Hugh Willmott. 2003. Re-Embedding Situatedness: The Importance of Power Relations in Learning Theory. *Organization Science* 14 (3): 283–296.

Crenshaw, Martha. 2000. The Psychology of Terrorism: An Agenda for the 21st Century. *Political Psychology* 21 (2): 405–420.

Cruz, Joelle. 2014. Memories of Trauma and Organizing: Market Women's Susu Groups in Postconflict Liberia. *Organization* 21 (4): 447–462.

Czarniawska, Barbara. 1997. *Narrating the Organization. Dramas of Institutional Identity*. Chicago: Chicago University Press.

———. 2004. *Narratives in Social Science Research*. Thousand Oaks: Sage.

———. 2007. *Shadowing and Other Techniques for Doing Fieldwork in Modern Societies*. Copenhagen: Copenhagen Business School Press.

———. 2008. *A Theory of Organizing*. Cheltenham: Edward Elgar Publishing.

Dany, Endres. 2011. *Parliament Politics. A Heterotopology of Liberal Democracy*. Ph.D. Dissertation, Lancaster University.

Dany, Charlotte, and Katja Freistein. 2016. Global Governance and the Myth of Civil Society Participation. In *Myths and Narrative in International Politics*, ed. Berit Bliesemann de Guevara, 229–248. London: Palgrave Macmillan.

Dauphinee, Elizabeth. 2010. The Ethics of Autoethnography. *Review of International Studies* 36 (3): 799–818.

———. 2013a. *The Politics of Exile*. London: Routledge.

———. 2013b. Writing as Hope: Reflections on the Politics of Exile. *Security Dialogue* 44 (4): 347–361.

Davies, Mathew. 2016. A Community of Practice: Explaining Change and Continuity in ASEAN's Diplomatic Environment. *The Pacific Review* 29 (2): 211–233.

Davis, Kevin E., Benedict Kingsbury, and Sally Engle Merry. 2012a. Indicators as a Technology of Global Governance. *Law & Society Review* 46 (1): 71–104.

Davis, Kevin, Angelina Fisher, Benedict Kingsbury, and Sally Engle Merry, eds. 2012b. *Governance by Indicators: Global Power Through Classification and Rankings*. Oxford: Oxford University Press.

De Certeau, Michel. 1984. *The Practice of Everyday Life*. Berkeley: University of California Press.

De Laet, Marianne, and Annemarie Mol. 2000. The Zimbabwe Bush Pump: Mechanics of Fluid Technology. *Social Studies of Science* 30 (2): 225–263.

De Volo, Lorraine Bayard, and Edward Schatz. 2004. From the Inside Out: Ethnographic Methods in Political Research. *PS: Political Science & Politics* 37 (2): 267–272.

Death, Carl. 2013. Governmentality at the Limits of the International: African Politics and Foucauldian Theory. *Review of International Studies* 39 (6): 763–787.

Devetak, Richard. 2009. After the Event: Don DeLillo's White Noise and September 11 Narratives. *Review of International Studies* 35 (4): 795–815.

Dittmer, Jason. 2016. Theorizing a More-Than-Human Diplomacy: Assembling the British Foreign Office, 1839–1874. *The Hague Journal of Diplomacy* 11 (1): 78–104.

Dodier, Nicolas. 1993. Action as a Combination of 'Common Worlds'. *Sociological Review* 41 (3): 556–571.

Doty, Roxanne Lynn. 1997. Aporia: A Critical Exploration of the Agent-Structure Problematique in International Relations Theory. *European Journal of International Relations* 3 (3): 365–392.

———. 2010. Autoethnography – Making Human Connections. *Review of International Studies* 36 (4): 1047–1050.

Down, Simon, and Michael Hughes. 2009. When the 'Subject' and the 'Researcher' Speak Together: Co-producing Organizational Ethnography. In *Organizational Ethnography. Studying the Complexities of Everyday Life*, ed. Sierk Ybema, Dvora Yanow, Harry Wels, and Frans Kamsteeg, 83–98. London: Sage.

Dreyfus, Hubert L., and Paul Rabinow. 1983. *Michel Foucault: Beyond Structuralism and Hermeneutics*. 2nd ed. Chicago: University of Chicago Press.

Drieschova, Alena. 2017. Peirce's Semeiotics: A Methodology for Bridging the Material–Ideational Divide in IR Scholarship. *International Theory* 9 (1): 33–66.

Dunne, Joseph. 1993. *Back to the Rough Ground: "Phronesis" and "Techne" in Modern Philosophy and Aristotle*. Notre Dame: University of Notre Dame Press.

Duvall, Raymond, and Arjun Chowdhury. 2011. Practices of Theory. In *International Practices*, ed. Emanuel Adler and Vincent Pouliot, 335–354. Cambridge: Cambridge University Press.

Eagleton-Pierce, Matthew. 2014. The Concept of Governance in the Spirit of Capitalism. *Critical Policy Studies* 8 (1): 5–21.

Eckl, Julian. 2008. Responsible Scholarship After Leaving the Veranda: Normative Issues Faced by Field Researchers-and Armchair Scientists. *International Political Sociology* 2 (3): 185–203.

Eder, Klaus. 2009. A Theory of Collective Identity: Making Sense of the Debate on a 'European Identity'. *European Journal of Social Theory* 12 (4): 427–447.

Edkins, Jenny. 2003. *Trauma and the Memory of Politics*. Cambridge: Cambridge University Press.

———. 2013. Novel Writing in International Relations: Openings for a Creative Space. *Security Dialogue* 44 (4): 281–297.

Eikeland, Olav, and Davide Nicolini. 2011. Turning Practically: Broadening the Horizon. *Journal of Organizational Change Management* 24 (2): 164–174.

Engert, Kornelia, and Björn Krey. 2013. Das lesende Schreiben und das schreibende Lesen. *Zeitschrift für Soziologie* 42 (5): 366–384.

Epstein, Charlotte. 2012. Stop Telling Us How to Behave. Socialization or Infantilization? *International Studies Perspectives* 13 (2): 135–145.

———. 2013. Norms. In *Bourdieu in International Relations: Rethinking Key Concepts in IR*, ed. Rebecca Adler-Nissen, 165–178. London: Routledge.

Erwin, Panofsky. 1970. *Meaning in the Visual Arts*. Harmondsworth: Penguin Books.

Faizullaev, Alisher, and Jerémie Cornut. 2017. Narrative Practice in International Politics and Diplomacy: The Case of the Crimean Crisis. *Journal of International Relations and Development* 20 (3): 578–604.

Fearon, James, and Alexander Wendt. 2002. Rationalism v. Constructivism: A Skeptical View. In *Handbook of International Relations*, ed. Walter Carlsnaes, Thomas Risse, and Beth Simmons, 52–72. London: Sage.

Fenton, Christopher, and Ann Langley. 2011. Strategy as Practice and the Narrative Turn. *Organization Studies* 32 (9): 1171–1196.

Fierke, Karin. 2002. Links Across the Abyss: Language and Logic in International Relations. *International Studies Quarterly* 46 (3): 331–354.

Fischer, Frank. 2003. *Reframing Public Policy: Discursive Politics and Deliberative Practices*. Oxford: Oxford University Press.

Fisher, Walter R. 1987. *Human Communication as Narration: Toward a Philosophy of Reason, Value, and Action*. Columbia: University of South California Press.

Flockhart, Trine. 2016. The Problem of Change in Constructivist Theory: Ontological Security Seeking and Agent Motivation. *Review of International Studies* 42 (5): 799–820.

Flyvbjerg, Bent. 2006. Five Misunderstandings About Case-Study Research. *Qualitative Inquiry* 12 (2): 219–245.

Fougner, Tore. 2008. Neoliberal Governance of States: The Role of Competitiveness Indexing and Country Benchmarking. *Millennium: Journal of International Studies* 37 (2): 303–326.

Fox, Stephen. 2000. Communities of Practice, Foucault and Actor-Network Theory. *Journal of Management Studies* 37 (6): 853–868.

Franke, Ulrich, and Ralph Weber. 2012. At the Papini Hotel – On Pragmatism in the Study of International Relations. *European Journal of International Relations* 18 (4): 669–691.

Freeman, Richard, and Maybin Jo. 2011. Documents, Practices and Policy. *Evidence & Policy: A Journal of Research, Debate and Practice* 7 (2): 155–170.

Frega, Robert. 2014. The Normative Creature: Toward a Practice-Based Account of Normativity. *Social Theory and Practice* 40 (1): 1–27.

Friedrichs, Jörg, and Friedrich Kratochwil. 2009. On Acting and Knowing: How Pragmatism Can Advance International Relations Research and Methodology. *International Organization* 63 (4): 701–731.

Frost, Mervyn, and Silviya Lechner. 2016a. Two Conceptions of International Practice: Aristotelian *Praxis* and Wittgensteinian *Language-Games*? *Review of International Studies* 42 (2): 334–350.

———. 2016b. Understanding International Practices from the Internal Point of View. *Journal of International Political Theory* 12 (3): 299–319.

Fuller, Alison. 2007. Critiquing Theories of Learning and Communities of Practice. In *Communities of Practice. Critical Perspectives*, ed. Jason Hughes, Nick Jewson, and Lorna Unwin, 17–29. London: Routledge.

Gad, Christopher, and Casper Bruun Jensen. 2009. On the Consequences of Post-ANT. *Science, Technology & Human Values* 35 (1): 55–80.

Gadinger, Frank. 2016. On Justification and Critique. Luc Boltanski's Pragmatic Sociology and International Relations. *International Political Sociology* 10 (3): 187–205.

Gadinger, Frank, and Taylan Yildiz. 2012. Unruhige Legitimität. Die Finanzkrise aus Sicht der pragmatischen Soziologie der Kritik. In *Der Aufstieg der Legitimitätspolitik. Rechtfertigung und Kritik politisch-ökonomischer Ordnungen*, eds. Anna Geis, Frank Nullmeier, and Christopher Daase, 302–318. Baden-Baden: Nomos.

Gadinger, Frank, Sebastian Jarzebski, and Taylan Yildiz. 2014a. Politische Narrative. Konturen einer politikwissenschaftlichen Erzähltheorie. In *Politische Narrative. Konzepte – Analysen – Forschungspraxis*, ed. Frank Gadinger, Sebastian Jarzebski, and Taylan Yildiz, 3–38. Wiesbaden: Springer VS.

———. 2014b. Vom Diskurs zur Erzählung: Möglichkeiten einer politikwissenschaftlichen Narrativanalyse. *Politische Vierteljahresschrift* 55 (1): 67–93.

Gadinger, Frank, Martina Kopf, Aysem Mert, and Christopher Smith, eds. 2016. *Political Storytelling: From Fact to Fiction*. Global Dialogues 12. Duisburg: Käte Hamburger Kolleg/Centre for Global Cooperation Research.

Galai, Yoav. 2017. Narratives of Redemption: The International Meaning of Afforestation in the Israeli Negev. *International Political Sociology* 11 (3): 273–291.

Galison, Peter. 1997. *Image & Logic: A Material Culture of Microphysics*. Chicago: University of Chicago Press.

Galtung, Johan. 1986. On the Anthropology of the United Nations System. In *The Nature of United Nations Bureaucracies*, ed. David Pitt and Thomas G. Weiss, 1–22. Boulder: Westview.

Garfinkel, Harold. 1967. *Studies in Ethnomethodology*. Englewood Cliffs: Prentice-Hall.

Gellman, Mneesha. 2017. *Democratization and Memories of Violence: Ethnic Minority Rights Movements in Mexico, Turkey, and El Salvador*. London: Routledge.

Gherardi, Silvia. 2012. *How to Conduct a Practice-Based Study: Problems and Methods*. Cheltenham: Edward Elgar Publishing.

Gherardi, Silvia, and Manuela Perrotta. 2010. Egg Dates Sperm: A Tale of a Practice Change and Its Stabilization. *Organization* 18 (5): 595–614.

Gilpin, Robert. 1981. *War and Change in World Politics*. Cambridge: Cambridge University Press.

Gilson, Julie. 2009. Learning to Learn and Building Communities of Practice: Non-governmental Organisations and Examples from Mine Action in Southeast Asia. *Global Society* 23 (3): 269–293.

Goldstein, Judith, and Robert Keohane. 1993. Ideas and Foreign Policy: An Analytical Framework. In *Ideas and Foreign Policy: Beliefs, Institutions, and Political Change*, ed. Judith Goldstein and Robert Keohane. Ithaca: Cornell University Press.

Golsorkhi, Damon, Linda Rouleau, David Seidl, and Eero Varaa, eds. 2010. *Cambridge Handbook of Strategy as Practice*. Cambridge: Cambridge University Press.

Græger, Nina. 2016. European Security as Practice: EU–NATO Communities of Practice in the Making? *European Security* 25 (4): 478–501.

———. 2017. Grasping the Everyday and Extraordinary in EU–NATO Relations. The Added Value of Practice Approaches. *European Security* 26 (3): 340–358.

Gray, Noella J. 2010. Sea Change: Exploring the International Effort to Promote Marine Protected Areas. *Conservation and Society* 8 (4): 331–338.

Greiffenhagen, Christian, Michael Mair, and Wes Sharrock. 2015. Methodological Troubles as Problems and Phenomena: Ethnomethodology and the Question of 'Method' in the Social Sciences. *The British Journal of Sociology* 66 (3): 460–485.

Gross Stein, Janice. 2011. Background Knowledge in the Foreground: Conversations About Competent Practice in 'Sacred Space'. In *International Practices*, ed. Emanuel Adler and Vincent Pouliot, 87–107. Cambridge: Cambridge University Press.

Guggenheim, Michael. 2012. Laboratizing and De-laboratizing the World. *History of the Human Sciences* 25 (1): 99–118.

Guggenheim, Michael, and Jörg Potthast. 2011. Symmetrical Twins: On the Relationship Between Actor-Network Theory and the Sociology of Critical Capacities. *European Journal of Social Theory* 15 (2): 157–178.

Guilhot, Nicolas. 2005. *The Democracy Makers. Human Rights and the Politics of Global Order*. New York: Columbia University Press.

Guillaume, Xavier. 2007. Unveiling the 'International': Process, Identity and Alterity. *Millennium: Journal of International Studies* 35 (3): 741–759.

Guzzini, Stefano. 1993. Structural Power: The Limits of Neorealist Power Analysis. *International Organization* 47 (3): 443–478.

———. 2000. A Reconstruction of Constructivism in International Relations. *European Journal of International Relations* 6 (2): 147–182.

———. 2012. The Ambivalent 'Diffusion of Power' in Global Governance. In *The Diffusion of Power in Global Governance. International Political Economy Meets Foucault*, ed. Stefano Guzzini and Iver B. Neumann, 1–37. Basingstoke: Palgrave Macmillan.

———. 2013. Power. Bourdieu's Field Analysis of Relational Capital, Misrecognition and Domination. In *Bourdieu in International Relations: Rethinking Key Concepts in IR*, ed. Rebecca Adler-Nissen, 78–92. London: Routledge.

Hafner-Burton, Emilie M., D. Alex Hughes, and David G. Victor. 2013. The Cognitive Revolution and the Political Psychology of Elite Decision Making. *Perspectives on Politics* 11: 368–386.

Hajer, Maarten. 2009. *Authoritative Governance.* Oxford: Oxford University Press.

Hajer, Maarten A., and Hendrik Wagenaar, eds. 2003a. *Deliberative Policy Analysis. Understanding Governance in the Network Society.* Cambridge: Cambridge University Press.

———. 2003b. Introduction. In *Deliberative Policy Analysis. Understanding Governance in the Network Society*, ed. Maarten A. Hajer and Hendrik Wagenaar, 1–30. Cambridge: Cambridge University Press.

Halkier, Bente. 2010. Focus Groups as Social Enactments: Integrating Interaction and Content in the Analysis of Focus Group Data. *Qualitative Research* 10 (1): 71–89.

———. 2011. Methodological Practicalities in Analytical Generalization. *Qualitative Inquiry* 17 (9): 787–797.

———. 2017. Questioning the 'Gold Standard' Thinking in Qualitative Methods from a Practice Theoretical Perspective: Towards Methodological Multiplicity. In *Methodological Reflections on Practice Oriented Theories*, ed. Michael Jonas, Beate Littig, and Angela Wroblewski, 193–204. Berlin, Heidelberg: Springer International Publishing.

Halkier, Bente, Tally Katz-Gerro, and Lydia Martens. 2011. Applying Practice Theory to the Study of Consumption: Theoretical and Methodological Considerations. *Journal of Consumer Culture* 11 (1): 3–13.

Hamati-Ataya, Inanna. 2014. Transcending Objectivism, Subjectivism, and the Knowledge In-between: The Subject In/of 'Strong Reflexivity. *Review of International Studies* 40 (1): 153–175.

Hanrieder, Tine. 2016. Orders of Worth and the Moral Conceptions of Health in Global Politics. *International Theory* 8 (3): 390–421.

Hansen, Lene. 2006. *Security as Practice. Discourse Analysis and the Bosnian War.* London: Routledge.

———. 2011. Theorizing the Image for Security Studies: Visual Securitization and the Muhammad Cartoon Crisis. *European Journal of International Relations* 17 (1): 51–74.

———. 2015. How Images Make World Politics: International Icons and the Case of Abu Ghraib. *Review of International Studies* 41 (2): 263–288.

Heath, Christian, and Jon Hindmarsh. 2011. Analysing Interaction: Video, Ethnography and Situated Conduct. In *Qualitative Research in Practice*, ed. Tim May. London: Sage.

Heaven, Corinne. 2017. A Visible College: The Community of Fact-Finding Practice. In *Commissions of Inquiry: Problems and Prospects*, ed. Christian Henderson, 337–359. London: Bloomsbury.

Heck, Axel, and Gabi Schlag. 2013. Securitizing Images: The Female Body and the War in Afghanistan. *European Journal of International Relations* 19 (4): 891–913.

Hellmann, Gunther. 2009. The Forum: Pragmatism and International Relations. *International Studies Review* 11 (3): 638–662.

Herschinger, Eva. 2011. *Constructing Global Enemies: Hegemony and Identity in International Discourses on Terrorism and Drug Prohibition.* London: Routledge.

Hillebrandt, Frank. 2009. Praxistheorie. In *Handbuch Soziologische Theorien*, ed. Georg Kneer and Markus Schroer, 369–394. Wiesbaden: Springer VS.

Hirschauer, Stefan. 2004. Praktiken und ihre Körper: Über Materielle Partzipanden des Tuns. In *Doing Culture. Neue Positionen zum Verhältnis von Kultur und Sozialer Praxis*, ed. Karl Hörning and Julia Reuter, 73–91. Bielefeld: Transcript.

Hitchings, Russell. 2012. People Can Talk About Their Practices. *Area* 44 (1): 61–67.

Hofius, Maren. 2016. Community at the Border or the Boundaries of Community? The Case of EU Field Diplomats. *Review of International Studies* 42 (5): 939–967.

Holmqvist, Caroline. 2013. Undoing War: War Ontologies and the Materiality of Drone Warfare. *Millennium: Journal of International Studies* 41 (3): 535–552.

Honneth, Axel. 2010. Dissolutions of the Social: On the Social Theory of Luc Boltanski and Laurent Thévenot. *Constellations* 17 (3): 376–389.

Hopf, Ted. 2002. *Social Construction of International Politics. Identities & Foreign Policies, Moscow 1955 & 1999.* Ithaca: Cornell University Press.

———. 2010. The Logic of Habit in International Relations. *European Journal of International Relations* 16 (4): 539–561.

———. 2017. Change in International Practices. *European Journal of International Relations.* Advance online publication. https://doi.org/10.1177/2F1354066117718041.

Hornborg, Alf. 2013. Technology as Fetish: Marx, Latour, and the Cultural Foundations of Capitalism. *Theory, Culture & Society*. Advance online publication. https://doi.org/10.1177/2F0263276413488960.

Huizinga, Johan. 1949. *Homo Ludens: A Study of the Play-Element in Culture*. Milton Park: Routledge.

Hülsse, Rainer. 2006. Imagine the EU: The Metaphorical Construction of a Supra-Nationalist Identity. *Journal of International Relations and Development* 9 (4): 396–421.

Humphreys, Michael, and Tony Watson. 2009. Ethnographic Practices: From 'Writing-up Ethnographic Research' to 'Writing Ethnography'. In *Organizational Ethnography. Studying the Complexities of Everyday Life*, ed. Sierk Ybema, Dvora Yanow, Harry Wels, and Frans Kamsteeg, 40–55. London: Sage.

Huysmans, Jef. 2006. *The Politics of Insecurity*. London: Routledge.

Ikenberry, G. John, ed. 2014. *Power, Order, and Change in World Politics*. Cambridge: Cambridge University Press.

Jackson, Peter. 2008. Pierre Bourdieu, the 'Cultural Turn' and the Practice of International History. *Review of International Studies* 34 (1): 155–181.

Jackson, Patrick Thaddeus, and Daniel Nexon. 1999. Relations Before States: Substance, Process, and the Study of World Politics. *European Journal of International Relations* 5 (3): 291–332.

Jaeger, Hans-Martin. 2008. 'World Opinion' and the Founding of the UN: Governmentalizing International Politics. *European Journal of International Relations* 14 (4): 589–618.

———. 2010. UN Reform, Biopolitics, and Global Governmentality. *International Theory* 2 (1): 50–86.

Jagd, Søren. 2011. Pragmatic Sociology and Competing Orders of Worth in Organizations. *European Journal of Social Theory* 14 (3): 343–359.

Jarvis, Lee, and Jack Holland. 2014. 'We (For)got Him': Remembering and Forgetting in the Narration of Bin Laden's Death. *Millennium: Journal of International Studies* 42 (2): 425–447.

Joas, Hans. 1996. *The Creativity of Action*. Chicago: University of Chicago Press.

Joas, Hans, and Wolfgang Knöbl. 2009. *Social Theory. Twenty Introductory Lectures*. Cambridge: Cambridge University Press.

Jonas, Michael, and Beate Littig, eds. 2017. *Praxeological Political Analysis*. London/New York: Routledge.

Jonas, Michael, Beate Littig, and Angela Wroblewski, eds. 2017. *Methodological Reflections on Practice Oriented Theories*. Berlin, Heidelberg: Springer International Publishing.

Joseph, Jonathan. 2016. Governing Through Failure and Denial: The New Resilience Agenda. *Millennium: Journal of International Studies* 44 (3): 370–390.

Kalthoff, Herbert, Stefan Hirschauer, and Gesa Lindemann, eds. 2008. *Theoretische Empirie. Zur Relevanz Qualitativer Forschung*. Frankfurt a. M.: Suhrkamp Verlag.

Kapiszewski, Diana, Lauren M. MacLean, and Benjamin L. Read. 2015. *Field Research in Political Science*. Cambridge: Cambridge University Press.

Keeley, James F. 1990. Toward a Foucauldian Analysis of International Regimes. *International Organization* 44 (1): 83–105.

Keens-Soper, Maurice. 1978. The Practice of a States-System. In *The Reason of States: A Study in International Political Theory*, ed. Michael J. Donelan, 25–44. London: Allen and Unwin.

Kenney, Michael. 2017. A Community of True Believers: Learning as Process Among "The Emigrants". *Terrorism and Political Violence*, online first, 30 August, https://doi.org/10.1080/09546553.2017.1346506.

Kessler, Oliver. 2016. The Contingency of Constructivism: On Norms, the Social, and the Third. *Millennium: Journal of International Studies* 45 (1): 43–63.

Khoury, Nadim. 2017. Plotting Stories After War: Toward a Methodology for Negotiating Identity. *European Journal of International Relations*. Advance online publication. https://doi.org/10.1177/2F1354066117711743.

King, Anthony. 2000. Thinking with Bourdieu Against Bourdieu: A 'Practical' Critique of the Habitus. *Sociological Theory* 18 (3): 417–433.

Knorr-Cetina, Karin D. 1981. *The Manufacture of Knowledge: An Essay on the Constructivist and Contextual Nature of Science*. Oxford: Pergamon Press.

Knorr Cetina, Karin. 1999. *Epistemic Cultures. How the Sciences Make Knowledge*. Cambridge: Harvard University Press.

———. 2001. Objectual Practice. In *The Practice Turn in Contemporary Theory*, ed. Theodore R. Schatzki, Karin Knorr Cetina, and Eike von Savigny, 175–188. London/New York: Routledge.

———. 2005. Complex Global Microstructures. The New Terrorist Societies. *Theory, Culture & Society* 31 (4): 213–234.

Knorr Cetina, Karin, and Urs Bruegger. 2002. Global Microstructures: The Virtual Societies of Financial Markets. *American Journal of Sociology* 107 (4): 905–950.

Koddenbrock, Kai. 2016. *The Practice of Humanitarian Intervention. Aid Workers, Agencies and Institutions in the Democratic Republic of the Congo*. Oxon: Routledge.

Koopman, Colin. 2013. *Geneaology as Critique. Foucault and the Problems of Modernity*. Bloomington: Indiana University Press.

Koopman, Colin, and Tomas Matza. 2013. Putting Foucault to Work: Analytic and Concept in Foucaultian Inquiry. *Critical Inquiry* 39 (4): 817–840.

Kornprobst, Markus. 2014. From Political Judgments to Public Justifications (and Vice Versa): How Communities Generate Reasons Upon Which to Act. *European Journal of International Relations* 20 (1): 192–216.

Koschorke, Albrecht. 2012. *Wahrheit und Erfindung: Grundzüge einer Allgemeinen Erzähltheorie*. Frankfurt a. M.: S. Fischer Wissenschaft.

Kratochwil, Friedrich. 1989. *Rules, Norms, and Decisions*. Cambridge: Cambridge University Press.

———. 2000. Constructing a New Orthodoxy? Wendt's 'Social Theory of International Politics' and the Constructivist Challenge. *Millennium: Journal of International Studies* 29 (1): 73–101.

———. 2011. Making Sense of 'International Practices'. In *International Practices*, ed. Emanuel Adler and Vincent Pouliot, 36–60. Cambridge: Cambridge University Press.

Krebs, Ronald. 2015a. How Dominant Narratives Rise and Fall: Military Conflict, Politics, and the Cold War Consensus. *International Organization* 69 (4): 809–845.

———. 2015b. *Narrative and the Making of US National Security*. Cambridge: Cambridge University Press.

Kreiswirth, Martin. 2000. Merely Telling Stories? Narrative and Knowledge in the Human Sciences. *Poetics Today* 21 (2): 293–318.

Kühn, Florian P. 2016. Afghanistan and the 'Graveyard of Empires': Blumenberg, Under-Complex Analogy and Basic Myths in International Politics. In *Myths and Narrative in International Politics*, ed. Berit Bliesemann de Guevara, 147–172. London: Palgrave Macmillan.

Kurowska, Xymena, and Benjamin Tallis. 2013. Chiasmatic Crossings: A Reflexive Revisit of a Research Encounter in European Security. *Security Dialogue* 44 (1): 73–89.

Kustermans, Jorg. 2016. Parsing the Practice Turn: Practice, Practical Knowledge, Practices. *Millennium: Journal of International Studies* 44 (2): 175–196.

Kuus, Merje. 2013. Foreign Policy and Ethnography: A Sceptical Intervention. *Geopolitics* 18 (1): 115–131.

———. 2015. Symbolic Power in Diplomatic Practice: Matters of Style in Brussels. *Cooperation and Conflict* 50 (3): 368–384.

Lachmann, Nils. 2011. In the Labyrinth of International Community: The Alliance of Civilizations Programme at the United Nations. *Cooperation and Conflict* 46 (2): 185–200.

Laffey, Mark, and Jutta Weldes. 1997. Ideas and Symbolic Technologies in the Study International Relations. *European Journal of International Relations* 3 (2): 193–237.

Lapid, Yosef. 1989. The Third Debate: On the Prospects of International Theory in a Post-Positivist Era. *International Studies Quarterly* 33 (3): 235–254.

Lapid, Yosef, and Friedrich Kratochwil, eds. 1996. *The Return of Culture and Identity in IR Theory*. Boulder: Lynne Rienner Publishers.

Latour, Bruno. 1987. *Science in Action. How to Follow Scientists and Engineers Through Society*. Cambridge, MA: Harvard University Press.

———. 1988. *The Pasteurization of France*. Cambridge, MA: Harvard University Press.

———. 1994. On Technical Mediation - Philosophy, Sociology, Genealogy. *Common Knowledge* 3 (2): 29–64.

———. 1996. *Aramis, or the Love of Technology*. Cambridge, MA: Harvard University Press.

———. 2004. Why Has Critique Run Out of Steam? From Matters of Fact to Matters of Concern. *Critical Inquiry* 30 (2): 225–248.

———. 2005. *Reassembling the Social. An Introduction to Actor-Network-Theory*. Oxford: Oxford University Press.

———. 2010. *The Making of Law. An Ethnography of the Conseil d'Etat*. Oxford: Polity Press.

Latour, Bruno, and Steven Woolgar. 1979. *Laboratory Life. The Social Construction of Scientific Facts*. Beverly Hills: Sage.

Lave, Jean, and Etienne Wenger. 1991. *Situated Learning: Legitimate Peripheral Participation*. Cambridge: Cambridge University Press.

Law, John. 1987. On the Social Explanation of Technical Change: The Case of the Portuguese Maritime Expansion. *Technology and Culture* 28 (2): 227–252.

———. 1994. *Organizing Modernity*. Oxford: Blackwell Publishers.

———. 2003. *Order and Obduracy*. Lancaster: Centre for Science Studies, University of Lancaster.

———. 2004. *After Method: Mess in Social Science Research*. London: Routledge.

———. 2009. Actor Network Theory and Material Semiotics. In *The New Blackwell Companion to Social Theory*, ed. Bryan S. Turner, 141–158. Oxford: Blackwell Publishing.

Law, John, and Michel Callon. 1992. The Life and Death of an Aircraft: A Network Analysis of Technical Change. In *Shaping Technology/Building Society: Studies in Sociotechnical Change*, ed. Wiebe E. Bijker and John Law, 21–52. Cambridge: MIT Press.

Leander, Anna. 2005. The Power to Construct International Security: On the Significance of Private Military Companies. *Millennium: Journal of International Studies* 33 (3): 803–825.

———. 2008. Thinking Tools. In *Qualitative Methods in International Relations: A Pluralist Guide*, ed. Audie Klotz and Deepa Praksah, 11–27. Basingstoke: Palgrave Macmillan.

———. 2011. The Promises, Problems, and Potentials of a Bourdieu-Inspired Staging of International Relations. *International Political Sociology* 5 (3): 294–313.

Lebow, Richard Ned. 2007. Social Science as an Ethical Practice. *Journal of International Relations and Development* 10 (1): 16–24.

Levitt, Peggy, and Nina Glick Schiller. 2004. Conceptualizing Simultaneity: A Transnational Social Field Perspective on Society. *International Migration Review* 38 (3): 1002–1039.

Lidskog, Rolf, and Goran Ran Sundqvist. 2002. The Role of Science in Environmental Regimes: The Case of LRTAP. *European Journal of International Relations* 8 (1): 77–100.

Lie, Sande, and Jon Harlad. 2013. Challenging Anthropology: Anthropological Reflections on the Ethnographic Turn in International Relations. *Millennium – Journal of International Studies* 41 (2): 201–220.

Lisle, Debbie. 2017. Learning How to See. In *Routledge Handbook of International Political Sociology*, ed. Xavier Guillaume and Pinar Bilgin, 295–304. London: Routledge.

Little, Paul E. 1995. Ritual, Power and Ethnography at the Rio Earth Summit. *Critique of Anthropology* 15 (3): 265–288.

Little, Richard. 2011. Britain's Response to the Spanish Civil War: Investigating the Implications of Foregrounding Practice for English School Thinking. In *International Practices*, ed. Emanuel Adler and Vincent Pouliot, 174–199. Cambridge: Cambridge University Press.

Lizardo, Omar. 2009. Is a 'Special Psychology' of Practice Possible?: From Values and Attitudes to Embodied Dispositions. *Theory & Psychology* 19 (6): 713–727.

Lok, Jaco, and Mark De Rond. 2013. On the Plasticity of Institutions: Containing and Restoring Practice Breakdowns at the Cambridge University Boat Club. *Academy of Management Journal* 56 (1): 185–207.

Löwenheim, Oded. 2007. The Responsibility to Responsibilize: Foreign Offices and the Issuing of Travel Warnings. *International Political Sociology* 1 (3): 203–221.

———. 2008. Examining the State: A Foucauldian Perspective on International 'Governance Indicators'. *Third World Quarterly* 29 (2): 255–274.

———. 2010. The 'I' in IR: An Autoethnographic Account. *Review of International Studies* 36 (4): 1023–1045.

Löwy, Ilana. 1992. The Strength of Loose Concepts—Boundary Concepts, Federative Experimental Strategies and Disciplinary Growth: The Case of Immunology. *History of Science* 30 (4): 371–396.

Lynch, Michael. 2001. Ethnomethodology and the Logic of Practice. In *The Practice Turn in Contemporary Theory*, ed. Theodore R. Schatzki, Karin Knorr Cetina, and Eike von Savigny, 131–148. London/New York: Routledge.

Mac Ginty, Roger. 2014. Everyday Peace: Bottom-Up and Local Agency in Conflict-Affected Societies. *Security Dialogue* 45 (6): 548–564.

MacIntyre, Alasdair. 1984. *After Virtue: A Study in Moral Theory*. Notre Dame: University of Notre Dame Press.

MacKenzie, Donald, Fabian Muniesa, and Lucia Siu, eds. 2007. *Do Economists Make Markets? On the Performativity of Economics*. Princeton: Princeton University Press.

Mahon, Kathleen, Susanne Kemmis, Stephen Francisco, and Annemaree Lloyd. 2017. Introduction: Practice Theory and the Theory of Practice Architectures. In *Exploring Education and Professional Practice – Through the Lens of Practice Architectures*, ed. Kathleen Mahon, Susanne Francisco, and Stephen Kemmis, 1–30. Singapore: Springer.

Marcus, George E. 1995. Ethnography in/of the World System: The Emergence of Multi-Sited Ethnography. *Annual Review of Anthropology* 24 (October): 95–117.

Marcus, George E., and Erkan Saka. 2006. Assemblage. *Theory, Culture & Society* 23 (2/3): 101–109.

Marks, Michael P. 2011. *Metaphors in International Relations Theory*. Basingstoke: Palgrave Macmillan.

Marshall, Judi. 2011. Images of Changing Practice Through Reflective Action Research. *Journal of Organizational Change Management* 24 (2): 244–256.

Marshall, Nick, and Jeanette Rollinson. 2004. Maybe Bacon Had a Point: The Politics of Interpretation in Collective Sensemaking. *British Journal of Management* 15 (S1): 71–86.

Martin-Mazé, Médéric. 2017. Returning Struggles to the Practice Turn: How Were Bourdieu and Boltanski Lost in (Some) Translations and What to Do About It? *International Political Sociology* 11 (2): 203–220.

Mayer, Maximilian. 2012. Chaotic Climate Change and Security. *International Political Sociology* 6 (2): 165–185.

Mayer, Frederick W. 2014. *Narrative Politics: Stories and Collective Action*. Oxford: Oxford University Press.

Mayer, Maximilian, Mariana Carpes, and Ruth Knoblich, eds. 2014. *International Relations and the Global Politics of Science and Technology*. Wiesbaden: Springer VS.

McCarthy, Daniel R., ed. 2017. *Technology and World Politics: An Introduction*. Abingdon: Routledge.

McCourt, David M. 2012. The Roles States Play: A Meadian Interactionist Approach. *Journal of International Relations and Development* 13 (3): 370–392.

McCourt, David. 2017. Practice Theory and Relationalism as the New Constructivism. *International Studies Quarterly* 60 (3): 475–485.

McDonald, Seonaidh. 2005. Studying Actions in Context: A Qualitative Shadowing Method for Organizational Research. *Qualitative Research* 5 (4): 455–473.

McEntee-Atalianis, Lisa J. 2011. The Role of Metaphor in Shaping the Identity and Agenda of the United Nations: The Imagining of an International Community and International Threat. *Discourse & Communication* 5 (4): 393–412.

———. 2013. Stance and Metaphor: Mapping Changing Representations of (Organizational) Identity. *Discourse & Communication* 7 (3): 319–340.

Merlingen, Michael. 2003. Governmentality. Towards a Foucauldian Framework for the Study of IGOs. *Cooperation and Conflict* 38 (4): 361–384.

———. 2006. Foucault and World Politics: Promises and Challenges of Extending Governmentality Theory to the European and Beyond. *Millennium: Journal of International Studies* 35 (1): 181–196.

———. 2011. From Governance to Governmentality in CSDP: Towards a Foucauldian Research Agenda. *JCMS: Journal of Common Market Studies* 49 (1): 149–169.

Miettinen, Reijo, Dalvir Samra-Fredericks, and Dvora Yanow. 2009. Re-Turn to Practice: An Introductory Essay. *Organization Studies* 30 (12): 1309–1327.

Mol, Annemarie. 2002. *The Body Multiple: Ontology in Medical Practice*. Durham/London: Duke University Press.

———. 2010a. A Letter to Georg Kneer. *Kölner Zeitschrift für Soziologie und Sozialpsychologie* 50 (1): 279–282.

———. 2010b. Actor-Network Theory: Sensitive Terms and Enduring Tensions. *Kölner Zeitschrift für Soziologie und Sozialpsychologie* 50 (1): 253–269.

Morgan, Patrick M. 2011. The Practice of Deterrence. In *International Practices*, ed. Emanuel Adler and Vincent Pouliot. Cambridge: Cambridge University Press.

Mørk, Bjørn Erik, Thomas Hoholm, Gunnar Ellingsen, Bjørn Edwin, and Margunn Aanestad. 2010. Challenging Expertise: On Power Relations Within and Across Communities of Practice in Medical Innovation. *Management Learning* 41 (5): 575–592.

Müller, Sophie Merit. 2016. Becoming the Phenomenon? An Alternative Approach to Reflexivity in Ethnography. *Qualitative Inquiry* 22 (9): 705–717.

Mutch, Alistair. 2003. Communities of Practice and Habitus: A Critique. *Organization Studies* 24 (3): 383–401.

Nachi, Mohamed. 2014. Beyond Pragmatic Sociology: A Theoretical Compromise Between 'Critical Sociology' and the 'Pragmatic Sociology of Critique'. In *The Spirit of Luc Boltanski. Essays on the Pragmatic Sociology of Critique*, ed. Simon Susen and Bryan Turner, 293–312. London: Anthem Press.

Navari, Cornelia. 2010. The Concept of Practice in the English School. *European Journal of International Relations* 17 (4): 611–630.

Neumann, Iver B. 2002. Returning Practice to the Linguistic Turn: The Case of Diplomacy. *Millennium: Journal of International Studies* 31 (3): 627–651.

———. 2005. To Be a Diplomat. *International Studies Perspectives* 6 (1): 72–93.

———. 2007. 'A Speech That the Entire Ministry May Stand For,' or: Why Diplomats Never Produce Anything New. *International Political Sociology* 1 (2): 183–200.

———. 2010. Autobiography, Ontology, Autoethnology. *Review of International Studies* 36 (4): 1051–1055.

———. 2012. *At Home with the Diplomats: Inside a European Foreign Ministry*. Ithaca: Cornell University Press.

———. 2013. *Diplomatic Sites. A Critical Enquiry*. Oxford: Oxford University Press.

Neumann, Iver B., and Ole Jacob Sending. 2010. *Governing the Global Polity: Practice, Mentality and Rationality*. Ann Arbor: The University of Michigan Press.

Nexon, Daniel H., and Vincent Pouliot. 2013. 'Things of Networks': Situating ANT in International Relations. *International Political Sociology* 7 (3): 342–345.

Nicolini, Davide. 2009. Articulating Practice Through the Interview to the Double. *Management Learning* 40 (2): 195–212.

———. 2012. *Practice Theory, Work, & Organization. An Introduction.* Oxford: Oxford University Press.

———. 2013. *Practice Theory, Work, & Organization: An Introduction.* Oxford: Oxford University Press.

———. 2017a. Is Small the Only Beautiful? Making Sense of 'Large Phenomena' from a Practice-Based Perspective. In *The Nexus of Practices. Connections, Constellations, Practitioners*, ed. Allison Hui, Theodore Schatzki, and Elizabeth Shove, 98–113. London/New York: Routledge.

———. 2017b. Practice Theory as a Package of Theory, Method and Vocabulary: Affordances and Limitations. In *Methodological Reflections on Practice Oriented Theories*, ed. Michael Jonas, Beate Littig, and Angela Wroblewski, 19–34. Berlin, Heidelberg: Springer International Publishing.

Niemann, Holger. 2015. *Justification and Critique in the UN Security Council: The Veto as Legitimacy Test.* Presented at the ISA Conference, New Orleans, February 18–21.

Niemann, Holger, and Henrik Schillinger. 2016. Contestation 'All the Way Down'? The Grammar of Contestation in Norm Research. *Review of International Studies* 43 (1): 29–49.

Nullmeier, Frank, and Tanja Pritzlaff. 2009. Zu einer Theorie politischer Praktiken. *Österreichische Zeitschrift für Politikwissenschaft* 38 (1): 7–22.

Olsson, Christian. 2015. Interventionism as Practice: On 'Ordinary Transgressions' and their Routinization. *Journal of Intervention and Statebuilding* 9 (4): 425–441.

Onuf, Nicholas. 2002. Worlds of Our Making: The Strange Career of Constructivism in International Relations. In *Visions of International Relations: Assessing an Academic Field*, ed. Donald J. Puchala, 119–141. Columbia: University of South Caroline Press.

———. 2015. *Theory Talk #70: Nicholas Onuf. Nicholas Onuf on the Evolution of Social Constructivsm, Turns in IR, and a Discipline of Our Making*, Thursday, 2 July 2015, available at http://www.theory-talks.org/2015/07/theory-talk-70.html.

Oppermann, Kai, and Alexander Spencer. 2016. Telling Stories of Failure: Narrative Constructions of Foreign Policy Fiascoes. *Journal of European Public Policy* 23 (5): 685–701.

Orange, Jennifer. 2016. Translating Law into Practice: Museums and a Human Rights Community of Practice. *Human Rights Quarterly* 38 (3): 706–735.

Ortner, Sherry B. 1984. Theory in Anthropology Since the Sixties. *Comparative Studies in Society and History* 26 (1): 126–166.

O'Toole, Paddy, and Steven Talbot. 2010. Fighting for Knowledge: Developing Learning Systems in the Australian Army. *Armed Forces & Society* 37 (1): 42–67.

Park-Kang, Sungju. 2014. *Fictional International Relations. Gender, Pain, and Truth*. London: Routledge.

Passoth, Jan-Hendrik, and Nicholas J. Rowland. 2010. Actor-Network State: Integrating Actor-Network Theory and State Theory. *International Sociology* 25 (6): 818–841.

Patterson, Molly, and Kristen Renwick Monroe. 1998. Narrative in Political Science. *Annual Review of Political Science* 1 (June): 315–331.

Pickering, Andrew, ed. 1992. *Science as Practice and Culture*. Chicago/London: University of Chicago Press.

———. 1995. *The Mangle of Practice. Time, Agency & Science*. Chicago: The University of Chicago Press.

Polkinghorne, Donald E. 1988. *Narrative Knowing and the Human Sciences*. Albany: State University of New York Press.

Porter, Tony. 2012. Making Serious Measures: Numerical Indices, Peer Review, and Transnational Actor-Networks. *Journal of International Relations and Development* 15 (4): 532–557.

Pouliot, Vincent. 2008. The Logic of Practicality: A Theory of Practice of Security Communities. *International Organization* 62 (2): 257–288.

———. 2010a. The Materials of Practice: Nuclear Warheads, Rhetorical Commonplaces and Committee Meetings in Russian–Atlantic Relations. *Cooperation and Conflict* 45 (3): 1–17.

———. 2010b. *International Security in Practice. The Politics of NATO-Russia Diplomacy*. Cambridge: Cambridge University Press.

———. 2013. Methodology. In *Bourdieu in International Relations. Rethinking Key Concepts in IR*, ed. Rebecca Adler-Nissen, 45–58. London: Routledge.

———. 2016. *International Pecking Orders. The Politics and Practice of Multilateral Diplomacy*. Cambridge: Cambridge University Press.

Pouliot, Vincent, and Jérémie Cornut. 2015. Practice Theory and the Study of Diplomacy: A Research Agenda. *Cooperation and Conflict* 50 (3): 297–315.

Pouliot, Vincent, and Frédéric Mérand. 2013. Bourdieu's Concepts. In *Bourdieu in International Relations: Rethinking Key Concepts in IR*, ed. Rebecca Adler-Nissen, 24–44. New York: Routledge.

Pratt, Simon Frankel. 2016. Pragmatism as Ontology, Not (Just) Epistemology: Exploring the Full Horizon of Pragmatism as an Approach to IR Theory. *International Studies Review* 18 (3): 508–527.

Prior, Lindsay. 2008. Repositioning Documents in Social Research. *Sociology* 42 (5): 821–836.

Prügl, Elisabeth. 2012. 'If Lehman Brothers Had Been Lehman Sisters…': Gender and Myth in the Aftermath of the Financial Crisis. *International Political Sociology* 6 (1): 21–35.

Pugh, Allison J. 2013. What Good Are Interviews for Thinking About Culture? Demystifying Interpretive Analysis. *American Journal of Cultural Sociology* 1 (1): 42–68.

Rabinow, Paul. 2011. *The Accompaniment. Assembling the Contemporary.* Chicago/London: University of Chicago Press.

Ralph, Jason, and Jess Gifkins. 2017. The Purpose of the United Nations Security Council Practice: Contesting Competence Claims in the Normative Context Created by the Responsibility to Protect. *European Journal of International Relations* 23 (3): 630–653.

Reckwitz, Andreas. 2002. Toward a Theory of Social Practices: A Development in Culturalist Theorizing. *European Journal of Social Theory* 5 (2): 243–263.

———. 2004a. Die Entwicklung des Vokabulars der Handlungstheorien: Von den zweck- und normorientierten Modellen zu den Kultur- und Praxistheorien. In *Paradigmen der akteurszentrierten Soziologie*, ed. Manfred Gabriel, 303–328. Wiesbaden: Springer VS.

———. 2004b. Die Reproduktion und die Subversion sozialer Praktiken. Zugleich ein Kommentar zu Pierre Bourdieu und Judith Butler. In *Doing Culture. Neue Positionen zum Verhältnis von Kultur und sozialer Praxis*, ed. Karl Hörning and Julia Reuter, 40–54. Bielefeld: Transcript.

———. 2008. Praktiken und Diskurse. Eine Sozialtheoretische Und Methodologische Relation. In *Theoretische Empirie. Zur Relevanz Qualitativer Forschung*, ed. Herbert Kalthoff, Stefan Hirschauer, and Gesa Lindemann, 188–209. Frankfurt a. M.: Suhrkamp Verlag.

———. 2010. *Unscharfe Grenzen. Perspektiven der Kultursoziologie.* Bielefeld: Transcript.

———. 2012. Affective Spaces: A Praxeological Outlook. *Rethinking History* 16 (2): 241–258.

Reus-Smit, Christian. 2007. International Crises of Legitimacy. *International Politics* 44 (2–3): 157–174.

Rhodes, R.A.W. 2011. *Everyday Life in British Government.* Oxford: Oxford University Press.

Riles, Annelise. 1998. Infinity Within the Brackets. *American Ethnologist* 25 (3): 378–398.

———. 2006. [Deadlines]: Removing the Brackets on Politics in Bureaucratic and Anthropological Analysis. In *Documents. Artifacts of Modern Knowledge*, ed. Annelise Riles, 71–94. Ann Arbor: University of Michigan Press.

———. 2008. Models and Documents: Artifacts of International Legal Knowledge. *International & Comparative Law Quarterly* 48 (4): 805–825.

Ringmar, Erik. 2014. The Search for Dialogue as a Hindrance to Understanding: Practices as Interparadigmatic Research Program. *International Theory* 6 (1): 1–27.

Roberts, Joanne. 2006. Limits to Communities of Practice. *Journal of Management Studies* 43 (3): 623–639.

Roberts, Nancy C. 2010. Spanning 'Bleeding' Boundaries: Humanitarianism, NGOs, and the Civilian-Military Nexus in the Post-Cold War Era. *Public Administration Review* 70 (2): 212–222.

Rose, Nikolas, and Peter Miller. 1992. Political Power Beyond the State: Problematics of Government. *The British Journal of Sociology* 43 (2): 173–205.

Rouse, Joseph. 1987. *Knowledge and Power: Toward a Political Philosophy of Science*. Ithaca: Cornell University Press.

———. 1996. *Engaging Science. How to Understand Its Practices Philosophically*. Ithaca: Cornell University Press.

———. 2006. Practice Theory. In *Philosophy of Anthropology and Sociology*, ed. Stephen Turner and Mark Risjord, vol. 15 of *Handbook of the Philosophy of Science*, ed. Dov M. Gabbay, Paul Thagard and John Woods, 499–540. Amsterdam: Elsevier BV.

Ruddin, Lee Peter. 2006. You Can Generalize Stupid! Social Scientists, Bent Flyvbjerg and Case Study Methodology. *Qualitative Inquiry* 12 (4): 797–812.

Ruggie, John G. 1975. International Responses to Technology: Concepts and Trends. *International Organization* 29 (3): 557–583.

Sandberg, Joergen, and Mats Alvesson. 2011. Ways of Constructing Research Questions: Gap-Spotting or Problematization? *Organization* 18 (1): 23–44.

Schäfer, Hilmar. 2013. *Die Instabilität der Praxis. Reproduktion und Transformation des Sozialen in der Praxistheorie*. Weilerswist: Velbrück Wissenschaft.

Schäfer, Franka, Anna Daniel, and Frank Hillebrandt, eds. 2015. *Methoden einer Soziologie der Praxis*. Bielefeld: Transcript.

Schatz, Edward. 2009. *Political Ethnography. What Immersion Contributes to the Study of Power*. Chicago: University of Chicago Press.

Schatzki, Theodore R. 1996. *Social Practices. A Wittgensteinian Approach to Human Activity and the Social*. Cambridge/New York: Cambridge University Press.

———. 2001. Practice Theory. In *The Practice Turn in Contemporary Theory*, ed. Theodore R. Schatzki, Karin Knorr Cetina, and Eike von Savigny, 1–14. London/New York: Routledge.

———. 2002. *The Site of the Social. A Philosophical Account of the Constitution of Social Life and Change*. University Park: Pennsylvania State University Press.

———. 2005. Peripheral Vision: The Sites of Organizations. *Organization Studies* 26 (3): 465–484.

Schatzki, Theodore R. 2012. A Primer on Practices. In *Practice-Based Education. Perspectives and Strategies*, Practice, Education, Work and Society, ed. Joy Higgs, Ronald Barnett, Stephen Billett, and Maggie Hutchings, vol. 6, 13–26. Rotterdam: Sense Publishers.

———. 2017. Sayings, Texts and Discursive Formations. In *The Nexus of Practices. Connections, Constellations, Practitioners*, ed. Allison Hui, Theodore R. Schatzki, and Elizabeth Shove, 126–140. London: Routledge.

Schatzki, Theodore R., Karin Knorr Cetina, and Eike von Savigny, eds. 2001. *The Practice Turn in Contemporary Theory*. London/New York: Routledge.
Scheper, Christian. 2015. 'From Naming and Shaming to Knowing and Showing': Human Rights and the Power of Corporate Practice. *The International Journal of Human Rights* 19 (6): 737–756.
Schindler, Sebastian, and Tobias Wille. 2015. Change in and Through Practice: Pierre Bourdieu, Vincent Pouliot, and the End of the Cold War. *International Theory* 7 (2): 330–359.
———. 2017. *Two Ways of Criticizing International Practices*. Paper Presented at the Pan-European Conference of the European International Studies Association, Barcelona, September 2017.
Schmidt, Robert. 2012. *Soziologie der Praktiken. Konzeptionelle Studien und empirische Analysen*. Berlin: Suhrkamp.
———. 2017. Sociology of Social Practices: Theory or Modus Operandi of Empirical Research? In *Methodological Reflections on Practice Oriented Theories*, ed. Michael Jonas, Beate Littig, and Angela Wroblewski, 3–17. Berlin, Heidelberg: Springer.
Schmidt, Sebastian. 2014. Foreign Military Presence and the Changing Practice of Sovereignty: A Pragmatist Explanation of Norm Change. *American Political Science Review* 108 (4): 817–829.
Schmitt, Olivier. 2017. International Organization at War: NATO Practices in the Afghan Campaign. *Cooperation and Conflict*. Advance online publication. https://doi.org/10.1177/2F0010836717701969.
Schmidt, Robert, and Jörg Volbers. 2011. Siting Praxeology. The Methodological Significance of 'Public' in Theories of Social Practices. *Journal for the Theory of Social Behaviour* 41 (4): 419–440.
Schouten, Peer. 2013. The Materiality of State Failure: Social Contract Theory, Infrastructure and Governmental Power in Congo. *Millennium: Journal of International Studies* 41 (3): 553–564.
———. 2014. Security as Controversy: Reassembling Security at Amsterdam Airport. *Security Dialogue* 45 (1): 23–42.
Schwartz-Shea, Peregrine, and Dvora Yanow. 2009. Reading and Writing as Method: In Search for Trustworthy Texts. In *Organizational Ethnography. Studying the Complexities of Everyday Life*, ed. Sierk Ybema, Dvora Yanow, Harry Wels, and Frans Kamsteeg, 56–83. London: Sage.
———. 2012. *Interpretive Research Design. Concepts and Processes*. Milton Park/New York: Routledge Press.
Sclavi, Marianella. 1989. *Ad Una Spanna Da Terra*. Milan: Feltrinelli.
Seale, Clive. 1999. *The Quality of Qualitative Research*. London: Sage.
Sending, Ole Jacob. 2002. Constitution, Choice and Change: Problems with the 'Logic of Appropriateness' and Its Use in Constructivist Theory. *European Journal of International Relations* 8 (4): 443–470.

———. 2015. Beyond the 'Here and Now' of Practice Theory. *International Studies Quarterly Online*. http://www.isanet.org/Publications/ISQ/Posts/ID/4960/Beyond-the-Here-and-Now-of-Practice-Theory.

Sending, Ole Jacob, and Iver B. Neumann. 2006. Governance to Governmentality: Analyzing NGOs, States, and Power. *International Studies Quarterly* 50 (3): 651–672.

———. 2011. Banking on Power. How Some Practices in an International Organization Anchor Others. In *International Practices*, ed. Emanuel Adler and Vincent Pouliot, 231–254. Cambridge: Cambridge University Press.

Sending, Ole Jacob, Vincent Pouliot, and Iver B. Neumann, eds. 2015. *Diplomacy and the Making of World Politics*. Cambridge/New York: Cambridge University Press.

Shapiro, Michael J., G. Matthew Bonham, and Daniel Heradstveit. 1988. A Discursive Practices Approach to Collective Decision-Making. *International Studies Quarterly* 32 (4): 397–419.

Sheeran, Paul. 2007. *Literature and International Relations: Stories in the Art of Diplomacy*. Milton Park/New York: Routledge.

Shenhav, Shaul R. 2006. Political Narrative and Political Reality. *International Political Science Review* 27 (3): 245–262.

Shim, David. 2017. Sketching Geopolitics: Comics and the Case of the *Cheonan* Sinking. *International Political Sociology*. Online First, doi: https://doi.org/10.1093/ips/olx016.

Shotter, John. 1993. *Cultural Politics of Everyday Life. Social Constructionism, Rhetoric and Knowing of the Third Kind*. Toronto: University of Toronto Press.

Shove, Elizabeth, Mika Pantzar, and Matt Watson. 2012. *The Dynamics of Social Practice: Everyday Life and How It Changes*. London: Sage.

Solomon, Ty, and Brent J. Steele. 2017. Micro-Moves in International Relations Theory. *European Journal of International Relations* 23 (2): 267–291.

Somers, Margaret R. 1994. The Narrative Construction of Identity: A Relational and Network Approach. *Theory and Society* 23 (5): 605–649.

Spaargaren, Gert. 2011. Theories of Practices. Agency, Technology, and Culture. *Global Environmental Change* 21 (3): 813–822.

Spiegel, Gabrielle M., ed. 2005a. *Practicing History. New Directions in Historical Writing After the Linguistic Turn*. London: Routledge.

———. 2005b. Introduction. In *Practicing History. New Directions in Historical Writing After the Linguistic Turn*, ed. Gabrielle M. Spiegel, 1–33. New York: Routledge.

Srnicek, Nick. 2017. New Materialisms and International Relations: Bodies, Brains and Complex Causality. In *Technology and World Politics: An Introduction*, ed. Daniel R. McCarthy, 84–99. Abingdon: Routledge.

Steinberg, Blema S. 2005. Indira Gandhi: The Relationship Between Personality Profile and Leadership Style. *Political Psychology* 26 (5): 755–790.

Stepputat, Finn, and Jessica Larsen. 2015. Global Political Ethnography: A Methodological Approach to Studying Global Policy Regimes. *DIIS Working Paper* (1): 1–30.

Stern, David G. 2003. The Practical Turn. In *The Blackwell Guide to the Philosophy of the Social Sciences*, ed. Stephen P. Turner and Paul A. Roth, 185–206. Malden: Blackwell Publishing.

Stone, Deborah A. 2002. *Policy Paradox. The Art of Political Decision Making*. New York: Norton.

Strömbom, Lisa. 2012. Thick Recognition: Advancing Theory on Identity Change in Intractable Conflicts. *European Journal of International Relations* 20 (1): 168–191.

Swidler, Ann. 2001. What Anchors Cultural Practices. In *The Practice Turn in Contemporary Theory*, ed. Theodore R. Schatzki, Karin Knorr Cetina, and Eike von Savigny, 74–92. London/New York: Routledge.

Sylvester, Christine. 2012. *War as Experience*. London: Routledge.

Thévenot, Laurent. 2007. The Plurality of Cognitive Formats and Engagements: Moving Between the Familiar and the Public. *European Journal of Social Theory* 10 (3): 409–423.

Thomas, Gary. 2010. Doing Case Study: Abduction Not Induction, Phronesis Not Theory. *Qualitative Inquiry* 16 (7): 575–582.

Trowler, Paul Richard. 2014. Practice-Focused Ethnographies of Higher Education: Method/ological Corollaries of a Social Practice Perspective. *European Journal of Higher Education* 4 (1): 18–29.

Tsing, Anna L. 2005. *Friction: An Ethnography of Global Connection*. Princeton: Princeton University Press.

Turner, Stephen P. 1994. *The Social Theory of Practice. Tradition, Tacit Knowledge and Presuppositions*. Cambridge: Polity Press.

———. 2001. Throwing Out the Tacit Rule Book. Learning and Practices. In *The Practice Turn in Contemporary Theory*, ed. Theodore R. Schatzki, Karin Knorr Cetina, and Eike von Savigny, 120–130. London: Routledge.

———. 2007. Mirror Neurons and Practices: A Response to Lizardo. *Journal for the Theory of Social Behaviour* 37 (3): 351–371.

van Munster, Rens, and Casper Sylvest. 2015. Documenting International Relations: Documentary Film and the Creative Arrangement of Perceptibility. *International Studies Perspectives* 16 (3): 229–245.

Vanderveen, Zach. 2010. Bearing the Lightning of Possible Storms: Foucault's Experimental Social Criticism. *Continental Philosophy Review* 43 (4): 467–484.

Vasilache, Andreas. 2014. Great Power Governmentality? Coincidence and Parallelism in the New Strategic Guidance for the US Department of Defense. *Security Dialogue* 45 (6): 582–600.

Vrasti, Wanda. 2008. The Strange Case of Ethnography and International Relations. *Millennium: Journal of International Studies* 37 (2): 279–301.

Wacquant, Louis. 2004. *Body and Soul. Notebooks of an Apprentice Boxer*. New York: Oxford University Press.
Wagenaar, Hendrik. 2004. 'Knowing' the Rules: Administrative Work as Practice. *Public Administration Review* 64 (6): 643–656.
———. 2011. *Meaning and Action: Interpretation and Dialogue in Policy Analysis*. Armonk/New York/London: M. E. Sharpe.
Wagner, Peter. 1999. After Justification: Repertoires of Evaluation and the Sociology of Modernity. *European Journal of Social Theory* 2 (3): 341–357.
Walker, R.B.J. 1993. *Inside/Outside: International Relations as Political Theory*. Cambridge: Cambridge University Press.
Walters, William. 2002. The Power of Inscription: Beyond Social Construction and Deconstruction in European Integration Studies. *Millennium: Journal of International Studies* 31 (1): 83–108.
———. 2012. *Governmentality: Critical Encounters*. London: Routledge.
———. 2014. Drone Strikes, Dingpolitik and Beyond: Furthering the Debate on Materiality and Security. *Security Dialogue* 45 (2): 101–118.
Watson, Matt. 2017. Placing Power in Practice Theory. In *The Nexus of Practices. Connections, Constellations, Practitioners*, ed. Allison Hui, Theodore R. Schatzki, and Elizabeth Shove, 169–182. London: Routledge.
Wedeen, Lisa. 2010. Reflections on Ethnographic Work in Political Science. *Annual Review of Political Science* 13 (1): 255–272.
Weisser, Florian. 2014. Practices, Politics, Performativities: Documents in the International Negotiations on Climate Change. *Political Geography* 40 (May): 46–55.
Wenger, Etienne. 1998. *Communities of Practice: Learning, Meaning and Identity*. Cambridge: Cambridge University Press.
Wenger, Etienne, and William W. Snyder. 2000. Communities of Practice: The Organizational Frontier. *Harvard Business Review* 78: 139–145.
White, Hayden. 1975. *Metahistory: The Historical Imagination in Nineteenth-Century Europe*. Baltimore: Johns Hopkins University Press.
Widmaier, Wesley W., Mark Blyth, and Leonard Seabrooke. 2007. Exogenous Shocks or Endogenous Constructions? The Meanings of Wars and Crises. *International Studies Quarterly* 51 (4): 747–759.
Wiener, Antje. 2008. *The Invisible Constitution of Politics. Contested Norms and International Encounters*. Cambridge: Cambridge University Press.
———. 2014. *A Theory of Contestation*. Wiesbaden: Springer.
Wight, Colin, Lene Hansen, and Tim Dunne. 2013. The End of International Relations Theory? *European Journal of International Relations* 19 (3): 405–665.
Wilcox, Lauren. 2017. Practising Gender, Queering Theory. *Review of International Studies*. Advance online publication. https://doi.org/10.1017/S0260210517000183.

Williams, Michael C. 2007. *Culture and Security: Symbolic Power and the Politics of International Security: The Reconstruction of Security in the Post-Cold War Era*. Oxon: Routledge.

Williams, Michael. 2012. The New Economy of Security. *Global Crime* 13 (4): 312–319.

Wilson, Gordon. 2006. Beyond the Technocrat? The Professional Expert in Development Practice. *Development and Change* 37 (3): 501–523.

Winch, Peter. 1958. *The Idea of Social Science and Its Relation to Philosophy*. London: Routledge and Kegan Paul.

Winner, Langdon. 1980. Do Artifacts Have Politics? *Daedalus* 109 (1): 121–136.

———. 1993. Upon Opening the Black Box and Finding it Empty: Social Constructivism and the Philosophy of Technology. *Science, Technology, and Human Values* 18 (3): 362–378.

Wittendorp, Stef. 2016. Conducting Government: Governmentality, Monitoring and EU Counter-Terrorism. *Global Society* 30 (3): 465–483.

Wittgenstein, Ludwig. 2009. *Philosophical Investigations*. Oxford: Wiley-Blackwell.

Wodak, Ruth. 2009. *The Discourse of Politics in Action: Politics as Usual*. Houndmills/New York: Palgrave Macmillan.

———. 2011. *The Discourse of Politics in Action: Politics as Usual*. Basingstoke: Palgrave Macmillan.

Wolcott, Harry F. 1973. *The Man in the Principal's Office. An Ethnography*. Walnut Creek: Altamira Press.

Wong, Theresa, and Joel Wainwright. 2009. Offshoring Dissent. *Critical Asian Studies* 41 (3): 403–428.

Yanow, Dvora. 2009. Dear Author, Dear Reader: The Third Hermeneutic in Writing and Reviewing Ethnography. In *Political Ethnography: What Immersion Contributes to the Study of Power*, ed. Edward Schatz, 275–302. Chicago/London: Chicago University Press.

Yanow, Dvora, and Haridimos Tsoukas. 2009. What Is Reflection-in-Action? A Phenomenological Account. *Journal of Management Studies* 46 (8): 1339–1364.

Yanow, Dvora, Marleen van der Haar, and Karlijn Völke. 2016. Troubled Taxonomies and the Calculating State: Everyday Categorizing and "Race-Ethnicity" – The Netherlands Case. *Journal of Race, Ethnicity, and Politics* 1 (2): 187–226.

Zahle, Julie. 2012. Practical Knowledge and Participant Observation. *Inquiry* 55 (1): 50–65.

Zanotti, Laura. 2005. Governmentalizing the Post–Cold War International Regime: The UN Debate on Democratization and Good Governance. *Alternatives: Global, Local, Political* 30 (4): 461–487.

Zwolski, Kamil. 2016. Integrating Crisis Early Warning Systems: Power in the Community of Practice. *Journal of European Integration* 38 (4): 393–407.

Index[1]

[1] Note: Page numbers followed by "n" refer to notes.

C. Bueger, F. Gadinger, *International Practice Theory*,
https://doi.org/10.1007/978-3-319-73350-0

E

F

G

H

I

O

P

R

S

T

U

V

W

Druck:
Customized Business Services GmbH
im Auftrag der
KNV Zeitfracht GmbH
Ein Unternehmen der Zeitfracht - Gruppe
Ferdinand-Jühlke-Str. 7
99095 Erfurt